sirous of seeing
of the HOUSE.
d to ring at the
nce and to
les
t th
e p

RUPERT THOMAS • ÉGLÉ SALVY

ANTIQUE & FLEA MARKETS OF LONDON & PARIS

Photographs by Rupert Thomas

with 332 color illustrations

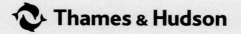 Thames & Hudson

FRONTISPIECE: John Goodison and Chris Paraskeva, Camden Passage

PAGE 2: LEFT TO RIGHT FROM THE TOP
M. Von Taubenheim, Bermondsey; Owen Hargreaves, Covent Garden;
Brick Lane; Posters for Collectors, Grays;
The Old Tool Chest, Camden Passage; Camden Lock;
Portobello; Catherine Wallis, Alfies; Old Crowther Market

All the information in this book relates to the period January–October 1998,
when it was compiled. Guidelines on stock and dealer specialities are subject to
change, as are locations and ownership of stalls.

First published in paperback in the United States of America in 1999 by Thames & Hudson Inc.,
500 Fifth Avenue, New York, New York 10110
Reprinted 2001

Library of Congress Catalog Card Number 98-61510
ISBN 0-500-28112-2

Printed and bound in Italy

LONDON CONTENTS

Using Your Guide   7

Author's Perspective   8

A History of London Antique Markets   11

Alfies Antique Market/Bell Street/Church Street   14

Bermondsey   24

Camden Lock   32

Camden Passage   38

Covent Garden   46

Grays Antique Markets   54

Old Crowther Market/Lillie Road/Antiquarius   62

Portobello   72

Spitalfields/Brick Lane/Columbia Road   94

Where to Buy Index   105

What to Buy Index   108

Where possible, we have provided telephone numbers for the
stalls themselves (in which case, you will only get a reply on trading days).
In other instances, the number listed is either the mobile or the home
telephone number of the dealer. Readers telephoning from abroad
should remember to replace the initial 'o' of the telephone number
with the country code for either England or France.

Where illustrations are not captioned, the stall photographed
is not mentioned in the book.

Maps by Hardlines

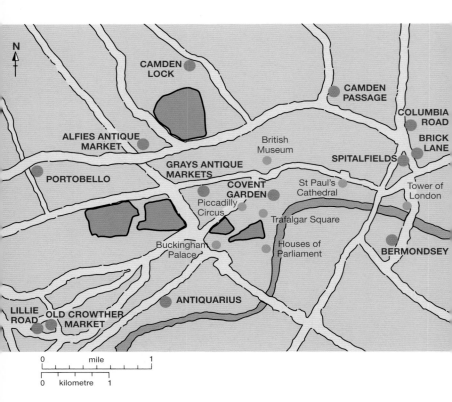

USING **YOUR GUIDE**

- Firstly, get your bearings. Look at the Contents Page for London (the one for Paris is at the other end of the book) to find a full list of the markets covered. The map opposite shows where the markets are situated within the city.

- If you know what you want, go straight to the Indexes. They will direct you both to dealers you may have heard of (Where to Buy Index, see p. 105) and to stands that specialize in the kind of stock you're looking for (What to Buy Index, see p. 108).

- If you simply want to explore, use the Contents Page to direct you to a particular market. Turn to the market in question to discover how it came into being, when trading takes place and what are the best ways of getting there; the maps are designed to make it as easy as possible.

- The following pages give you the facts, as well as anecdotes, about some of the stallholders you will encounter. ● indicates a stall that is a particular favourite of the author.

- When you get there, be sure to hunt around, to talk to the dealers and perhaps try a spot of bargaining. If you're tired and need a break, turn to your guide's Nearbuys for advice on local cafés – and for a list of other shops in the area.

AUTHOR'S PERSPECTIVE

AUTHOR'S **PERSPECTIVE**

Ever since I came to London in 1977 at the age of twelve, I have been addicted to antique and junk markets. I started off at Winchester Market in Swiss Cottage, moved on to Camden Lock, where I briefly ran a stall, and as my disposable income increased and my taste developed, I progressed to Portobello Road and Bermondsey. When, despite a string of petitions, Winchester Market was closed down in the early 1980s by Camden Council, I was struck by the precarious position that markets occupy. Seemingly robust, they are surprisingly fragile, relying on supportive landlords and, more acutely than other commercial enterprises, on a healthy worldwide stock market. Independent dealers are on the cutting edge of the economic chopping block: the knock-on effects of a financial crisis can rob them of their best customers overnight.

This half of the book focuses on antiques markets in central London and will steer you towards individual dealers specializing in an enormous range of stock (see the What to Buy Index, p. 108). While the introductions provide a brief history of each market and its surrounding streets, the photographs, taken on the hoof over several months, capture the atmosphere of each location and convey some of its vivacity and subversive charm.

So this is not simply a list of antiques dealers in the capital. Though many recognized specialists are featured, so too are traders whose eye for the curious (and not always that old) seemed to me relevant, exciting and unmissably individual. I have included a jewelry designer who makes tiaras for adult Tinkerbells and a number of committed young dealers selling classic 20th-century design, along with more established sellers of antiquities, early ceramics, flatware and textiles; it is precisely this eccentric mix of stock that gives markets their edgy glamour. The London markets are not systematically laid out and some of the stands are not numbered; they are therefore listed alphabetically. When you arrive at the market, ask for the stall or arcade you're looking for; as most of the stallholders tend to know each other, they should be able to point you in the right direction. A Nearbuys section concludes each market, offering a selection of good cafés and interesting shops in the vicinity.

Although some independent shops thrive around markets, many of London's small antique shops have been forced out of business over the past decade by ever-increasing rents. Markets have therefore become the most reliable places for collectors to find and discuss what they are passionate about. They have a more rapid turnover of stock than salerooms and dealers are under pressure to produce new

ESTER CHIGINE, PORTOBELLO

treasures every week. The potential of the unexpected is what makes the places so compulsive.

The spotlight that television programmes, books and magazines have thrown on the antiques trade has added to the allure of buying, but has also given rise to a number of misconceptions. Most relevant here is the idea that dealers make vast profits. Some undoubtedly do. However, as good stock becomes scarcer and more highly prized, most specialists find themselves buying from other dealers, at auction or at antiques fairs. Their prices therefore represent only a small profit on what they have already had to shell out. It is fair to say that many dealers, particularly the ones I have chosen, are motivated as much by a passion for what they sell as by pure profit.

Remember this when you decide you want something and start to bargain down its price. Haggling comes naturally, almost compulsively, to some people; there are relatively few who are willing to pay the initial asking price, even if they think it's fair. There are no hard and fast rules and you should never be embarrassed to talk about price, since dealers do it all the time among themselves. If you are planning to barter, a few stock phrases – 'What is the best price on…?' or 'What is the trade price on…?' – will help you make the point. Paying in cash, rather than by cheque or credit card, may also reduce the price. If a dealer suggests a figure that you feel is still too high, you may be able to bring them down a little further, but don't expect a great drop. Some guidebooks claim that walking away, then coming back and looking again will help. Do it at your peril. My most vivid memories are of returning to things I wanted to buy, only to find that

they had been sold. If you like something and you can afford it, don't be mean.

It goes without saying that you should always examine carefully what you're intending to buy. Most dealers will point out damage and restoration, but you need to satisfy yourself. Dealers may also make mistakes and not always to their advantage, particularly if they are selling an object outside their field, which is why you can still come across amazing finds at antiques markets. When I was researching this book, a picture-dealer friend at Portobello told me about a primitive-looking drawing signed 'VG' that was on display for two weeks before someone took a chance on it. It turned up later at auction with a firm attribution to Van Gogh. 'Good luck to [the person who bought it]', said my friend, 'we'd all looked at it and thought that it was too good to be true.'

A HISTORY OF **LONDON ANTIQUE MARKETS**

London's reputation as a centre of trade is preserved in the tell-tale names of some of its surviving medieval streets. You could buy timber in Wood Street and, according to the antiquarian John Stow (1525–1605), Silver Street took its name from the 'siluer smithes dwelling there'.

Alongside this network of individual trade centres, London continued to support a number of weekly food markets, as it had done since its foundation as a Roman garrison. The majority of these were based around Westcheap (now Cheapside) and Eastcheap (*ceap* being the Saxon word for market). The capital also hosted annual fairs where imported luxuries were sold: textiles from Constantinople, spices from Italy and fur from Russia. Smithfield's Bartholomew Fair, founded in 1133 by Rahere, the court jester to Henry I, was initially a cloth fair and attracted sellers from France and Flanders.

During the 13th and 14th centuries, craftsmen and merchants formed guilds and livery companies and began to exert increasing power over the City and its markets. But it was the Great Fire of 1666 that brought decisive rationalization. The fire destroyed most of the City (over four hundred acres), leaving a charred wasteland in its wake. (Smoke from the inferno reached Oxford sixty miles away.) Town planning began immediately and, as open stalls were considered a fire hazard, markets such as Billingsgate and Newgate were rehoused in covered buildings. Spitalfields, the fruit and vegetable market, was granted its charter by Charles II in 1682 and was held there until 1991.

The post-fire property boom encouraged new landowners to earn revenue by allowing markets to set up on their land. Covent Garden, Newport Market (near Leicester Square) and St James's Market, Piccadilly (which diarist Samuel Pepys visited in 1699 to call on two Dutch painters) were all established in the late 17th century. 150 years later, Henry Mayhew, in his survey of the capital *London Labour and the London Poor*, listed thirty-seven markets and 3,911 traders, many of them selling the Victorian equivalent of fast food.

But as shops took hold, markets dwindled. In recent decades, a combination of changing shopping habits, traffic, building development and general indifference has forced many of them to uproot and relocate. Antiques markets have had to adapt too. Bermondsey, for instance, which in the Middle Ages was connected to Smithfield, moved to its present site after World War II and dealers at Portobello relocated after the closure of the Caledonian Market in 1948 (see p. 73). The resounding feature of markets, however, is their ability to redefine themselves and carry on trading regardless of climate or council legislation. London is the richer for it.

ALFIES ANTIQUE MARKET

BELL STREET · CHURCH STREET

Although Lisson Grove is not mentioned in the rate-book until 1783, it is clear that the site was inhabited long before. According to the Domesday Book, eight families were living in the area in 1086 and the name itself originates from the pre-Norman Conquest manor of Lileston, which in turn derives from Lille's *tun* or farm. The sculptor Charles Rossi (1762–1839) and the painter Benjamin Haydon (1786–1846) had studios at no. 116, but today little of the Grove's polite Georgian charm remains, since much of the area has been cleared to make way for a medley of post-war housing projects.

There's a rather grim clothes and junk market in nearby Bell Street on Saturdays. Though a friend once bought a striking sub-Picasso canvas here for £5, you are more likely to find old shoes, grimy kitchen utensils and well-thumbed soft porn.

Church Street is the reliable alternative. There has been a market on the site since the 1830s and it continues to flourish today. The western end (Edgware Road) sells fruit and vegetables, while the eastern half (Lisson Grove) is home to a thriving community of antique traders. Some of these have their own shops (see Nearbuys) but most trade from Alfies Antique Market, which was set up in 1976 in the defunct Jordans department store. There are around two hundred permanent dealers (plus a café and a bureau de change), specializing in decorative antiques, garden paraphernalia, upholstered furniture, jewelry, toys, ceramics, prints and 20th-century design classics. Alfies has always been open to the public, but has somehow remained predominantly a dealers' market and is therefore competitively priced. Only ten minutes' walk from Baker Street tube station and from major attractions such as Madame Tussaud's and the Planetarium, it is not yet on the tourist trail. Buying there remains an antidote to the push-and-shove of Portobello.

HOW & WHEN TO GO TO

ALFIES ANTIQUE MARKET

BELL STREET • CHURCH STREET

ALFIES ANTIQUE MARKET

13–25 CHURCH STREET, NW8 8DT

✆ **0171-723 6066**

OPEN

Tuesday to Saturday, 10am–6pm. Most of the nearby shops are open Monday to Saturday, 10am–5.30pm.

BELL STREET

NW1

OPEN

Saturday, 8am–1pm

CHURCH STREET

NW8 AND W2

OPEN

Monday to Saturday, 8am–6pm

BY TUBE

Edgware Road and **Marylebone** (Bakerloo Line)

BY BUS

6, 16, 16A, 18, 98, 139 and 189

PARKING

There are parking meters in nearby streets and an NCP car park in Penfold Street.

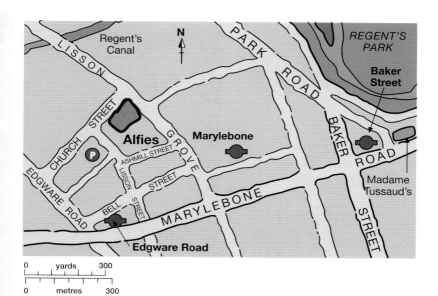

BEBE SECOND FLOOR, S012. ℃ 0171-724 4639

Peachy-pink walls and a French sofa make Bebe feel more like a boudoir than a boutique. The decor is the perfect foil to the Twenties, Thirties and Forties dresses that ex-fashion designer Sue Evans sells, alongside hats, handbags and other 'ditsy bits'.

BIBLIOPOLA FIRST FLOOR, F017. ℃ 0171-724 7231

Antiquarian and illustrated books, many of them produced for children.

S. BRUNSWICK FIRST FLOOR, F001–12. ℃ 0171-724 9097

Modern and period garden and conservatory furniture, accessories and oddities. From metal tables and loungers to terracotta forcers and flowerpots.

DAVID BURROWS SECOND FLOOR, F046–47. ℃ 0171-723 0429

Reconditioned mirrors and lighting from the 1800s to the early 20th century.

CRISTOBAL GROUND FLOOR, G125–27. ℃ 0171-724 7789

Steven Miners, founder of Cristobal, specializes in the best costume jewelry (by Chanel, Trifari, Stanley Hagler and others) and particularly in examples by Joseff of Hollywood, the designer who put the glitter into classic movies, such as *Cleopatra,* and who shrewdly launched limited-edition ranges of his creations to coincide with film releases (even patenting the dull gold-coloured alloy he used, to give his pieces extra exclusivity). Miners showed me a snake bracelet identical to the one Elizabeth Taylor wore when playing the Egyptian Queen.

GILLIAN DANZ FIRST FLOOR, F048–49. ℃ 0171-723 0678

Danz used to display her stock in the window of Alfies before she moved upstairs to become one of a group of decorative dealers who sell in this part of the

ROBIN GARDINER   S. BRUNSWICK

market. She is the only one to specialize exclusively in English and French curtain poles, tassels, tie-backs and finials.

DUDLEY AND GENIE SECOND FLOOR, S054–58. ℂ 0171-723 2548
Reconditioned telephones dating from the 1890s to the 1950s; anglepoise lamps; electric fans; and a whole stand devoted to brass and nickel-plated fittings, including door handles, bathroom accessories and candlesticks.

FURNITURE + DESIGNS 1870–1970 BASEMENT, B02–20
ℂ 0171-724 9761
Fiona Wicks has been dealing from these stands since Alfies first opened. 'I run it like a business', she says, 'I'm open from ten to six every trading day [unlike some dealers here].' Her taste is for dark Gothic and Arts and Crafts furniture (from individual footstools to dining tables), which she often mixes with lighter modern pieces.

ROBIN GARDINER GROUND FLOOR, G045–46. ℂ 0171-723 0449
An inspiring selection of prints from 1880 to 1970. Gardiner's own taste leans 'heavily towards French abstraction', but he buys almost anything he likes. When we met, he was selling Chagalls and Mirós 'off the block', but also had interesting, reasonably priced things for the first-time buyer: a John Nash print for £30; a woodcut by Jean Arp for only £20; and a pochoir (a limited-edition screen print) after Ben Nicholson at £50.

GARDINER & GARDINER FIRST FLOOR, F013 AND F24
ℂ 0171-723 5595
'I sell proper things', says Helen Gardiner as I browse around her cosy and seductive shop, crammed with early English ceramics, leather-bound books, pieces of small furniture and piles of 19th-century woven Paisley shawls. Although small-scale, her objects have an authenticity and grandeur that other stock here lacks. Her stand opposite is more countrified, with French tickings, pottery, linens and painted wares.

ANNE GORMLEY SECOND FLOOR, S104. ℂ 0171-723 5731
Gormley manages to unearth the kind of rare and early oddities it's become increasingly hard to find, among them a set of naively painted American dolls ('one is supposed to be George Washington') and the top of an alcove removed from an English country house which, now cleaned, reveals elaborately painted mythological figures.

DAVID HUXTABLE SECOND FLOOR, S003 AND S005. ℂ 0171-724 2200
Lined from floor to ceiling with old packaging, tins, advertising showcards and cardboard signs, Huxtable's shop is strangely captivating: 'it's the nostalgia side of it that attracts people', he says. His stock, most of which dates from around 1880 to 1930, is some of the best you'll find. Though most of it is British, he also has equally evocative European examples.

JONES AND CAMPBELL BASEMENT, B028–32. ℂ 0171-723 7730
Frame dealers Rod Jones and William Campbell were in competition before they started selling together. Now Jones finds the stock (from gilded 18th-century examples to painted modern British ones), while Campbell restores and

adapts it to their customers' requirements as well as traditionally handmaking frames from scratch. When I saw him last, he was engrossed in framing a whole series of immaculately detailed Forties designs by the illustrator Eric Fraser.

KITCHEN BYGONES BASEMENT, B051–53. ℂ 0171-258 3405
Seductively displayed working and decorative kitchen wares from the early 1800s to the 1940s, most of them English. From jars and sieves to small furniture and entire sets of kitchen china.

BARRY LANDSMAN FIRST FLOOR, F103–4. ℂ 0171-723 1370
A pleasing selection of small-scale 18th- and 19th-century watercolours. From scenes of rural English life to images of the Roman Campagna by those on the Grand Tour.

SARAH LEWIS AND JUNE VICTOR SECOND FLOOR
S040 AND S042–45. ℂ 0171-723 6105
Lewis and Victor's stands are a favourite haunt of film and theatre designers, who come to browse through their enormous stock of 19th- and early 20th-century fabrics and trimmings; I encountered one haggling over a bundle of silk velvets. They are not strictly a team, but 'buy and sell together' and share an eye for everything from pelmets and beadwork to lace and chenille.

GREG LI AND EDWARD HOLDEN FIRST FLOOR, F122–25
ℂ 0171-723 1370
Greg and Shelley Li collected paintings before they began selling them. Their taste is for traditional landscapes, portraits and still lifes, 'the earlier, the better', some of which are copies of old masters. Their long, narrow stand is shared with Edward Holden, who specializes in small 18th- and 19th-century cabinet pictures in oil; he manages to find curious and impressive things that retain a sense of grandeur despite their dimensions.

CONNIE MARGRIE FIRST FLOOR, F050–51. ℂ 0171-723 0678
Margrie specializes in upholstered chairs and drop-arm sofas: 'I always have a back-up stock of them.' The upholsterer in the basement (see Textilean, p. 22) restores pieces that have seen better days. Some large-scale furniture also.

MARIE-LOUISE OF MARYLEBONE SECOND FLOOR, S052
ℂ 0171-724 8383
Marie-Louise has been making hats since the mid-1980s and both Ava Gardner and Sir John Gielgud have sported her creations. She specializes in reusing designs from the early 20th century and in Twenties-style cloches, which are handmade using period fabrics and trimmings. She also makes modern hats to order.

FRANCESCA MARTIRE FIRST FLOOR, F131–37. ℂ 0171-724 4802
Francesca Martire deals in decorative art from 1880 to 1960 but admits to making room for other things, 'if they are particularly wonderful'. Vintage Fornasetti, 'no new stuff', and lights, ceramics and accessories by other influential Italian designers, such as Gae Aulenti and Vico Magistretti, give her shop genuine glamour. She also has a good eye for costume jewelry and is now importing an exclusive range of contemporary glass beads from Murano.

KITCHEN BYGONES   KITCHEN BYGONES

BRUNA NAUFAL BASEMENT, BOI. ✆ 0181-346 1387

Although the classic 20th-century furniture Bruna Naufal sells is often featured in glossy magazines, her basement shop remains little known outside the trade. She specializes in furniture made in bent plywood (the early modernists' favourite medium) and stocks pieces by names such as Breuer and Aalto, plus good unattributed examples from the Thirties through to the Seventies. A large wire rack holds her selection of interesting textiles from the same period. 'Not many people ask about them', she says, 'they're more like my private collection.'

PAOLA AND IAIA GROUND FLOOR, G087–88. ✆ 0171-723 0449

Bakelite isn't necessarily brown. Paola and Iaia's stock of mostly English and American accessories in the plastic dates from the Twenties to the Fifties and comes in every imaginable shade, including a number of wild marbled colours.

PERSIFLAGE SECOND FLOOR, S006–8. ✆ 0171-724 7366

Women's clothes from the 1800s to the 1970s. It is particularly good for late Victorian and Edwardian white linen dresses.

LARAINE PLUMMER SECOND FLOOR, S131–32. ✆ 0171-723 5731

Plummer has been selling here since the early 1990s and is sandwiched between seven other interesting decorative dealers. 'We're all affordable', she says, 'we want people to get this look at a reasonable price.' She specializes in country furniture, much of which (like the 18th-century Irish mule chest she showed me) retains its original paint.

KATHERINE POLE SECOND FLOOR, S105. ✆ 0171-723 5731

A casual but elegant mix of small country furniture, rustic French weaves and things with a decorative impact.

GEOFFREY ROBINSON GROUND FLOOR, G077–78 AND G091–92
✆ 0171-723 0449
Geoffrey Robinson says, with a groan, that he has been dealing here for 'eighteen years'. His stand remains a good source for Art Deco lighting and accessories, 1950s glass and 1960s Whitefriars.

ROJEH ANTIQUES BASEMENT, B022–27 AND B033–34
✆ 0171-724 6960
A sparkling selection of English and French Art Deco mirrored and veneered furniture, lamps and wall mirrors, many of which are by recognized designers such as Maurice Adams or the manufacturer Hille. They will also take on French polishing, gilding and general restoration.

SPARKLE MOORE GROUND FLOOR, G100 AND G116
✆ 0171-724-8984 (ALSO AT THE STABLES, CAMDEN LOCK.)
Sparkle Moore's address card boasts an airbrushed Fifties blonde bombshell, bending over to reveal polkadot stockings and a tutu petticoat, and the slogan 'The Girl Can't Help It'. It captures Moore's taste for Fifties glamour garb, which she sells, hires, and wears herself. Most of her stock comes from America and much of it is in mint condition. Fifties underwear is a speciality and, when we met, she had just found a ruched gold-lamé swimsuit – 'It's so Esther Williams.'

SUSIE COOPER CERAMICS GROUND FLOOR
G069–74 AND G093–95. ✆ 0171-723 0449
Nick Jones and Geoffrey Peake's vast array of pristine Art Deco ceramics (by Clarice Cliff, Shelley and Susie Cooper, as the name suggests) takes up a whole corner of Alfies. They also have a stash of Lalique glass and lights, plus a unit devoted to Keith Murray's plain architectural wares which were designed for Wedgwood in the Forties and Fifties.

TEXTILEAN BASEMENT, B058–59. ✆ 0171-723 4990
Samantha Peters, the driving talent behind this reliable upholstery shop, has worked for everyone from the fashion designer Lulu Guinness to Benazir Bhutto. Besides 'straight' upholstery (blinds, curtains, loose covers), she also restores beadwork and Aubusson tapestries and conserves early upholstered furniture using period trimmings and traditional techniques and materials, such as horsehair. 'I put back exactly what comes off the original', she explains, pointing to a 19th-century French chair she is working on.

CATHERINE WALLIS FIRST FLOOR, F052–53. ✆ 0171-723 0678
A keen-eyed decorative dealer who mixes rustic country antiques with finer oddities. When I visited, some roughly painted gates were propped next to part of a panelled room decorated with gilded carvings. Much of her stock comes from France.

JESSICA WARD SECOND FLOOR, S100–1. ✆ 0171-723 5731
A wild and witty mix of stock that can include anything from a bald rocking horse to the richly jewelled crowns used to celebrate Spanish saints' days. Camp heaven.

NEARBUYS

ARCHIVE BOOKSTORE
83 BELL STREET
NW1 6TB
☎ 0171-402 8212
Antiquarian and secondhand books, plus a good selection of sheet music: scores, chamber sets and songsheets.

A. BINDER
34 CHURCH STREET
NW8 8EP
☎ 0171-723 0542
Specializes in shop counters and showcases salvaged from old-fashioned haberdashers, shoe shops, chemists, etc.

MADELINE CRISPIN ANTIQUES
95 LISSON GROVE (CORNER OF BROADLEY STREET), NW1 6UP
☎ 0171-402 6845
This green-painted corner shop has a dependable mix of English and Continental furniture, 18th- and 19th-century pictures and other oddities.

STEPHEN FOSTER'S BOOKSHOP
95 BELL STREET
NW1 6TL
☎ 0171-724 0876
One of London's best selections of secondhand books (both recent publications and out-of-print standard works) on art, design, architecture and antiques.

GALLERY OF ANTIQUE COSTUME & TEXTILES
2 CHURCH STREET
NW8 8ED
☎ 0171-723 9981
Seriously impressive selection of clothes and fabrics from around the world, from 18th-century cut velvets and Nigerian *kente* cloth to Thirties curtains. Unmissable.

LISSON GALLERY
67 LISSON STREET
NW1 5DA
☎ 0171-724 2739
Nicholas Logsdale's gallery is dedicated to work by minimalist and installation artists. It represents some big names, among them Anish Kapoor.

THE SEA SHELL
49 LISSON GROVE
NW1 6UH
☎ 0171-723 8703
Award-winning fish and chip shop that has made an art form out of batter and the deep-fat fryer.

23

DAVID HUXTABLE

BERMONDSEY

Henry VIII's dissolution of the monasteries in the 1530s augmented royal power and removed objections to his divorce from Catherine of Aragon; it also marked the end of medieval life in London. At the time, the capital supported about twelve monasteries, one of which was Bermondsey Abbey (Cluniac order, founded in 1082). Its lands were surrendered to the king in 1537 and the buildings passed to Sir Thomas Pope, one of Henry's chief agents and supporters. Pope razed the abbey and used the stone to build Bermondsey House, the grounds of which covered twenty acres and included outbuildings, orchards and ponds; Elizabeth I visited the Earl of Sussex there in 1570. (Pope also founded Trinity College, Oxford, and books from the monastic libraries he helped ravage, possibly including works from Bermondsey, are now there.)

Nothing remains of these early structures, except one side of a late medieval gatehouse in Grange Walk and the 12th-century carved capitals in the vestibule of St Mary Magdalene in Bermondsey Street, opposite the market. Rebuilt *c.* 1680 and remodelled in 1830, the interior of the church retains a late 17th-century simplicity. The weekly outdoor antiques market now occupies the abbey's former site and in 1998 there were council plans to uproot the two hundred sellers in an attempt to excavate the foundations. But Bermondsey dealers are no strangers to being pushed around. Traders only moved here after World War II, when bomb damage had robbed them of their original pitches at the Caledonian Market in Islington (see Camden Passage, p. 39).

Although much of the surrounding area is architecturally depressing, Bermondsey retains a strong sense of identity and history. Neighbouring streets, such as Morocco Street and Tanner Street, recall its ancient links to the leather industry and the walk to the market from London Bridge station (the capital's earliest railway terminus, *c.* 1836–1851) evokes a sense of the past. Tower Bridge, a potent tourist image of London but actually a Victorian creation (J. Wolfe Barry and Horace Jones, 1886–1894), is on your left-hand side.

Many of today's traders helped their parents establish their stands when dealing began here in 1948. Indoor markets have since sprung up in the immediate vicinity and along Tower Bridge Road. One is housed in a defunct bacon factory at the junction of Bermondsey Street and Long Lane and some dealers store stock in its old smoking ovens.

Bermondsey is still a dealers' market but deserves to attract a wider public. Part of the problem has been its reputation for handling stolen goods. Silver and jewelry remain its mainstay and many dealers whom I visited were suspiciously reluctant to talk about themselves or their stock. But this turned out to be for fear of publicizing their goods to thieves rather than to the police.

HOW & WHEN TO GO TO
BERMONDSEY

BERMONDSEY
**BERMONDSEY
SQUARE, SE1 3UN**
☎ 0171-351 5353

OPEN
Friday, 4am–2pm

BY TUBE
London Bridge
(Northern Line)

BY BUS
1, 42, 78, 188, 199
and N1 night bus

PARKING
Parking in the area is
mostly unrestricted, but if
you do decide to park on a
single yellow line, check the
time plate carefully or you
may end up with a fine.

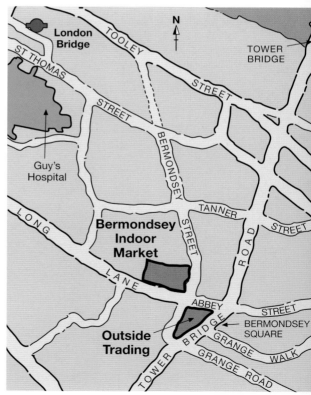

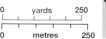

CHRIS BENNETT STAND 3 (BERMONDSEY STREET SIDE)

A compelling and curious mixture of small stock: Delft tiles, an early 20th-century hot-water bottle, 'one of the first in rubber', and a pristine-looking Betty Boo doll balancing on a crocheted stand! He has sold similar delights here since the Seventies.

CHARLIE BERMONDSEY SQUARE (TOWER BRIDGE ROAD SIDE)

℅ 01702-473619

This knowledgeable and helpful dealer specializes in drawings and watercolours. He trained as a bookbinder, 'It gave me an eye for this stuff', and has a true appreciation of draughtsmanship. Consequently, the pictures he sells tend to be representational rather than abstract. A number of works are framed, but more interesting are the piles of plastic folders crammed with everything from a naive late 19th-century view of a mill to a fine pen drawing for *Costumes of the World* on Whatman paper, watermarked 1820.

N. DAVALOU CARPETS CORNER OF BERMONDSEY SQUARE

AND ABBEY STREET. ℅ 0171-724 4142

Thrown over parked cars, piled on tables and laid out on the pavement, this stand's impressive selection of Persian rugs takes up more space than any other stock at Bermondsey. Ali, their owner, also sells Aubusson tapestries and the occasional *suzani*.

FANTASTICKS STAND 2 (BERMONDSEY STREET SIDE)

℅ 01892-523994 (ALSO AT PORTOBELLO.)

A good stock of mostly 19th-century walking sticks, some of them incorporating ingenious extras, such as measuring devices or tiny liqueur flasks.

CHARLIE   PETER LAURIE

KAY BOOKS STAND G36, BERMONDSEY INDOOR MARKET (LONG LANE ENTRANCE). ℂ 0171-491 0223

A Bond Street dealer who specializes in 'leather bindings by the yard' (in other words, affordable sets of traditionally bound books used by interior designers to decorate rooms); he has supplied 2,500 of them to redecorate the library of County Hall. He also sells travel, topographical and plate books, plus prints and old photographs.

PETER LAURIE STAND 89, CORNER OF BERMONDSEY SQUARE AND ABBEY STREET. ℂ 0181-853 5777

Greenwich-based dealer who specializes in good, early nautical antiques.

ROSSLYN NEAVE STAND 213 (ABBEY STREET SIDE) ℂ 0181-785 2464 (ALSO AT PORTOBELLO.)

The first breadboard Rosslyn Neave sold was a harvest board from the 1880s. She has now been specializing in them for twenty-five years. 'They were made for all kinds of occasions', she explains, 'weddings, holidays, investitures….' Droll lead model figures from the turn of the 20th century – farms, animals and villagers – form the other part of her pleasing, if eccentric, mixture of stock.

MICHAEL OLIPHANT STAND 174 (ABBEY STREET SIDE) ℂ 01424-882142

'Art and gambling are the two things I like best', says Michael Oliphant when I ask how he came to deal in gaming equipment and old artists' materials. His stand is one of the most attractive in Bermondsey, with mother-of-pearl fish-shaped counters from the 1820s piled up alongside tin paint boxes, ceramic mixing trays, palettes, brushes and lay figures; his earliest art supplies date from the 1700s. A painter himself, 'I do big, bold things like Van Gogh. Little old ladies are frightened by them', he is also a good source for new paints and materials.

SUE PERKS STAND 3, BERMONDSEY STREET (BY THE BAKED POTATO) ℂ 0181-769 1427

A reliable source for Georgian and Victorian silver and silver-plate cutlery and flatware, such as pastry forks, butter knives and fish servers. Many of the pieces are still in their original presentation boxes.

RICHARD PERRY STAND 25, CORNER OF BERMONDSEY SQUARE AND TOWER BRIDGE ROAD. ℂ 01273-728610

Perry started coming to Bermondsey with his father in the 1950s; Sterry's, the trading name of his stand, refers to his dad's old dealing partner. He has a partic-ular eye for small oddities, but also stocks arms, armour and metalware; when we met, he was on the floor sorting through piles of ormolu curtain tie-backs. His stall looks genuinely exciting, crammed with everything from pieces of Chinese export porcelain to a car bumper.

PL-B 12A, BERMONDSEY INDOOR MARKET (LONG LANE ENTRANCE) ℂ 01303-260726

Pauline Leath-Butler sold jewelry at Bermondsey before turning to textiles and has vivid memories of the market's heyday. 'I used to have a queue of buyers waiting to see what I'd bring. Now it's two people.' Dealing may be tougher now, but she continues to find a great range of period textiles: white work, lace, towels. When I arrived, she was unpicking beaded motifs from a perished 1860s ballgown so that they could be reused.

PRINT DEALER BERMONDSEY INDOOR MARKET
(LONG LANE ENTRANCE)

Look out for this narrow stand below the café. It has a good, varied selection of small framed and unframed prints and is shared by a dealer specializing in interesting oddities, among them glass, ceramics and metalware.

CHAD SANSEAN STAND 222 (TOWER BRIDGE ROAD SIDE
NEXT TO THE SYCAMORE TREE). ✆ 0181-882 5804

Sansean usually deals from beneath two large black umbrellas: 'It looks like a Bedouin encampment [but] actually I'm just sensitive to sunlight.' His stock can be equally surprising, with metalware and early photographs displayed side by side with car-boot-sale kitsch.

MOYA SMITH STAND 235 (TOWER BRIDGE ROAD SIDE)
✆ 01604-880514 (ALSO AT PORTOBELLO.)

'Years of practice' have given Moya Smith an eye for how to display things. Her stock of pristine-looking 19th-century cutlery is therefore suspended by clothes pegs from lengths of twine and even hung from plastic drying racks, which are 'meant for your smalls', she laughs. Along with cut forks, strainers and fruit spoons, she also sells military buttons.

BARBARA SPRINGALL BERMONDSEY INDOOR MARKET
(CORNER OF BERMONDSEY STREET ENTRANCE). ✆ 0181-647 5643

This fan dealer has lost none of her enthusiasm for the stock she 'has always specialized in'. When she holds up a blond-tortoiseshell Chinese brisé fan from the 1820s, so intricately cut that it looks like lace, it's hard not to be captivated as well. Her stock is from the 18th and 19th centuries and mostly European, but sometimes Oriental or Indian. 'It's the incredible variety [of styles and materials]', she says, 'that fascinates me.'

M. VON TAUBENHEIM STAND 12 (BERMONDSEY STREET SIDE)
✆ 01993-822780

Most Fridays Von Taubenheim is here selling English and Continental china and accessories that are decorative, 'without being too fluffy'. Blue-and-white china is a staple and, when I visited, there were piles of French enamel door numbers and a box of 19th-century specimen eggs carved in hard stone.

NEARBUYS

There are three catering vans in Bermondsey Square selling tea, coffee, burgers and butties to eat on the hoof.

DELFINA STUDIOS
50 BERMONDSEY STREET SE1 3UD
📞 **0171-357 6600**
An old warehouse converted into studios for young artists by the philanthropic Delfina Entrecanales; its good café is open to the public.

ROSIE'S DINING ROOM CAFÉ
BERMONDSEY STREET (NEAR BERMONDSEY INDOOR MARKET) SE1 3UD
The dealers' favourite greasy-spoon café.

MICHAEL OLIPHANT

CAMDEN LOCK

Of all London's markets, those around Camden Lock are the most successful but the least enjoyable. Since dealing began here in the early 1970s, the atmosphere has changed from hippie heaven to theme park. The Lock is now on every tourist itinerary, with visitors encouraged to come and gawp at the orchestrated street life; they will certainly smell the market's mixture of joss sticks and fried food before they see anything to buy.

However, in the 19th century, when most of Camden Town was laid out, it was a rather refined place. It still consists of terraces of moderately sized, and now immensely desirable, houses; the façades and interiors of some were recorded by the Camden Town Group of painters (formed *c*. 1911), which included Walter Sickert, Spencer Gore, Harold Gilman and Charles Ginner. Pianos, which Camden Town specialized in making, were produced in the Circular Factory (*c*. 1860) on Oval Road, and Arlington House (*c*. 1905) on Arlington Road, built by the philanthropic Lord Rowton, is one of the few surviving working men's hostels. The Regent's Canal, which Camden Lock straddles, was opened in 1820 and you can still walk along most of it; head west, passing Regent's Park Zoo and St John's Wood, to reach Lisson Grove and Alfies Antique Market (see p.15). The area was gentrified in the 1960s when a number of writers, artists and journalists converted Camden's plethora of lodging houses back into individual homes.

There are now various markets in the area, of which The Stables is the best. A number of good, often young, dealers sell classic modern furniture, accessories, clothes and even the odd antique on the cobblestones, from defunct railway sheds and under the arches. On Chalk Farm Road is the Round House (*c*. 1847), built to house the engine turntable at one end of the London to Birmingham railway. The Round House's *raison d'être* stopped running in 1869 and the building became a warehouse until 1964. Despite repeated attempts to convert it into an arts centre, the Round House's future remains uncertain.

HOW & WHEN TO GO TO
CAMDEN LOCK

THE STABLES
CHALK FARM ROAD
NW1 8AH
✆ 0171-485 5511

OPEN
Saturday and Sunday,
8am–6pm

BY TUBE
Camden Town (Northern
Line) and Chalk Farm
(Northern Line). Camden
Town tube station tends
to get very crowded,
so use Chalk Farm to
avoid the scrum.

BY BUS
24, 27, 29, 31, 134, 135,
168, 214, 253, 274 and C2

PARKING
Arriving by car is not
advisable as parking
is a problem. There is a
small underground car
park (100 spaces) at
38–40 Pratt Street,
off Camden High Street,
which is open from 9am
to 7pm at the weekends.

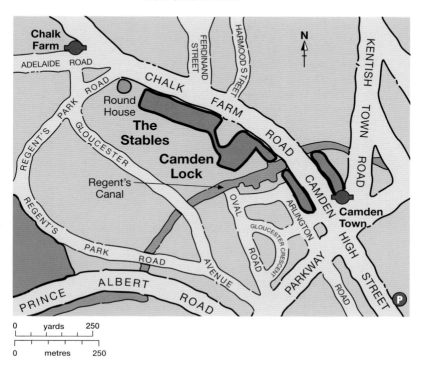

PAUL ARNOLD UNIT H36, THE STABLES. ℃ 0181-482 2745
A good selection of old advertising material from 1920s Huntley & Palmer tins to contemporary Coca-Cola classics. Some slot machines too, for those with large corners to fill.

CO$_2$ UNIT 98, THE STABLES. ℃ 0171-609 0857
Modern living on a grand scale. There is plenty of room to display large-scale furniture by modern masters and contemporary designers in the cavernous, brick-vaulted space of this gallery. Carlo Holdener, one of its founders, pointed out work by the architect Ron Arad and the glass designer Danny Lane, as well as Verner Panton's classic 'living' shelving system from the 1960s. If you're yet to be convinced by modern furniture, come here and see how impressive it can look.

THE HOME SERVICE UNIT H34, THE STABLES. ℃ 0171-267 0620
Paul Hughes's stand has real panache. He dressed the windows of London's best-known country antiques shop, The Lacquer Chest, and did a stint at Portobello (where his colour-coordinated stock was the envy of other traders), before taking on this space. Initially dealing 'mainly in 19th-century stuff', he now concentrates on classic 20th-century furniture, ceramics and accessories.

36

PLANET BAZAAR UNIT H10, THE STABLES. ℃ 0171-387 8326
Planet Bazaar is Maureen Silverman's well-stocked outlet for designer furniture, ceramics, glass, books and art dating from the Fifties to the Eighties. She sells everything from classic Alvar Aalto chairs and smart Swedish glass to Barbarella calendars and those terrible long-haired troll dolls that were *de rigueur* in the Seventies. Go for the classic or the camp.

KEITH ROUGHTON UNIT 89, THE STABLES. ℃ 0171-482 1498
Roughton's low-key, traditional oak furniture is a surprising and welcome find amid the mass of modern designs that crowd the rest of the market. Most of his stock is English and ranges from 19th-century neo-Gothic and Arts and Crafts to sturdy Twenties examples; he restores every piece by hand – 'It's really the only way you can do it.' Chairs are hung Shaker-style around the walls, making his barn-like shop seem even larger.

STABLE FIVE UNIT 5, THE STABLES. ℃ 01666-504462
'I'm allergic to people in silly hats', says Roger Denman, summing up the kind of tourists who now traipse through The Stables. His in-laws have dealt here since the market began in the early 1980s and, together with them, he specializes in reconditioned nickel- and chrome-plated accessories and fittings from the Twenties to the Fifties: towel rails, typewriters, fans. The family are philosophical about the changes here and ensure that their stock, at least, remains first-rate.

UNIT 78 THE STABLES. ℃ 0181-567 1296
Nick Cash and Sharaz Karim specialize in 20th-century furniture and accessories, from sofas and standard lamps to individual plastic egg cups. Look out for the selection of sleek Seventies watches with LEDs (light-emitting diodes) on the right as you enter.

NEARBUYS

Regent's Park Road and Primrose Hill (on which the Prince Regent intended to build the pavilion he eventually sited in Brighton) are a short walk from The Stables. The area is still extremely smart, but retains vestiges of a village atmosphere and is crammed with cafés, restaurants and interesting little shops. Tourists to Camden Market proper never seem to venture this far.

CAFÉ SEVENTY-NINE
79 REGENT'S PARK ROAD NW1 8UY
✆ 0171-586 8012
Particularly cosy café with a good selection of home-made cakes.

GRAHAM & GREEN
164 REGENT'S PARK ROAD NW1 8XN
0171-586 2960
Well-chosen furniture and decorative accessories. See also Portobello Nearbuys, p. 93.

LEMONIA
89 REGENT'S PARK ROAD NW1 8UR ✆ 0171-586 7454
Award-winning Greek restaurant. Hugely popular and always full.

IAN MANKIN
109 REGENT'S PARK ROAD, NW1 8UR
✆ 0171-722 0997
Mankin has single-handedly turned ticking stripes into the nation's favourite furnishing fabric. His designs are available by the yard in an unchanged

19th-century shop that was once a library.

MARINE ICES
8 HAVERSTOCK HILL NW3 2BL
✆ 0171-482 9003
Family-run ice-cream parlour and pizzeria.

NEAL'S YARD REMEDIES
68 CHALK FARM ROAD NW1 8AN
✆ 0171-284 2039
Old-fashioned health shop that sells essential oils, traditionally made soaps and other irresistible lotions and potions; liquids are packaged in distinctive blue glass bottles.

VICTORY MOTORCYCLES
49 KENTISH TOWN ROAD NW1 8NX
✆ 0171-284 2074
A specialist biker shop tucked away in a vacant railway arch. As well as classic Fifties and Sixties English bikes, such as Triumphs and Nortons, and Italian scooters, it also sells all the associated gear: original boots, goggles, badges and vintage and reproduction jackets by the likes of Lewis Leathers, 'the Louis Vuitton of biker jackets'.

KEITH ROUGHTON

CAMDEN PASSAGE

By the 16th century, the hilltop village of Islington was noted for its handsome manor houses with their gardens and orchards; Henry VIII owned properties in the area and reputedly installed his mistresses in one of them. In the 18th century, the village was also commended for its dairy farms, pure spring water and plethora of tea gardens and amusements. Sadly the borough as a whole is now considerably run down, but many fine early houses remain, the oldest of which, built *c.* 1657, are in Newington Green. Those in Cross Street, designed by James Spiller between 1774 and 1779, are particularly grand.

In 1855 the Metropolitan Cattle Market moved to Islington from Smithfield. Out of this developed the great Caledonian bric-a-brac Market, which the painter Walter Sickert, who owned or rented studios in the area, claimed to be his idea of heaven. The market, which is now remembered with great nostalgia for the quality and quantity of its goods, closed during World War II. Local bomb damage prevented it from reopening here and forced it south of the river to Bermondsey (see p. 25). The area was cleared for housing in 1965, but the old market's original iron railings (in Market Road), taverns and a clock tower remain.

Camden Passage, the Caledonian Market's successor, is a far more recent development. Established in the early 1960s, when the regentrification of central Islington began, it is already internationally renowned. Narrow and flagstoned, the once-quiet alley is now home to hundreds of smart antique dealers selling everything from whole suites of fine furniture to individual spoons, breadboards and thimbles. Trading takes place in shops and galleries, on the street and in the Mall – a classical, two-storey brick building that used to be a tramshed. On Saturdays, a specialist military market with over thirty-five dealers is also held in the Angel Arcade. Behind the Passage are Duncan Terrace (essayist Charles Lamb lived at no. 64 with his notoriously insane sister, Mary) and Colebrook Row, both the pride of 18th-century residential Islington. The house and chapel of John Wesley, the founder of Methodism, can be found further down City Road at no. 47; he is buried in the churchyard.

HOW & WHEN
TO GO TO
CAMDEN PASSAGE

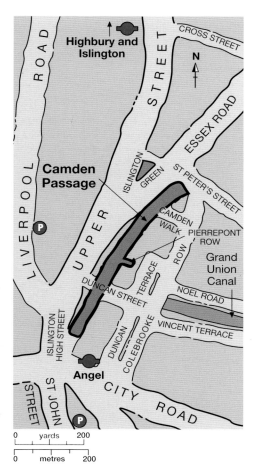

CAMDEN PASSAGE
UPPER STREET, NI
✆ 0171-359 9969

OPEN
Wednesday, 7am–2pm
Saturday, 8am–4pm

LONDON MILITARY MARKET
ANGEL ARCADE
CAMDEN PASSAGE, NI
✆ 01628-822503

OPEN
Saturday, 8am–2pm

BY TUBE
Angel (Northern Line)

BY BUS
4, 19, 30, 38, 43, 56, 73, 153, 171A, 214 and 274

PARKING
There are a limited number of spaces at the NCP car park on Layton Road, off Liverpool Road. If not, try the 24-hour car park on Owen Street, off Goswell Road.

ANNIE'S VINTAGE COSTUME AND TEXTILES
10 CAMDEN PASSAGE. ✆ 0171-359 0796

'I'm particularly interested in the Twenties', says Annie, 'I suppose it was the age of "the party."' Her rails of exquisitely beaded flapper dresses and silk-velvet coats reflect her passion for women's fine period evening wear and attract the most discerning and knowledgeable buyers, plus scouts from John Galliano and Alexander McQueen.

RAUL ARANTES **FRONT STAND, THE GEORGIAN GALLERIES**
✆ 0171-704 2322

Jewelry and glass by the renowned French maker René Lalique, who is best remembered for adopting the favourite motifs of Art Nouveau artists (among them, dragonflies, flowers and impossibly sinuous female nudes) and applying them to everything from scent bottles to screens.

IAN AULD **1 GATEWAY ARCADE, CAMDEN PASSAGE.** ✆ 0171-359 1440

Auld feels more like an enthusiatic collector than a hardened dealer. He was Head of Ceramics at London's Camberwell School of Art before he began to sell tribal art and early pottery. He still seems to have a potter's response to objects and forms, dotting his white-painted shop with satisfyingly sculptural pieces, such as African neck rests and Sokoto terracottas. His particular area of speciality is Nigeria, where he taught in the Seventies.

THE CORNER ROOM **3 THE GEORGIAN GALLERIES**
✆ 0171-704 2322

'That wall's never normally bare', explains Tracey White, the eye and energy behind this seductive little shop which is regularly crammed with frothy French furniture, lights, decorative accessories and toile de Jouy. 'At home', she laughs, 'I try to be a minimalist, but it's harder than giving up smoking.'

NIC COSTA **30 CAMDEN PASSAGE.** ✆ 0956-370506

Costa's slip of a shop was built before World War II as an entrance hall to the house above, but was never finished. It has since been used as a bookshop and even as an outlet for cat food, which was sold through a window at the front. Now it is home to Costa's impressive selection of coin-operated slot machines, on which he is a recognized authority, which date from 1880 to 1960. These line either side of the narrow space and are piled with his stock of tin toys, lead figures, board games and comics.

TONY D'ALMEIDA **STAND 6, ANGEL ARCADE.** ✆ 01304-611364

A pleasing mixture of decorative textiles, furniture and curiosities transforms this potentially unpromising brick-walled stand into a strangely cosy space.

CARLTON DAVIDSON ANTIQUES **33 CAMDEN PASSAGE**
✆ 0171-226 7491

Davidson explains that he first moved to this site when he was only seventeen, and he's now thirty-six: 'I can't remember a time when I wasn't here.' Though his glittering selection of reconditioned late 19th-century chandeliers, wall lights and lamps looks intimidatingly smart from outside, his shop feels remarkably casual. There are also some large-scale pieces of furniture (bureaux and uphol-stered chairs) among the ormolu and crystal.

DECODENCE 21 THE MALL, 359 UPPER STREET. ℂ 0171-354 4473

Gad Sassower's shop is 'the only one dealing exclusively in early plastics'. Dating from the turn of the 20th century to the 1940s, his stock of bold, brightly coloured everyday wares, such as radios, telephones, lamps and egg cups, comes from all over the world, although 'fifty per cent is English'. Bakelite and celluloid gave designers new freedom in mass production and many of Sassower's goods still feel fresh and modern.

JOHN GOODISON AND CHRIS PARASKEVA
16 CAMDEN PASSAGE. ℂ 0171-226 2423

A painted-metal table and a French horse-butcher's sign stood outside Goodison and Paraskeva's shop when I visited, seeming to typify its mix of bold, quirky stock. Though it specializes in lighting, leather club chairs, painted tin and papier mâché, the shop's three floors and garden can be crammed with anything from individual shells to a life-size lay figure.

GORDON GRIDLEY 28 AND 41 CAMDEN PASSAGE. ℂ 0171-226 0643

When I saw Gordon Gridley, he was laying out a 19th-century dinner service for a potential client. He finds serious and rare things – a set of six Delft plates rather than just one, for example. His 17th-, 18th- and 19th-century furniture, paintings and decorative objects have scale and honesty, like the George III corner cupboard I saw which still had its original paint inside and out.

43

PAM HEBBS 5 THE ANNEXE. ℂ 0181-361 3739

Pam Hebbs is something of a leading light in the teddy-bear field. She started dealing in 1979, long before the cult of the teddy took off, and now boasts regular clients in Japan, Singapore – and Harrogate. Besides period bears and

JUDITH LASSALLE   ANNIE'S VINTAGE COSTUME AND TEXTILES

golliwogs, she also commissions and stocks limited-edition 'artists' bears', which come dressed as anything from French waiters to mermaids.

JONATHAN'S BELOWSTAIRS STANDS 26 AND 33, BASEMENT
THE GEORGIAN VILLAGE. ℂ 0171-226 7835

Most of the basement of this three-floor arcade is given over to dealers in small collectables, but it is also home to these two stands of brightly coloured kitchen wares. The stock – enamel jars, coffee pots, breadboards, pottery – fills every inch of shelf space and even hangs from the ceiling.

JUDITH LASSALLE 7 PIERREPONT ARCADE. ℂ 0171-607 7121

Lassalle was on Portobello Road for thirty-five years before moving to this pleasing corner shop; on her last day there she put out huge bowls of sweets, decked her old stall with balloons and 'didn't sell a thing'. Her current site is equally distinctive and is painted a rich chalky pink – a colour advised by her friend Geoffrey Bennison, the legendary decorator. Her fortes are optical toys and games (the earliest one she has sold dates from 1693) and she can't resist rocking horses, which she loves doing up.

SHANE MEREDITH OUTSIDE THE GEORGIAN VILLAGE
ℂ 0370-737186

Most of Meredith's decorative mirrors, candlesticks and small-scale furniture now come from France. When we met, he had just returned from buying there: 'I came back last night, then got up at 4am to come here.' Decorators and other dealers buy regularly from him, so his affordable stock turns up elsewhere with higher price tags.

CHRISTOPHER PEARCE STAND 6, FIRST FLOOR
THE GEORGIAN VILLAGE. ℂ 0171-359 4560

A good stock of glass from the 1700s to the 1900s.

TEMPLAR ANTIQUES 28 THE MALL, 359 UPPER STREET
ℂ 0171-704 9448

18th- and 19th-century glass, from individual rummers to whole sets of drinking goblets, plus decanters and jugs.

YESTERDAY CHILD FRONT OF ANGEL ARCADE. ℂ 0171-354 1601

In the Seventies and Eighties, London was full of doll shops, but David and Gisela Barrington's is one of the few to survive. They continue to find and sell an astounding array of mostly 19th-century dolls, from German and French bisque examples to English wax dolls. All are sold in their original clothes or in period costumes made by the shop's dressmakers using authentic fabrics and patterns. They also run a doll clinic, where owners can have their charges repaired, restored and even rewigged. Miniature dolls' houses are also a speciality.

NEARBUYS

AFTER NOAH
121 UPPER STREET, N1 1QP
☎ 0171-359 4281
Sells new homewares with
a Forties and Fifties feel:
clocks, lights, furniture
and bedding.

ALFREDO'S SNACK BAR
**4 AND 6 ESSEX ROAD
N1 8LN**
☎ 0171-226 3496
It's worth choosing
something from the chips-
with-everything menu in
order to sit in the wipe-
clean Art Deco interior
of this café that has been
serving since 1920.

CRITERION AUCTION ROOMS
53 ESSEX ROAD, N1 2SF
☎ 0171-359 5707
A local auction house that
has furniture sales every
Monday.

MANUELA HOFER
**29–30 ST ALBANS PLACE
(OFF UPPER STREET), N1 0NX**
☎ 0171-930 1904
Hofer uses her own
photographic studio to display
original prints by a range of
contemporary British and
European photographers.

LIMONCELLO
**402 ST JOHN STREET
EC1V 4NJ**
☎ 0171-713 1678
Fresh Italian-style food
made using the best and
most authentic ingredients.
Eat lunch alfresco in the
back garden.

THE OLD TOOL CHEST
41 CROSS STREET, N1 2BB
☎ 0171-359 9313
Old-fashioned shop, tucked
away in one of Islington's least-
touched 18th-century streets
(see p. 39), which specializes
in 'ancient and modern tools
for all trades'.

TWENTYTWENTYONE
274 UPPER STREET, N1 2UA
☎ 0171-288 1996
The area's best source for
classic chairs, tables and
lamps by formative modern
designers.

THE OLD TOOL CHEST

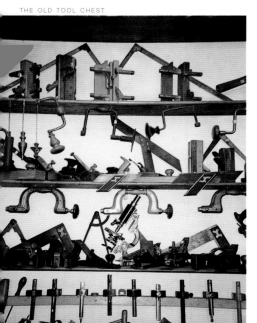

COVENT GARDEN

St. PAUL'S CHURCHYARD, COVENT GARDEN

Visitors are invited to enjoy the peace of these consecrated
grounds and to behave with consideration for others.
Please respect the many people who are buried beneath the
stones and lawns including some who perished in the
Great Plague of London in 1665.

NO DOGS · NO TRADERS · NO RADIOS

COVENT GARDEN

Though the crowds of visitors to Covent Garden seem like a late 20th-century phenomenon, this area has long been popular. It was once a convent garden belonging to the Abbey of St Peter but was granted to John Russell, first earl of Bedford, in 1553 following Henry VIII's dissolution of the monasteries (see p. 25). The fourth earl commissioned the great piazza and church of St Paul's from Inigo Jones, the king's surveyor of works, in the 1630s. Jones's revolutionary plan of an open square surrounded by tall houses (all now destroyed) was based on Italian models and shocked many Londoners; it was branded 'very imperfectly persu'd' by the contemporary diarist John Evelyn. Nevertheless, the piazza – the name applied to the residential arcades as well as to the square – soon became immensely sought after and by the end of the 17th century boasted the royal portrait painters Sir Peter Lely and Sir Godfrey Kneller among its residents.

A fruit and vegetable market was established here in the 1670s and functioned until 1974, when traders were moved to Battersea. By the mid-18th century, shops had sprung up and coffee houses appeared, including The Bedford, in which William Hogarth, Alexander Pope and David Garrick regularly met. In 1732, Covent Garden Theatre opened (the present Royal Opera House was constructed on its Bow Street site in 1857), cementing the area's popularity with actors and artists. Simultaneously, Covent Garden grew increasingly shameless, becoming home to gambling dens, taverns and a number of brothels, such as the notorious Mother Douglas's.

The market had taken over the area by the 19th century and new structures were needed to house the traders. Charles Fowler's Central Market buildings were completed in the 1830s, and although they are now crammed with boutiques and cafés, they retain their elegance and grandeur. There is a small antiques market here on Monday mornings which, despite the tourist clamour for tat, still throws up interesting things. Even more surprising is the Jubilee Market (opened in 1904) on the south side of the piazza, which attracts about a hundred dealers from Bermondsey and Portobello and is largely aimed at the trade. It too opens on Monday.

Try not to miss the garden at the west front of St Paul's, beneath which lie some of the victims of the 1665 Great Plague; it is an oasis of calm in the centre of the city.

HOW & WHEN TO GO TO
COVENT GARDEN

APPLE MARKET
(ALSO KNOWN AS CENTRAL MARKET)
THE PIAZZA, COVENT GARDEN, WC2
℡ 0171-240 7405

JUBILEE MARKET
JUBILEE HALL (OFF SOUTHAMPTON STREET) COVENT GARDEN, WC2
℡ 0171-836 2139

OPEN
Monday, 8am–4pm

BY TUBE
Covent Garden
(Piccadilly Line)

BY BUS
6, 9, 11, 13, 15, 23, 24, 29, 68, 77A, 91, 168, 171, 176, 188, 501, 505 and 521

PARKING
The closest NCP car park is off Upper St Martins Lane, but there is another one on Drury Lane (between Macklin Street and Parker Street).

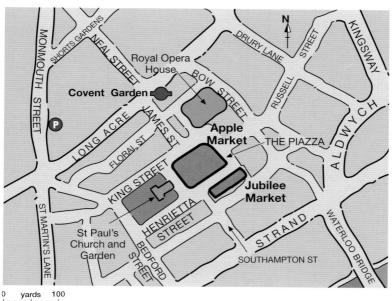

0   yards   100

0   metres   100

CHERYL ALL STALL 37, JUBILEE MARKET (EAST SIDE)
✆ 0181-813 8557

Though the postcards All sells here are just a sample of the full range she stocks, the number of subjects on offer is nevertheless impressive. Along with early embossed cards produced at the turn of the 20th century, there are categories for everything from topography and archaeology to Marilyn Monroe and silk textiles; even a number of cards for dog lovers, indexed by breed.

CAROL STALL 2, OUTSIDE JUBILEE MARKET
Carol has been here since the early 1980s selling all-white Twenties and Thirties lace, voiles and bedspreads that look appealingly home-made. Other dealers buy the fragments she piles on her stand to make period dolls' clothes and even wedding dresses.

SANDY FIELD STALL 12, JUBILEE MARKET
(CORNER OF SOUTHAMPTON STREET)
Prime source for affordable prints. Find work by Modern British masters, such as Eric Ravilious and William Nicholson, alongside topographical views and maps dating from 1850 to the turn of the 20th century. Field also has a selection of decorative prints (from *c.* 1900) for as little as £1 each.

H & C JUBILEE MARKET (EAST SIDE)
(ALSO AT CAMDEN PASSAGE ON SATURDAY.)
Double stand crowded with baskets and Twenties and Thirties domestic wares: brightly coloured tea and coffee jars, blue-and-white striped mugs, old kitchen utensils. Also a selection of Victorian and later buttons.

OWEN HARGREAVES

HEATHER'S TEDDIES

OWEN HARGREAVES STALL 16, APPLE MARKET. ☏ 0171-729 6491
(ALSO AT PORTOBELLO AND SPITALFIELDS.)

Every two or three months, Owen Hargreaves travels to the most remote reaches of West, Central and Southern Africa in search of small-scale tribal domestic wares and decorations; his stock feels genuinely exciting as a result. His supplies of well-rusted bracelets, trade-bead necklaces, rings, pitchers and masks are laid out on textiles from the same areas.

HEATHER'S TEDDIES STALL 28, APPLE MARKET. ☏ 0181-204 0106
(ALSO AT PORTOBELLO.)

An endearing array of unrestored early soft toys. Give a home to a teddy or golly by well-known makers such as Steiff, Merry Thought and Chiltern, or take pity on a Peter Rabbit who's seen better days.

HILARY KASHDEN STALL 138, BACK OF JUBILEE MARKET
☏ 0181-958 1018 **(ALSO AT PORTOBELLO.)**

A specialist in pewter plates, tankards and wares which date 'from Romano-British right up to the 1850s'. She shares the stand with her husband, whose expertise lies in early deeds and documents, some of which date back to the 1200s.

NIGEL MILLS STALL 119, JUBILEE MARKET
(SOUTHAMPTON STREET SIDE). ☏ 0181-504 2569

A fantastic and affordable source for antiquities and coins. Before he began dealing, Mills trawled the banks of the River Thames for long-lost relics; the first thing he found was a Charles II farthing, which 'turned out to be worth about 50p'. He was a founder member of the Society of Mud Larks, which enthusiasts formed in 1980 (see also Jane Stewart, p. 60), and is currently involved in the battle to legitimize metal detecting. Here he sells mainly medieval antiquities

SANDY FIELD   SANDY FIELD

(pilgrims' badges, horse adornments, thimbles, brooches, pins), but also has some Celtic and Roman pieces. He is fascinated by, but refreshingly unprecious about, the items he sells: 'I never forget that this stuff has come out of the ground.'

KIT SMITH STALL 8, JUBILEE MARKET (ALSO AT BERMONDSEY.)

'They're not valuable', says Kit Smith, looking down at her table of neatly arranged beads, bags, Twenties Bakelite and jewelry, 'they're all just pretty.' Displayed on one of the shawls or Oriental textiles she also sells, her quirky and interesting stock has a particular charm.

STEVEN WHEELER STALL 111, JUBILEE MARKET. (ALSO AT THE LONDON MILITARY MARKET, CAMDEN PASSAGE.)

Wheeler's impressive stock of medals and military decorations occupies two stands. He has been specializing in them since 1982 and handles orders from all over the world. The earliest pieces date from 1750, but others are later and commemorate such recent conflicts as the Gulf War of 1991.

NEARBUYS

ARAM DESIGNS
3 KEAN STREET
WC2B 4AT
✆ 0171-240 3933
Housed in a former
warehouse, Aram Designs
is devoted to modern
furniture. It also owns
the exclusive rights to
reproduce the furniture
designs by the formative
Twenties architect
Eileen Gray.

THE DOVER BOOKSHOP
18 EARLHAM STREET
WC2H 9LN
✆ 0171-836 2111
A brilliantly quirky
shop that specializes

in black-and-white
illustrated books about
patterns, graphics and
costume.

THE DUFFER OF ST GEORGE
29 SHORTS GARDENS
WC2H 9AP
✆ 0171-379 4660
Trend-setting men's
clothes shop where
English tailoring meets
urban sportswear.

MONMOUTH COFFEE HOUSE
27 MONMOUTH STREET
WC2H 9DD
✆ 0171-836 5272
Specialist coffee shop.

THE PHOTO-GRAPHERS' GALLERY
5 GREAT NEWPORT STREET
WC2H 7HY
✆ 0171-831 1772
London's premier space for
showing work by both new
photographic talents and
established names. There is
a print sales room upstairs.

SIR JOHN SOANE'S MUSEUM
13 LINCOLN'S INN FIELDS
WC2A 3BP
✆ 0171-405 2107
The house of the distinguished
architect Sir John Soane
(1753–1837) has one of the
most evocative interiors in
London. He transformed
the building into a fantastic
repository for his antiquities,
statuary and pictures (Hogarths
and Turners among them),
using mirrored panels and
hidden light sources to intensify
the delights of his collection.
A jewel; don't miss it.

WORLD
27 LITCHFIELD STREET
WC2A 9NW
✆ 0171-379 5588
Strangely pleasant shop selling
global oddities; popular with
clubbers craving ethnic glitter
to have at home or to wear out.

ZWEMMERS
24 LITCHFIELD STREET
WC2H 9NJ
✆ 0171-379 7886
London's best-known
art bookshop.

GRAYS ANTIQUE MARKETS

Oxford Street is the capital's best-known, busiest and arguably least-pleasurable shopping street. Built on the site of a Roman road that ran from Hampshire to the Suffolk coast, it was not until the 19th century that it began to develop into the serious shopping experience it is today. Selfridges, the grand, confident and imposing department store, designed by R.F. Atkinson and the Chicago architect Daniel Burnham, is the only Temple of Retail to survive from those earlier days; a chiming clock with an eleven-foot-high figure of The Queen of Time by Gilbert Bayes still stands over the shop's main entrance.

From Marble Arch to Regent Street, the south side of Oxford Street borders Mayfair, which takes its name from the cattle market authorized by James II in 1686 that was held there every May until the 1730s. This area was severely expanded in the 18th century, but, surprisingly, retains an air of Georgian refinement with its three squares (Hanover, Berkeley and Grosvenor), its porticoed church of St George's (1721–1724, Hanover Square) and its collection of tall town houses. Good examples of these can be found in Upper Brook Street and no. 25 Brook Street, where the composer Handel lived and wrote his *Messiah*, hopes to open as a museum in the year 2000.

Arriving at Bond Street tube station, you are on Mayfair's doorstep. South Molton Street, behind the station, was rebuilt in the 1900s but still has many of its original small Georgian houses; William Blake lived (in squalor) on the second floor of no. 17 in 1803. The street is now pedestrianized and one of London's best for designer clothes.

Grays Antique Markets, in nearby South Molton Lane, are housed in the glorious brick-built former showrooms and factory of John Boulding & Sons, the water-closet manufacturers. Occupying two separate sites, Grays and Grays Mews, the antique markets opened in 1976. Over two hundred specialists deal here in a range of small, precious stock: jewelry, silver, clocks, watches, dolls and antiquities. Although it is only a short step from Oxford Street, Grays is relatively unknown. Smart and glamorous, it can initially feel intimidating; one dealer implied that it was deliberately kept secret to attract high-profile customers. But for many stallholders who also sell at Portobello or Bermondsey (so beware of coming on a Friday morning, when Bermondsey takes priority), this is simply a useful West End base and prices are as reasonable here as at other markets.

HOW & WHEN TO GO TO
GRAYS ANTIQUE MARKETS

GRAYS ANTIQUE MARKETS
**58 DAVIES STREET
AND 1–7 DAVIES MEWS
W1Y 2LP**
✆ 0171-629 7034

OPEN
Monday to Friday,
10am–6pm
Closed weekends

BY TUBE
Bond Street (Jubilee
and Central Lines)

BY BUS
6, 7, 8, 10, 12, 13, 15, 23,
73, 94, 98, 113, 135, 137,
139, 159 and 189

PARKING
There is an underground car
park at the London Marriott
hotel, off Balderton Street. If
not, try the multi-storey car
park on Welbeck Street.

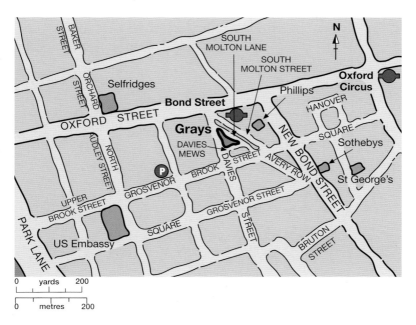

AURA ANTIQUES STANDS L10–11. ✆ 0171-495 6083

Aura has been specializing in Far Eastern art and artefacts since the early Eighties; before that she studied photography and went to Japan to learn wood carving. She is particularly interested in Tibetan Bhuddism, so regularly stocks Tibetan meditative pictures, or *tankas*, but also sells Mughal jewelry, amber and old ivory bracelets from Ethiopia and Nagaland.

DON BAYNEY STANDS C22–23. ✆ 0171-629 3644

Bayney became interested in Japanese swords after studying martial arts and has been collecting them for thirty years; the examples he sells date from the 15th to the 19th century. Traditionally, he explains, swords were handed down from generation to generation, but at the end of World War II, despite their antiquity, many were confiscated and destroyed by the Allies, which accounts for their rarity today.

LINDA BEE STANDS J20–21. ✆ 0171-629 5921

The vintage fashion accessories on this unmissable Schiaparelli-pink stand have attracted everyone from Joan Rivers to the vice-president of the United Nations. Owner Linda Bee was born in Soho and explains that she acquired her eye for colour from the Georgian doors in nearby Bedford Square. Visit for Fifties designer jewelry, handbags and a slice of Hollywood heyday glamour.

BILL BENNETT AND KEITH THOROGOOD
STANDS C31–32. ✆ 0171-408 1880

A useful, and surprisingly rare, partnership who engrave on glass and metal.

PATRICK BOYD-CARPENTER STAND 127. ✆ 0171-491 7623

Boyd-Carpenter began dealing in the late 1980s, giving up his place at the Courtauld Institute when he became hooked. He started selling watercolours and prints, which at the time were underrated, but has gradually diversified his stock, much of which he buys on the Continent. He finds rare and interesting small works of art and occasionally things on a larger scale; when we met, he had just invested in a Romanesque tympanum.

BRITANNIA STANDS 101–2 AND 159–60. ✆ 0171-629 6772

Majolica – Léon Arnoux's vividly glazed and madly inventive pottery – was launched at London's Great Exhibition of 1851; it was produced until 1890. Britannia specialize in the ware as well as selling contemporary Minton, Wedgwood and commemorative pieces.

CHRISTOPHER CAVEY STANDS 177–78. ✆ 0171-495 1743

A collector's cabinet of a shop selling 'all sorts of strange things' to do with gem stones: lumps of quartz, pieces of jade, disks of moss agate, even lava cameos from the late 1700s.

A. DOUCH STANDS L22–23. ✆ 0171-493 9413

Douch specializes in English flatware (cutlery) and interesting small jewelry, largely 18th-century. 'We get more excited [if silver is] earlier than the English stamp duty of 1784', he explains, casually pulling table forks (*c.* 1705) and pistol-handled knives (*c.* 1745) from plastic bags. I first came across him at an antiques fair; his stock of fine, early objects stood out as vividly there as it does here.

BRITANNIA

J. FIRST STAND 310. ℂ 0171-409 2772

Old-fashioned and enviously knowledgeable silver dealer who concentrates more on good stock than on flashy display. He specializes in Chinese and Japanese silver (one culture will never buy silver made by the other, he explains), but also has fine English examples. Among other things that I came across, when I visited, were a set of mid-18th-century candlesticks made for the German market; an unusual three-piece wine funnel; and a simple Regency teapot with its date engraved on the bottom.

PETER GAUNT STANDS 120–21. ℂ 0171-629 1072

There's a wonderfully old-fashioned feeling to this shop selling fine silver and objects of vertu. Some pieces are displayed in glass cabinets, others are just piled on the floor.

THE GILDED LILY STANDS 144–45. ℂ 0171-499 6260

'I don't really mind what age things are', says Korin Harvey of her distinctive selection of signed designer jewelry. Some pieces are old, while others, such as a Lalaounis bracelet inspired by classical Greek gold work (*c.* 1970), simply appeal to her eye for the dramatic. She also stocks South Sea pearls the size of marbles, which are strung specially for her.

GORDONS MEDALS LTD STANDS G16–17. ℂ 0171-495 0900

A wide selection of medals, most of which come with exhaustively researched details of their recipients, and general militaria: helmets, photographs, even a rare German paratrooper's folding bike of *c.* 1941.

GUEST & GRAY STANDS H25–28 AND J10–13. ℂ 0171-408 1252

Deals in Oriental ceramics and works of art, but also often has good European ceramics in stock.

HARRISON'S BOOKS STANDS J20–21. ℐ 0171-629 1374

Fishing books, illustrated children's classics, travel, literature and rare or interesting bindings, such as *The Yellow Book*, and a limited-edition portfolio by Wyndham Lewis of personalities from the Thirties.

POSTERS FOR COLLECTORS STANDS 1–7.
℮ 0171-355 2488

Allie and John Barnicoat collected posters before they began dealing in them (he is also the author of a standard work on the subject). They specialize in European posters in near-perfect condition; I saw one by Henri Ibels (the man credited with encouraging Toulouse-Lautrec to take up lithography), dated 1894, that was entirely perfect.

RADFORD-MUIR STAND 108. ℐ 0171-499 0269

Chris Radford was 'evading school' when he saw Brighton Pavilion's 1972 exhibition of Susie Cooper's boldly decorated Art Deco ceramics. He has been selling the wares she designed ever since.

SHAPIRO & CO. STAND 380. ℐ 0171-491 2710

Sheldon Shapiro has been dealing since the age of ten, when he began helping his father at Portobello. He stocks interesting and unusual jewelry, silver and works of art, but occasionally buys and sells goods outside his regular field, such as a complete bolt of Art Nouveau printed cotton. 'Important people have been buying here for years', he says of Grays. 'They just don't tell anyone. It's a well-kept secret.'

SHIRAZ ANTIQUES STANDS L10–11. ℐ 0171-495 0635

Ancient and Islamic works of art.

JANE STEWART STANDS L25–27. ℐ 0171-355 3333

Jane Stewart became interested in pewter when she met some of the enthusiasts who regularly dig for early remains on the banks of the River Thames – 'mud larks' as they're known (see Nigel Mills, p. 51). Now, from her cosy terracotta-coloured stand, she sells early oak chests, tapestry cushions and Delft, but specializes in pewter platters, tankards and vessels. She is also fascinated by the lead badges medieval pilgrims wore on their excursions. The one she showed me, with an intricate Gothic arch and figures, was cast in honour of the shrine of Our Lady of Walsingham and dated from the 14th century.

SULTANI ANTIQUES STANDS K28–31. ℐ 0171-491 3847

Enticingly arranged jumble of Islamic and Roman antiquities, from trade beads and coins to large-scale sculpture. Be prepared for a language barrier.

THE THIMBLE SOCIETY STANDS 134–36. ℐ 0171-493 0560

A stall devoted to thimbles and other fine sewing tools, run by the director of the Thimble Society (yes, there is one), Bridget McConnel.

WHEATLEY ANTIQUES STAND 106. ℐ 0171-629 1352

A good selection of Oriental works of art and ceramics, including, when I visited, a pair of 18th-century polychrome-decorated porcelain barbers' bowls made for the European market.

NEARBUYS

There are two good cafés in the market, one in Grays and the other in Grays Mews. Both are downstairs.

BROWNS
SOUTH MOLTON STREET
WIY IHE ✆ **0171-491 7833**
One of the capital's premier designer clothes shops; it is famous for buying and displaying Galliano's first collection. Among others, it stocks Helmut Lang and Comme des Garçons, for men and women.

CHRISTIE'S
8 KING STREET
ST JAMES'S, SWIY 6QT
✆ **0171-839 9060**
This, the grandest of the salerooms, was established in 1766. Van Gogh's *Sunflowers* sold here for a record £24 million.

JO'S CAFÉ
SECOND FLOOR
FENWICKS
63 NEW BOND STREET
WIA 3BS
✆ **0171-495 5402**
The elegant department store has an equally smart café serving fresh food with an Italian flavour.

PAUL SMITH SALE SHOP
23 AVERY ROW, WIX 9HB
✆ **0171-493 1287**
Samples, seconds and last season's must-haves by the famous British tailor.

PHILLIPS
IOI NEW BOND
STREET, WIY OAS
✆ **0171-629 6602**
Reliable auction house with branches nationwide; far more approachable than some of its rivals.

SOTHEBY'S
34 NEW BOND STREET
WIA 2AA ✆ **0171-493 8080**
The world-renowned auction house's monthly Colonnade sales (where estimates range from £200 to £2,000) are surprisingly affordable.

VINCI ANTIQUES
27 AVERY ROW, WIX 9HD
✆ **0171-499 1041**
This old curiosity shop of jewelry, ceramics and oddments is a surprising find in the middle of the West End.

LINDA WIGGLESWORTH
34 BROOK STREET
LONDON, WIY IYA
✆ **0171-408 0177**
Leading specialist in antique Chinese textiles and costume.

HARRISON'S BOOKS

OLD CROWTHER MARKET
LILLIE ROAD
ANTIQUARIUS

At the beginning of the 20th century, the stonemason Thomas Crowther bought a grand 1840s villa set back from North End Road from which to sell garden ornaments, statuary, furniture and architectural salvage. World War II threatened to close the business, but it survived by making parts for weapons and, after 1945, began to thrive again. As bomb-damaged buildings were cleared away all over Britain, Crowther's was able to buy vast quantities of fine fittings from country houses and buildings in London, including some in Mayfair's Grosvenor Square (see p. 55), which were pulled down to make way for the American Embassy. The company's notebook from the period lists hundreds of clearance sales and records how it purchased panelling and fire surrounds from, among others, 4 South Quay, Great Yarmouth, the house in which the death warrant of Charles I was signed.

Although Crowther's left in 1992, the building remains, complete with open gallery, ornate Coade-stone frieze and Italianate garden; it is a surprising and surreal site in this dingy, traffic-logged part of Fulham. A market was set up in the house (now painted a vibrant blue) a year later. Small and undistinguished, it nevertheless has two or three interesting dealers and is worth visiting for the surroundings alone.

In buying terms, nearby Lillie Road is a better bet. Crowther's founded an ironworks here in the 1900s, but today much of its length is taken up with public-housing projects. At the far end, however, is a red-brick terrace of shops which are now almost entirely devoted to selling antiques: a kind of collectors' Golden Mile. Twenty-four independent decorative dealers sell here, and although their shops cannot constitute a market, there is a dynamism and sense of community in Lillie Road that many true markets lack.

A ten-minute drive takes you to the Kings Road and the polite face of Chelsea. 'The King's Road' was begun in the late 17th century as Charles II's private route to Hampton Court. Its transformation into

TITANIC

a main artery started in around 1830, and over a century later, in the Sixties, it developed into London's most swinging shopping street. Surprisingly, some early 18th-century houses survive, such as nos. 211, 213 and 215, in which Dr Thomas Arne lived and possibly composed 'Rule Britannia'. But, in recent years, even the Kings Road has succumbed to chain-store mediocrity and many of the independent shops on which its reputation was founded have now closed. There used to be various antiques centres here too – Antiquarius remains and is home to 120 specialists (and a bureau de change) and in 1997 the Bourbon-Hanby Antiques Centre opened in Sydney Street (see Nearbuys, p. 71).

G WHIZZ

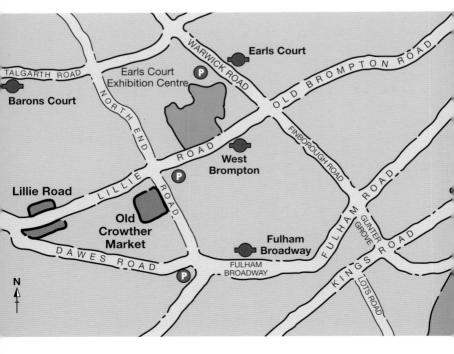

HOW & WHEN TO GO TO

OLD CROWTHER MARKET
LILLIE ROAD
ANTIQUARIUS

OLD CROWTHER MARKET
282 NORTH END ROAD
SW6 INH
☎ 0171 385 8481

OPEN
Monday and Wednesday to Saturday, 10.30am–5pm Sunday, 11am–4.30pm

LILLIE ROAD
sw6. ☎ 0171-381 2500

OPEN
Most shops open Monday to Saturday, 10am–5pm

ANTIQUARIUS
131–141 KINGS ROAD
SW3 4PW
☎ 0171-351 5353

OPEN
Monday to Saturday, 10am–6pm

OLD CROWTHER MARKET & LILLIE ROAD

BY TUBE
Fulham Broadway (District Line)

BY BUS
11, 14, 28, 74, 190, 211, 295, 391 and C4

PARKING
There are parking meters in the area or car parks at the Earls Court Exhibition Centre, at the Earls Court Park Inn and also off the North End Road, between the Fulham Road and Dawes Road.

ANTIQUARIUS

BY TUBE
Sloane Square (Circle and District Lines)

BY BUS
11, 19, 22, 49, 211, 249, 319 and 345

PARKING
Mainly metered, but there is also a car park in Sydney Street.

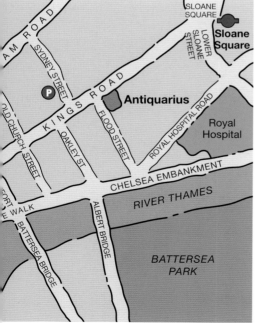

OLD CROWTHER MARKET

G WHIZZ REAR OF GARDEN. ℰ 0171-386 5020 (THURSDAY–SATURDAY)
'I sell secondhand bikes to get around London on', says owner Gordon Davey
from beneath the mass of spare wheels hanging from the ceiling of his secluded
workroom. Stock, new models as well as vintage, is lined up outside.

TITANIC THE LONG GALLERY. ℰ 0171-385 8481
Denis Cochrane has been fascinated by the *Titanic* since he was a child and now
lectures and prepares exhibitions on the subject, using his own collection of
objects from the doomed ship, such as a life jacket and a chess table made out
of wood salvaged from the wreck. Here he sells memorabilia related to the vessel
and to other ocean liners, from flags to menus.

TNT ENTRANCE
Tass and Tarnya are the only dealers who have remained here since the market
opened in 1995. Selling Levis, leathers and assorted retro clothing at charity-shop
prices, their space attracts a string of regular buyers.

LILLIE ROAD

BAROQUE 'N' ROLL 291 LILLIE ROAD, SW6 7LL. ℰ 0171-381 5008
If Catherine the Great had designed sets for pop-music videos, they would look
like the interior of this shop. A seriously theatrical creation, it is packed with
early textiles (damasks, velvets, even a piece of 18th-century Russian brocade),
chandeliers and striking furniture. 'Scale and texture are my forte', its interior-
designer owner Alyson tells me, as Elvis classics play in the background.

AT THE MOVIES   BAROQUE 'N' ROLL

ANDREW BEWICK AND JONATHAN LEE

287 LILLIE ROAD, SW6 7LL. ✆ 0171-385 9025

There is a distinctive, quietly English feel to the painted furniture, upholstered chairs, foxed mirrors and oddities that Bewick and Lee sell. 'Lots of it's country stuff', Lee tells me, 'but vicarage bedroom rather than cottage.' Much of their stock is 19th-century, but they also have later decorative pieces, such as a 1930s screen based on an 18th-century Chinoiserie original.

ZAL DAVAR 273 LILLIE ROAD, SW6 7LL. ✆ 0171-381 2500

Davar has been a driving force behind the promotion of Lillie Road and, I'm told, 'is one of the last gentlemen dealers left'. For forty years he kept a shop on the Kings Road that specialized in 19th-century furniture, but his stock has grown to encompass a more diverse range, 'anything from a 16th-century coffer to a piece made between the wars'.

DECORATIVE ANTIQUES 284 LILLIE ROAD, SW6 7PX. ✆ 0171-610 2694

Long, narrow shop packed with large-scale French or English country furniture and punchy decorative items.

HELRAY LTD 295 LILLIE ROAD, SW6 7LL. ✆ 0171-381 5277

Helray's owner Andrew Harley had a flat on Portobello Road in the 1980s and sold things from his doorstep; I bought a deckchair from him there for £5. He was one of the first dealers to move to Lillie Road and now has a whole shop to display his oddly pleasing combination of stock: old terracotta pots, an Eames lounger, a French Art Deco washbasin, and lots of leather chairs.

CATHERINE NIMMO 277 LILLIE ROAD, SW6 7LL. ✆ 0171-385 2724

There is a particular elegance to the mainly 18th-century French painted furniture that Nimmo sells along with contemporary mirrors, old French pottery, lights and textiles. Her window and shop displays are as subtle as the goods she deals in.

ANTIQUARIUS

AT THE MOVIES STAND V3. ✆ 0171-376 7670

Liza Tesei collected film posters before she began dealing in them. Most of her stock dates from the Fifties and Sixties and, though the majority is American or English, she also manages to find slick examples from the Continent: a Belgian poster for *Breakfast at Tiffany's* and a German one announcing *Steve McQueen ist Bullitt*. All are backed on either paper or linen, 'depending on the size'.

BRIAN GORDON STAND G1. ✆ 0171-351 5808

Gordon moved here from the now-defunct Chenil Gallery to continue specializing in (mostly English) antique silver and old Sheffield plate. He gets good simple pieces (Georgian coffee pots and cream jugs), but also has an eye for more decorative curiosities, such as the late 19th-century Austrian table decoration in the form of a chick that he showed me.

HAYMAN & HAYMAN STAND K3. ✆ 0171-351 6568

A good selection of small photograph frames from the Twenties to the Fifties and a range of Art Deco-style diamanté designs, which are made to order.

EMERICH VIDICH

70

DON KELLY STAND M3. ℂ 0171-352 4690 (ALSO AT PORTOBELLO.)

Kelly has always dealt in books on the applied arts, which means his stock is one of the most comprehensive in London. As well as new titles on specialist subjects, such as ceramics, silver, upholstery and textiles, his stock also includes rare trade catalogues that date back as far as the 1780s. If he hasn't got, or can't find, what you're looking for, it's unlikely that anyone can.

SUE NORMAN STAND L4. ℂ 0171-352 7217

Norman sells only 19th-century blue-and-white transfer-printed earthenware; displayed en masse, it looks bold and pleasing. As well as plates, platters and jugs, she has rarer pieces: drainers, knife rests, even miniatures made for dolls' houses.

EMERICH VIDICH STANDS A14–17. ℂ 0171-376 4252

Vidich opens the definitive book on British prints to reveal that its endpapers are decorated with the same scene of *The Gloucester Coffee House, Piccadilly* that he currently has in stock. 'And if you want a Goltzius', he continues, 'I can bring you a Goltzius.' His range of old-master and decorative prints is impressive and he also restores and traditionally frames works to order.

GEOFFREY WATERS STANDS F1–6. ℂ 0171-376 5467

Smart, and potentially intimidating, stand of fine Chinese porcelain. Many of the pieces were made for export in the 1700s, but others were intended for the home market. The range of decoration on the wares is staggering, from wild, polychrome Imari patterns to monochrome figure scenes based on early Western prints.

X.S. BAGGAGE CO. STANDS B1–6. ℂ 0171-376 8781 (ALSO AT GRAYS.)

The spectacular selection of antique Vuitton trunks, crocodile-skin suitcases and leather hat boxes piled in and around this double stand convey quite how glamorous travel must have been before the days of the plastic hold-all.

NEARBUYS

BONHAMS LOTS ROAD
65–69 LOTS ROAD
SW10 0RN
🕾 0171-393 3900
This is where the Knightsbridge-based auction house holds less grand sales of pictures, frames, ceramics and architectural fittings.

BOURBON-HANBY ANTIQUES CENTRE
151 SYDNEY STREET
SW3 6NT
🕾 0171-352 2106
Opened in 1997, the Bourbon-Hanby Antiques Centre supports forty dealers and a courtyard café. Worth a browse.

CHELSEA FARMERS MARKET
SYDNEY STREET
(BETWEEN THE BOURBON-HANBY ANTIQUES CENTRE AND THE CHELSEA GARDENER), SW3 6NR
A clutch of small cafés and restaurants, many with tables alfresco.

CHELSEA GARDENER
125 SYDNEY STREET
SW3 6NR
🕾 0171-352 5656
Essentials for the smart urban gardener, from seeds and plants to conservatory furniture and outside lighting.

DELITALIA
325 LILLIE ROAD
SW6 7NR
Old-fashioned and well-stocked Italian deli that

prepares takeaway sandwiches on a variety of good breads, such as ciabatta and oregano rolls.

FLOWER STALL
CORNER OF CHELSEA MANOR STREET
(OPPOSITE OLD TOWN HALL)
Reasonably priced fresh flowers (a well-kept Chelsea secret).

GREEN & STONE
259 KINGS ROAD
SW3 5EL
🕾 0171-352 0837
Pleasingly old-fashioned art shop and framers that opened in 1934 to cater for the plethora of local artists. It now also sells small-scale antiques, particularly 19th-century glasses and ceramics.

HABITAT CAFÉ
UPSTAIRS IN HABITAT
206 KINGS ROAD
SW3 5XP 🕾 0171-351 1211
The nation's smoothest chain store now sells not only good design, but also irresistible Italian food.

LOTS ROAD GALLERIES
71 LOTS ROAD
SW10 0RN
🕾 0171-351 7771
Small auction house that has sales of furniture, pictures, etc., every Monday.

PICASSO
127 KINGS ROAD
SW3 4PW
🕾 0171-352 4921
Café-cum-institution. Sit inside or watch the action

from one of the tables on the street.

PIMLICO ROAD
SW15
This street behind Sloane Square is packed with smart, inspiring antique shops. Good for window-shopping even if you can't afford to buy.

STEINBERG & TOLKEIN
193 KINGS ROAD
SW3 5EB
🕾 0171-376 3660
Serious, and frequently stunning, vintage clothing and costume jewelry, from a three-tiered diamanté tiara from the Folies-Bergère to a fur-trimmed coat owned by Mandy Rice-Davies.

THE STOCK POT
273 KINGS ROAD
SW3 5EN
🕾 0171-823 3175
The cheapest place to get a square meal in Chelsea. Popular with the Prada-handbag set as well as with impoverished students.

PORTOBELLO

Notting Hill Gate was down at heel thirty years ago but is now one of the most fashionable – and consequently most expensive – areas in London. Its centrality, fine early Victorian houses and market subculture, combined with a vivacious ethnic identity, have made it irresistible to everyone from politicians to thrusting young media stars.

Portobello Road, which runs north from grand Notting Hill Gate to Golborne Road (its poorer relation) was originally a track leading to Porto Bello farm, named in honour of Admiral Vernon's capture of the city of Porto Bello in the Gulf of Mexico in 1739. The writer George Orwell lodged at no. 10 Portobello Road from 1927 to 1928 with a Mrs Craig. You pass the house with its blue plaque if you walk from Notting Hill Gate tube station. The Electric Cinema at no. 191 is also worth noting, being one of Britain's oldest purpose-built cinemas; it was designed by G.S. Valentin in 1910–1911.

A market was established here in the early 1870s, selling mainly fruit and vegetables. The antiques market did not get under way until 1948, when dealers were displaced by the closure of the legendary Caledonian Market in Islington (see p. 39). Today, however, it is the antiques that attract tourists to Portobello.

On Friday, trading runs between Westway and Golborne Road. Dealers turn up to complain that they can never find anything any more and, paradoxically, to buy stock for their stands at other markets or for 'up the road' on Saturday. You may come across good antiques on Friday (remnants of a Coptic cope were once unearthed among some Seventies curtains), but it is better for modern design classics, interesting textiles and covetable junk. Wiser to come for the atmosphere, which is the best of any central London market, and to learn what you should be wearing from the secondhand clothes dealers who sell here.

Saturday is more reliable, with about two thousand specialists housed in arcades and on pitches in the street; but be warned, it gets seriously crowded. You will find experts in every field and stock as varied as you could imagine, from early aboriginal boomerangs to Bow porcelain. Guidebooks always tell you not to expect bargains here, but neither should you presume you are going to be conned. With so many stalls, dealers need to price their stock competitively.

HOW & WHEN TO GO TO
PORTOBELLO

PORTOBELLO
**PORTOBELLO ROAD
AND NEIGHBOURING
STREETS, W10 AND W11**
✆ 0171-727 7684

OPEN
Friday, 7.30am–1pm,
from Westway to
Golborne Road
Saturday, 6am–2pm,
from Chepstow Villas
to Blenheim Crescent
The antique shops on
Westbourne Grove and
Golborne Road tend to
open earlier on market
days, but also trade during
the week (many close on
Mondays).

BY TUBE
Notting Hill Gate (Central,
Circle and District Lines)
Westbourne Park
(Metropolitan Line)
Ladbroke Grove
(Metropolitan Line)

BY BUS
12, 27, 28, 31, 52,
70, 94 and 302
to **Notting Hill Gate**;
23, 28 and 31
to **Westbourne Park**;
7, 23, 52, 70, 295 and
302 to **Ladbroke Grove**

PARKING
Portobello is a popular and
crowded residential area
and parking is often for
residents only. There are
some parking meters (and
a large number of traffic
wardens) but spaces get
taken early, so it's best
not to arrive by car.

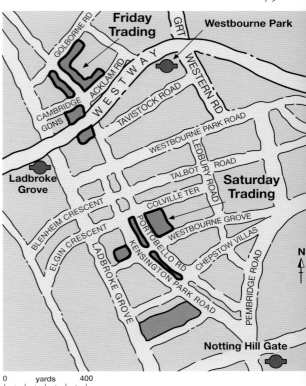

PORTOBELLO – FRIDAY

AFFINITY UNDER WESTWAY. ℂ 0956-368461

Initially, Fiona Carenza wanted to sell new clothes by young designers. When no one bought any on her first day here, she swapped to selling her own cast-offs which 'sold out' immediately; she has been dealing in secondhand women's wear ever since. Trained at St Martins College of Art and Kingston Polytechnic, she has a sharp, clever eye and sells fashionably chic Thirties to Seventies clothing and updates vintage pieces to fit with current tastes, turning men's trousers into pedal pushers or dying silk slips so that they can be worn as dresses. New makers sometimes share her stand. When we met, Claire, a milliner, was selling her feathery hair pieces in the corner.

VIVA BARNETT CORNER OF ACKLAM ROAD (OPPOSITE WESTWAY). ℂ 0181-333 9580

When a buyer from Donna Karan saw this stand she branded it her favourite in the market. Barnett's stock of secondhand women's clothes, bags and shoes has become increasingly refined since she started here; she now treats her pitch like a shop window and colour coordinates her display each week. Contemporary designer labels are sometimes stocked, but she is particularly good at finding interesting Sixties and Seventies wear.

LES COUSSIS DU CHIEN 65 GOLBORNE ROAD ℂ 0181-964 8192

Jerome Dodd designed and made furniture before buying this green-tiled corner shop that used to be a bakery in the 19th century. 'They made cakes here for Queen Victoria', he explains, 'the ovens are still downstairs.' His stock of furniture, architectural salvage and classic modern lighting (much of which spills on to the pavement outside) is distinctive and strangely focused, although it can include anything from a stone trough or a typesetter's desk to a set of Fifties chairs. 'I never know what I'm going to buy', he says, 'so you never know what you'll find.'

GRAHAM AND DANI UNDER WESTWAY (CORNER OF CAMBRIDGE GARDENS). ℂ 0171-633 0503

This couple used to sell the smartest secondhand men's suits in the market – Savile Row quality at a fraction of cost price – plus shirts, cashmere jumpers and coats. Increasingly they are also importing new work- and sportswear from America, such as classic Carhartt, and limited numbers of Nike trainers. Consignments of interesting unused pieces also turn up, such as the stock of Sixties sports bags I saw.

HARRY ACKLAM ROAD (OFF PORTOBELLO ROAD)

Harry's collection of reconditioned old domestic and garden tools are immaculately laid out by category: chisels, saws, hammers, even a group of parrot-beak secateurs. He only sells here once a fortnight, but his stock and prices (little costs more than £5) are worth waiting for.

IDENTITY JUNCTION OF PORTOBELLO ROAD AND CAMBRIDGE GARDENS. ℂ 0171-792 4604

Clothes by Vivienne Westwood. From early Let it Rock pieces, c. 1971 ('they go for thousands'), to Buffalo Girl garb, Pirate shirts and bits from recent collections.

MARGARET AND KIM   LES COUSSIS DU CHIEN

PAUL LAU PITCH 170, PORTOBELLO ROAD
(JUNCTION OF OXFORD GARDENS). ℂ 0171-633 0503

Lau's distinctive and unpredictable mixture of design classics means that the Valentine typewriter that Ettore Sottsass designed for Olivetti (*c.* 1969) can be found alongside a money box in the shape of ET.

MARGARET AND KIM UNDER WESTWAY
(OPPOSITE 9 THORPE CLOSE). ℂ 01273 624006

Other traders look forward to the arrival of this pair of Brighton textile dealers who come to Portobello on the first Friday of every month. I have been buying from Margaret since she started coming here in the early Eighties, selling everything from sets of velvet curtains and Thirties household linens to wonderful fragments of early lace or scraps of 18th-century Spitalfields silk. The things she finds always have an appealing honesty and never feel fussy. Kim's eye is equally reliable, but her taste is more for the Fifties: dresses, headscarves, prints.

STEPHEN OSBORN UNDER WESTWAY (OPPOSITE SANABEL TAKEAWAY)

A good source for modern lamps, from sturdy Thirties Bakelite examples to classic Sixties anglepoises, and the occasional electric fan. Each one is reconditioned or 'revived', as Osborn says.

SARAH AND JO JUNCTION OF PORTOBELLO ROAD AND WESTWAY
ℂ 0181-341 5343

A gaggle of textile dealers have made this spot under the Westway their home. Sarah and Jo have both been dealing here for twenty years, selling interesting fabrics, curtains, rugs, ribbons and decorative pieces. Stock dates from the 1890s on, but there is particular emphasis on the Twenties and Thirties: underwear, hats and the kind of bizarre oddities that women were encouraged to make by early good-housekeeping magazines. Always worth a scout.

SERVICE *you don't forget*
FROM
PEACHEYS
(OLDHAM) LTD.
FEATHERSTALL RD. NORTH

The Largest Stockist in the north
OBTAINABLE

M^cCHRISTIANS

CHEESE OF THE WEEK

Pecorino fresh from Tuscany

A delicious cheese made from sheeps
milk, it has a light fresh taste
which changes slightly as it matures

ANDY'S TIN CITY

PORTOBELLO – SATURDAY

ANDY'S TIN CITY BASEMENT, 282 WESTBOURNE GROVE
✆ 0171-727 2027
A varied and interesting selection of old advertising and packaging material: tins, showcards, enamels.

APPLEBY ANTIQUES STAND 18, GEOFFREY VAN ARCADE
105–7 PORTOBELLO ROAD. ✆ 01452-741540
Mike and Sue Witts deal in the kind of honest 18th- and 19th-century British pottery that it has become increasingly hard to find: Delft, salt-glaze, Jackfield, creamware and lustre. They are particularly interested in early food moulds – 'We're compiling a book on them at the moment' – and their stock of moulds is displayed to the right of the stand; en masse, they look extraordinary and abstract.

ATLAM STANDS 1–3, 282 WESTBOURNE GROVE. ✆ 0171-371 6960
A serious and impressive selection of English, European and American pocket watches dating from 1680 to 1930. Some are reconditioned, others are not, such as the late 18th-century shagreen-covered example I looked at, but all are kept as original as possible.

R.A. BARNES STANDS D3, D5 AND D6, ROGERS GALLERY
65 PORTOBELLO ROAD. ✆ 0181-789 3371
A dealer here for thirty years, Barnes remembers the arcade when it had a large garden in front, which has now been roofed over to create space for more stalls. He has three stands, 'I got them because they couldn't let them then', each catering to different tastes: one has English and Continental ceramics; another Chinese export porcelain; and the last is packed with highly polished brass wares.

SUSAN BILTCLIFFE GALLERY 289, WESTBOURNE GROVE
✆ 0181-740 5326

Biltcliffe has an eye for antiquarian books that give an insight into the way people lived, worked and played, predominantly in the 19th century. She is strong on works relating to science, technology and social and economic conditions and also has a stock of lavishly illustrated trade catalogues (*c.* 1880–1930) for everything from paintbrushes to Indian weaves.

HEATHER AND CLIFFORD BOND FIRST FLOOR, PORTOBELLO
STUDIOS (PINK TEAPOT SIGN), 101 PORTOBELLO ROAD. ✆ 01737-249525

As a child, Heather Bond created her own museum and displayed a Roman pot her father had given her, a pair of Victorian boots and an ostrich egg: 'I labelled them and imagined people came in to look round.' From this upstairs shop, she sells fine antique dolls and dolls' houses; each one, she explains, is a piece of social history. She showed me two German character dolls that had their own trousseaux of home-made miniature clothes. 'I tend to go for good original dolls', she says, 'ones of museum quality.'

BILL BROWN BACK STAND, 153 PORTOBELLO ROAD. ✆ 0181-650 3933

Brown's stand is an amazing find. The acknowledged authority on the history of cutlery, his own collection, from 'razor-sharp' Stone Age flints to 18th-century pistol-handled knives and forks, has been exhibited at Sotheby's and Sheffield's Mappin Art Gallery. He has dealt for forty years and now sells from the back of one of Portobello's least flashy indoor markets. He has trays of interesting cutlery, 'the older, the better', from 16th- and 17th-century knives dug up on the banks of the River Thames to standard-issue sets made for officers during World War I, and even pieces produced for the department store Heals in the 1950s.

HENRY BROWNRIGG STANDS 2 AND 21, 287 WESTBOURNE GROVE
✆ 0171-381 5407

'I always look forward to Saturday', says Henry Brownrigg. His two stalls are an effective outlet for his Indian, Islamic and South-East Asian art and antiques (which include miniatures, metalwork, colonial paintings and jewelry) and spare him having to deal with the grand 'decorator-type' clients his reliable and interesting stock would attract in smarter surroundings.

PETER CAMERON PASH'S GALLERY, 135 PORTOBELLO ROAD
✆ 0836-210759

This double stand at the back of one of the market's least-hyped arcades is home to perhaps the best selection of early English and European silver at Portobello. Cameron has been dealing since the mid-Seventies and has a hoard of saleable pieces (tea and coffee pots, dining wares, canteens of cutlery), plus more remarkable one-offs, such as the intricately engraved George I buckle he showed me.

AUREA CARTER FRONT STAND, BURTON'S ARCADE
296 WESTBOURNE GROVE. ✆ 0171-731 3486

From early printed creamware to Bow-handled cutlery, Aurea Carter's selection of English 18th- and early 19th-century pottery and porcelain is as good as you can hope to find. Many of the more colourful wares – Staffordshire, pearl, lustre, Whieldon, even the odd piece of Delft – are displayed on a large pine dresser, making them feel like part of a personal collection, rather than just stock.

CARTER & BRADY BACK OF CROWN ARCADE
119 PORTOBELLO ROAD. ✆ 0181-870 8996

James Brady was at Hornsea School of Art in the Sixties, so was a painter before he began to deal in pictures. The things he buys often have a modern British feel, but his stock actually dates from 1880 to the present day and comes from Europe, America and even Australia. St Ives and the Newlyn School are a particular speciality.

ESTER CHIGHINE SITE 40, PORTOBELLO ROAD
Chighine's stock of period prints and watercolours is spread over a large table outside the butcher's shop at no. 140 Portobello Road. She prefers prints with original colour, particularly those with 'decorative, architectural and classical subjects'.

CRANBORNE ANTIQUES STANDS 32A AND 33A
113 PORTOBELLO ROAD. ✆ 0181-675 4699

This narrow stall specializes in unframed natural history and botanical prints from the 1700s to the early 1900s. 'I'm very particular about original colour', explains its owner, Deborah Carter, 'there is no modern colour at all.' The stand also has a good selection of gardening bygones (forcers, trugs, cloches, tools and terracotta pots) with which to grow the prize specimens that the prints record.

CHARLES DAGGETT GALLERY FIRST FLOOR
153 PORTOBELLO ROAD. ✆ 0171-229 2248

Before he became a picture dealer and framer, Daggett was a historian, 'but you don't make money doing that, so I stopped'. Now, from his crowded first-floor gallery/workshop, he sells old-master British pictures (many repatriated from America) and mainly 19th-century frames, while also handmaking frames to order, using traditional techniques.

DELEHAR 146 PORTOBELLO ROAD. ✆ 0171-727 9860
At a glance, Delehar looks much like other Portobello arcades. In reality, it is a single shop, run by the Delehar family (who have been dealing since 1919), and the quality of stock is staggering. At the front, it is packed with the kind of European works of art, objects of vertu, early textiles and jewelry that you seldom find under one roof; at the rear, Peter Delehar sells rare scientific and medical instruments.

JO DE SOUSA MACEDO STAND 17, GRAYS ARCADE
138 PORTOBELLO ROAD. ✆ 0171-602 1266

De Sousa Macedo has been selling at Portobello for twenty-five years 'on and off'. She deals in English, Continental and Oriental ceramics, but also takes chances on interesting things outside her field. She had just bought a 'restored... but wonderful' fragment of a 4th-century wall painting from Afghanistan when we met.

NICHOLAS DONN FRONT STAND, GRAYS ARCADE
138 PORTOBELLO ROAD. ✆ 0171-609 0786

A specialist in ethnographic objects and jewelry, Nicholas Donn points out opium weights from Burma, amber from Morocco and even a small collection of Javanese pots dating from *c.* 1000 BC. He is particularly reliable for African trade beads, which he often restrings.

MARC-ANTOINE DU RY WESTBOURNE ANTIQUES ARCADE
113 PORTOBELLO ROAD. ✆ 0171-224 1259

Though there were three large and impressive pieces of 15th-century statuary and a cluster of Roman bronzes on Du Ry's stand when we met, he actually specializes in medieval manuscripts. He finds extraordinary things, such as an illuminated twelve-page calendar produced in Paris in the early 1400s, some of which come directly from the families for whom they were originally made.

EUREKA ANTIQUES STAND 6, GEOFFREY VAN ARCADE
105 PORTOBELLO ROAD. ✆ 0161-941 5453

Largest selection of tartanware in Britain, plus papier-mâché snuff and patch boxes.

LIZ FARROW STAND 26, BASEMENT, ADMIRAL VERNON ARCADE
141–49 PORTOBELLO ROAD. ✆ 0171-706 1545 (ALSO AT ALFIES.)

In 1960 Liz Farrow opened Dodo, the first shop in Britain to specialize in advertising art; she sold to Terence Conran and commissioned Peter Blake's enamel of *Babe Rainbow*. She now concentrates on European posters from the 1900s to the 1940s, 'everything except film and war', and has a particularly good eye for colourful, quirky and amusing images. All her posters are backed on linen, 'so people can pick them up and look at them properly'.

AGNES FOX STAND 21, ADMIRAL VERNON ARCADE
141–49 PORTOBELLO ROAD. ✆ 016284-73088

'I buy mostly in country auctions', explains Fox, which means that her stock of fine European ceramics and works of art hasn't passed endlessly through the London trade. She doesn't specialize and can stock anything from a Syrian tile to an English apothecary box of *c.* 1850.

CHARLES DAGGETT GALLERY   NICHOLAS DONN

CARLO FULLER JEWELRY SECTION, ADMIRAL VERNON MARKET
141–49 PORTOBELLO ROAD

Fuller's stock may include Georgian lockets, inlaid boxes or finely painted Indian miniatures on ivory. 'I don't specialize', he says, but his stock of bibelots is always distinctive.

GARLAND ANTIQUES FRONT STAND, BURTON'S ARCADE
296 WESTBOURNE GROVE. ✆ 0171-603 1161

A huge tôle boot, advertising a mid-19th-century cobbler's shop, was occupying a chunk of Garland Antiques when I visited. It seemed typical of the interesting, and entirely authentic, early English pottery, folk and decorative art that its owner stocks.

PHYLLIS GORLICK-KING STAND I, PORTWINE GALLERIES
175 PORTOBELLO ROAD. ✆ 0171-584 2688 (ALSO AT JUBILEE MARKET COVENT GARDEN.)

A small stand crammed with original fountain pens and magnifying glasses. Gorlick-King also has a good selection of original drawings, many of which come from Cecil Beaton's estate.

84 DEREK GREENGRASS CHELSEA GALLERIES
67, 69 AND 73 PORTOBELLO ROAD. ✆ 01276-857582

Greengrass's stand is located at the back of this good, reasonably sized arcade. He always has an interesting selection of walking sticks, which he shows alongside pictures, metalware, works of art and oddities, such as the extraordinary mid-19th-century articulated female figure that he had just bought when we met; she was eerily fascinating.

DEREK GREENGRASS   DAVID IRELAND

JULIE GREGORY BACK OF WORLD FAMOUS MARKET
177 PORTOBELLO ROAD. ℂ 0171-727 8781

A good range of 18th- and 19th-century prints and original works on paper, plus a conservation and restoration service.

COLIN GROSS STAND 17, GEOFFREY VAN ARCADE
105–7 PORTOBELLO ROAD. ℂ 0171-229 5577

Gross concentrates on scientific instruments and ethnographical material, but also sells woolwork pictures, glass paintings and examples of Napoleonic prisoner-of-war work. He had two narwhal horns when we met. These come from a type of tusked Arctic whale, but were traditionally believed to be from unicorns: 'I know it sounds corny', he says, 'but I like that unusual sort of thing.'

MIKE HANDFORD JONES ARCADE, 113 PORTOBELLO ROAD
ℂ 0171-352 9435

As a child, Handford remembers putting his parents' last Georgian silver teaspoon 'down a crack in the floorboards'. Growing up amid early objects, and with a watchmaker for a father, he developed a sharply refined eye and a taste for small, interesting things, such as shards of architectural carving and woodwork, portrait miniatures, gardening objects and Delft tiles. Most of his stock is undisguisedly worn: 'I'm much more comfortable with things that have got honest scars', he says.

HELIOS GALLERY BASEMENT, 292 WESTBOURNE GROVE
ℂ 0973-730 843

Dealing since 1995, Rolf Kiar and Samantha Neal are relative newcomers to the antiquities field. They specialize in small-scale works from the classical and European world (coins and oil lamps) but also have some Asian and Egyptian pieces, such as the stucco mummy mask from the Ptolemaic period that they showed me.

ERNA HISCOCK AND JOHN SHEPHERD CHELSEA
GALLERIES, 67, 69 AND 73 PORTOBELLO ROAD. ℂ 01233-661407

An unmissable stand that combines Hiscock's stock of samplers with Shepherd's early English pottery. Hiscock has a private collection of rare miniature samplers, embroidered in places such as Cheltenham Orphanage, but here concentrates on larger-scale pieces, including white work dating from the 1680s, vibrant mid-18th-century examples and 19th-century darning samplers. Shepherd's ceramics provide the perfect complement, as most of them (Bellarmine jugs, Leeds creamwares, blue-and-white Staffordshire, tiles and figures) date from the same period as the textiles and have a similarly honest appeal.

HISTORICAL IMPRESSIONS PORTWINE GALLERIES
175 PORTOBELLO ROAD. ℂ 0171-727 4681

John Benjafield's interest in the history of photography means that he sells books on the subject as well as individual prints, albums, daguerreotypes and cartes de visite. Mostly 19th-century, his stock ranges from images of early English architecture to hand-coloured prints of Japan made in the 1880s.

DAVID IRELAND WESTBOURNE ANTIQUES ARCADE
283 WESTBOURNE GROVE. ℂ 0181-968 8887

Ireland's stock of 18th- and 19th-century costumes and textiles is astounding; scouts from Gaultier, Galliano and Prada visit for inspiration and to buy bolts of early Chinese silk, printed cottons and weaves. When I visited, he had a piece of fine French embroidery from the 1700s that had been intended as a waistcoat. Sent to England to be decorated with silver thread and sequins, it was seized on arrival at Dover and therefore never made up.

ANTHONY JACK ENTRANCE, ANTIQUE ARCADE
293 WESTBOURNE GROVE. ℂ 0171-272 4982

Jack has been dealing at Portobello since 1971 and, refreshingly, doesn't feel its character has changed beyond recognition. He continues to specialize in the ethnography of North Africa, but concentrates on tribal weaponry and objects of everyday use, rather than on masks or figures. Most of his stock was 'brought back [to England] in colonial times'.

JOHN KING STAND 43, GOOD FAIRY MARKET, 100 PORTOBELLO ROAD
ℂ 0181-868 8363

King's stock of old woodworking tools is immaculately laid out. His stand, with its neat rows of hammers and polished brass plumb-line weights, feels more like an old-fashioned ironmonger's than a stall in one of Portobello's less glamorous markets. He also stocks watchmaking equipment.

86

DAVID LEVI ANTIQUES BASEMENT, STANDS 3 AND 4
LIPKA'S ARCADE, 282 WESTBOURNE GROVE. ℂ 0171-272 2664

Levi is the only dealer here to specialize in treen (turned-wood objects). His richly patinated bowls, coffee grinders, candlesticks and snuff boxes date from the 1400s to the 1800s. 'Really, I'd love to deal only in Elizabethan treen, but you just can't find it', he says. He has also recently branched outside his field to stock early objects with a similar presence: metalwares, frames, decorative oddities.

DAVID LEWIN STAND 15, GEOFFREY VAN ARCADE
105–7 PORTOBELLO ROAD. ℂ 0410-319809

Lewin came to London from South Africa in 1987 and expected, he admits, 'to go straight to working in Bond Street'. Instead, he found himself in Portobello and now occupies the front window of the market's smartest gallery. There is a distinctive, sculptural quality to his stock, and though he now concentrates on tribal art and artefacts (African staffs and war clubs, huge ivory bracelets and North American beadwork), other well-worn personal objects can also turn up: English folk pieces, textiles and the occasional piece of European pottery. 'What makes [the things I sell] beautiful', says Lewin, 'is that they have been used. They were treasured objects in their own culture.'

BEN MAURICE-JONES 293 WESTBOURNE GROVE. ℂ 0181-452 6193

Besides selling fishing rods and reels from the 1830s to the early 1900s, all of which are restored to use rather than to be treated as decorative objects, Maurice-Jones lovingly handmakes split-bamboo wet and dry rods in exactly the same way as the American rodmaker Philips the Younger first did in 1855. 'My nephews have [my rods] and tell me they're very good.'

ALAN MILFORD STANDS 5–6, DOLPHIN ARCADE
155 PORTOBELLO ROAD

An inspiring range of early glass (decanters, bottles, barley-twist stemmed drinking glasses and engraved rummers), Delft, European and Chinese pottery. With

DAVID LEWIN   DAVID LEWIN

a permanent cluster of buyers around the stand, it may take time to get a proper look at the stock.

SUSANA MONTIEL FRONT STANDS, 286 WESTBOURNE GROVE
✆ 0171-823 4388

Montiel had a shop on the Kings Road during the Seventies where she mixed 'the best' tribal artefacts with European works of art and Thirties pictures. She still deals in similar fine, serious things, particularly in 17th- and 18th-century Spanish colonial objects which have increasingly fascinated her. The calibre of her stock, be it an African staff or an Art Deco silver tea service, means that museums such as the V&A are among her customers.

NADIA STAND H, CENTRAL GALLERY, 125 PORTOBELLO ROAD
✆ 0171-243 8027

Appealing Victorian and Edwardian jewelry, pocket watches and trinkets.

THE NANKING PORCELAIN COMPANY UNIT L21–24
BASEMENT, ADMIRAL VERNON MARKET, 141–49 PORTOBELLO ROAD
✆ 0171-243 3030

A vast selection of 17th-, 18th- and 19th-century Chinese export porcelain, much of it made for the Portuguese market. Stock ranges from individual coffee cans to whole dinner services: 'We try to have at least three or four at a time.' Although decoration is mainly *famille rose*, armorial or blue-and-white, there are also pieces painted with rarer European subjects. The stall is named after the Chinese port from which cargo loads of porcelain were exported in the 1700s.

B.A. NEAL STANDS D2 AND D7, ROGERS GALLERY
65 PORTOBELLO ROAD. ✆ 01202-763324

'I started off part-time', says Neal, who has been 'hanging round salerooms and markets since [he] was about twenty'. He has now been selling at the back of this lesser-known arcade for twenty-seven years. He deals mainly in scientific and marine objects (sextants, theodolites, model boats), with some medical equipment and 'the odd clock'.

PAT NOVISSIMO STAND C, CENTRAL GALLERY
125 PORTOBELLO ROAD. ℭ 0181-878 6858

Novissimo has one of the finest selections of early jewelry in the market. 'I do 17th- and 18th-century', she says, 'but that's not to say I don't go earlier.' When we met, she had a particularly good stock of memorial rings, one of which bore an enamel inscription to the memory of one Katherine Bull 'Ob. 12 Oct, 1738'; she died at the age of sixty-one. She also regularly stocks clasps for necklaces, 'no other dealer sells them', such as the pair of 18th-century ivory fixings I saw; both were finely decorated with hairwork scenes.

THE OLD FATHER TIME CLOCK CENTRE
FIRST FLOOR, PORTOBELLO STUDIOS (PINK TEAPOT SIGN)
101 PORTOBELLO ROAD. ℭ 0181-546 6299

19th- and early 20th-century clocks are sold and repaired, and there is also a good stock of glass domes.

88

THE OLD HABERDASHER STAND 19, ADMIRAL VERNON MARKET
141–49 PORTOBELLO ROAD. ℭ 0181-907 8684

Corner stand, crammed with period ribbons, braids, laces, textiles and tassles, that also manages to stock antique dolls' hats, needlework and even artificial flowers.

JACQUELINE OOSTHUIZEN STANDS 10–11, ADMIRAL VERNON
MARKET, 141–49 PORTOBELLO ROAD. ℭ 0171-352 6071

London's biggest dealer in Staffordshire figures.

DALE ROGERS   KIM SINCLAIR

PAST TIME WRISTWATCHES 101 PORTOBELLO ROAD
℗ 0171-794 3336
Good selection of Rolex, Cartier, Patek Philippe and, more interestingly, British military wristwatches.

NEIL PHILLIPS 99 PORTOBELLO ROAD. ℗ 0171-229 2113
Neil Phillips's family has been making and restoring stained glass and church furnishings since 1838. He sells similar stock at this distinctive, cavernous shop, from whole sets of windows to individual panes.

JUDITH POLLITT CHELSEA GALLERIES, 67 PORTOBELLO ROAD
℗ 0831-454225
Pollitt is one of the few dealers specializing in early sewing equipment; she even lectures on the subject, albeit only at Women's Institute meetings she points out with a smile. She has an impressive stock of tools (thimbles, pincushions, etc.) and other small pretty objects, such as chatelaines, buttons and delicate 19th-century posy holders, which were, she explains, 'standard equipment if you moved in certain circles'.

NOEL AND ELIZABETH PULLMAN STAND 1, DOLPHIN ARCADE
155 PORTOBELLO ROAD. ℗ 01892-724236
'There's nothing more useless than bellows that don't blow', laughs Noel Pullman. He has been specializing in 18th- and 19th-century brass and copper for twenty years and is particularly good for fireplace pieces, such as bellows (which he has restored to perfect working order) and firedogs, but also smaller wares, such as bells, candlesticks and handles.

DALE ROGERS 88 PORTOBELLO ROAD. ℗ 0973-655514
This fossil specialist, who collects all over the world, was fresh back from tracking down stock in Madagascar when we spoke. 'A modern-day Indiana Jones' is how one friend described him.

KIM SINCLAIR STILL TOO FEW, 300 WESTBOURNE GROVE
℗ 0171-727 7752
A corridor-like stand that, says Sinclair, 'is one of the most photographed in Portobello'. She always has a good selection of small kitchen and country wares (watering cans, enamels, breadboards), plus the odd quilt and larger piece of pine furniture, all heaped together to seductive effect.

COLIN SMITH AND GERALD ROBINSON
STAND 2, GEOFFREY VAN ARCADE, 105–7 PORTOBELLO ROAD
℗ 0171-225 1163
Smith and Robinson have been dealing here for twenty years and specialize in fine and decorative accessories made in silver, ivory and shagreen; 'objects of vertu is too narrow a definition', says Smith. There is a refined glamour to all their stock, be it an 18th-century tortoiseshell-and-gold box or a 1930s dressing case made by Asprey.

MARTYN STAMP JEWELRY SECTION, ADMIRAL VERNON MARKET
141–49 PORTOBELLO ROAD. ℗ 0171-384 3441
Stamp has a good eye for interesting classic modern watches.

RITA STEPHENSON STAND 2, ADMIRAL VERNON MARKET
141–49 PORTOBELLO ROAD. ℂ 01753-642067

Stephenson found her vocation in buttons: 'After them, nothing seemed interesting.' She is particularly fascinated by the range of materials used to make buttons and stocks examples from the 18th century to the 1960s in enamel, satsuma, paste, brass, Bakelite and carved pearl.

SWIFT ANTIQUE LACE STAND 1, PORTOBELLO ROAD
(JUNCTION OF WESTBOURNE GROVE). ℂ 0171-370 6589

Annie Swift's stall is one of only a handful of council-managed outdoor pitches on Portobello; she has been here since the late Eighties. Although the stand is on the road, the stock of mostly 18th- and 19th-century lace and related items (bobbins, lacemakers' lamps, etc.) is as fine as anything you will find in a shop: from large pieces of early gros point to babies' bonnets and lappets, the decorative lace panels worn at the back of the head in the 1700s.

MICHAEL TELFER-SMOLLETT 88 PORTOBELLO ROAD
ℂ 0171-727 0117

Telfer-Smollett was buying in the Middle East, Africa and India forty years ago: 'It was far easier in those days.' His stock of ethnic textiles and artefacts, spilling from his shop on to an outside pitch, still feels fresh and exciting. Go to buy African masks and beadwork and natural history oddities, such as narwhal horns, framed insects and bright-green emu eggs.

TETRAGON ANTIQUITIES 293 WESTBOURNE GROVE
ℂ 0171-486 6739

'I deal in ancient Tupperware and dead gods' is the disconcerting, if truthful, way the owner of Tetragon describes the fantastic selection of everyday antiquities she has been selling here for the past nineteen years. Her stock of commonplace objects dates from the Egyptian to the early medieval period and encompasses everything from flint axe heads to carved-bone Roman hairpins. 'I even have three shelves of things for under £10. No one does that any more.'

ALASTAIR THOMAS DOLPHIN ARCADE, 155 PORTOBELLO ROAD

Whereas many dealers rely on glass shelves to display their stock, Thomas's stand of Chinese, Indian and South-East Asian art and artefacts is more imaginatively arranged. He has even collaged together a model of a grand 19th-century woman from Manchu to show exactly how the kingfisher-feather headdresses, platform shoes and spiky nailguards he sells would have originally been worn.

BRYONY THOMASSON 283 WESTBOURNE GROVE. ℂ 0171-731 3693

Thomasson specializes in the kind of rustic textiles that were once the preserve of French peasants. Her linen and hemp sheets, clothes, tickings and woven horse-blankets are now the height of shabby chic and, when we met, her stock had been severely depleted by buyers from Ralph Lauren. Clothes with darns, holes and patches, 'the more the better', are a particular quirk.

PAUL TREADAWAY STAND 4A, 113 PORTOBELLO ROAD
ℂ 0850-621507

Treadaway hand-reproduces 18th- and 19th-century picture frames to order,

BRYONY THOMASSON   TURNING WORMS

using traditional techniques. His range of stock designs (from plain Georgian to ornate neoclassical mouldings) are gessoed, water- or sand-gilded and subtly patinated: 'People say our finishes are the most authentic.' He is also one of the few framers who can supply *verre églomisé* (gilded glass) rather than relying on modern cardboard mounts. A real find.

TURNING WORMS STAND 42, GOOD FAIRY MARKET
100 PORTOBELLO ROAD 01473-215650
A good source for affordable corkscrews. 'We're on the bottom rung', says its owner, but the calibre of stock 'is climbing steadily'.

VINTAGE PISCATORIANA STAND 15A, 113 PORTOBELLO ROAD
0171-253 4611
19th-century rods, reels and fishing accessories for the collector, decorator and aesthetically minded fisherman.

WYNYARD R.T. WILKINSON RED LION ARCADE
165–69 PORTOBELLO ROAD. 0171-229 0539
Wilkinson has been selling silver 'in this particular spot' since the early 1980s. The acknowledged authority on Indian colonial silver and author of the definitive book on the subject, he also has stock from Britain, America, Australia and even Burma. The items he displays here (flatware and small pieces mainly) tend to be from the 18th and 19th centuries, but he will source earlier pieces to order. Seriously knowledgeable and helpful with it.

BETTY AND LEN WILTSHIRE STAND 9, GOOD FAIRY MARKET
100 PORTOBELLO ROAD. 0181-668 2418
Betty Wiltshire's stock of costume jewelry dates from the Twenties to the Sixties, with the odd bit of Seventies sparkle mixed in. Diamanté from the Thirties, which she restores and restuds, is also a forte.

NEARBUYS

Most of Portobello's antique arcades have cafés, although some, like the stock, are less pristine than others. If you want to take a break from buying, there are plenty of good, and usually packed, cafés in the surrounding streets.

A.P.C.
40 LEDBURY ROAD
W11 2AA ℭ **0171-229 4933**
Smart, wearable clothes for men and women from French designers with an eye for industrial detailing.

BAZAR ANTIQUES & DECORATIVE ITEMS
82 GOLBORNE ROAD
W10 5PS ℭ **0181-969 6262**
Useful and good-looking French country furniture, ceramics, glass and lighting. Find the table, chairs or shelves you need at affordable prices and then blow any extra cash on a decorative oddity.

EMMA BERNHARDT

EMMA BERNHARDT
301 PORTOBELLO ROAD
W10 5TD ℭ **0181-960 2929**
Shop-cum-shrine dedicated to the Mexican taste for all things bright, beautiful and plastic. Track down luminous shopping bags, tin trays, feathers, glitter, and other kitsch pickings.

BOOKS FOR COOKS
4 BLENHEIM CRESCENT
W11 1NN ℭ **0171-221 1992**
London's best selection of new and secondhand books devoted to food. There are sometimes cookery demonstrations on Saturday;

the results are served in the tiny café.

MR CHRISTIAN'S
11 ELGIN CRESCENT
W11 2JA ℭ **0171-229 0501**
Delicatessen and charcuterie with a wide variety of home-baked specialist breads sold outside.

SHEILA COOK TEXTILES
184 WESTBOURNE GROVE
W11 2RH ℭ **0171-792 8001**
A vast selection of textiles, costumes and fashion accessories from the 1700s to the 1970s, for sale or to hire.

CHRISTOPHER FARR
212 WESTBOURNE GROVE
W11 2RH ℭ **0171-792 5761**
Romeo Gigli and Rifat Ozbek are two of the fashion designers Farr has commissioned to design rugs. Here he sells his carpets alongside hard-edged modern furniture by Italian manufacturers Cappellini.

FELICITOUS
19 KENSINGTON PARK ROAD, W11 2EU
ℭ **0171-243 4050**
Gourmet grocery shop with a distinctive aqua-blue interior. Seriously tasty food (prepared by chefs who used to work at the exclusive Kensington Place restaurant) to take away or eat in at the one and only table.

BAZAR ANTIQUES & DECORATIVE ITEMS

PORTOBELLO LONDON

GRAHAM & GREEN
**4 ELGIN CRESCENT
W11 2HX**
C 0171-727 4594
Antonia Graham has three
shops on this small street
selling clothes, homewares
and furniture, each with its
own distinctive flavour.

LACY GALLERY
**203 WESTBOURNE GROVE
W11 2SB**
C 0171-229 6340
An impressive selection
of 18th-, 19th- and 20th-
century picture frames.

LISBOA
**57 GOLBORNE ROAD
W10 5NR**
C 0181-968 5242
A Portuguese café that
has become a Portobello
institution. Dealers come here
on a Friday morning for a
galou (milky coffee in a glass)
and a sticky custard tart.

MIKE'S CAFÉ
**12 BLENHEIM
CRESCENT, W11 1NN**
C 0171-229 3757
A post-modern greasy-
spoon café with clean white

walls and American diner-
style seating. The food,
however, hasn't had a
makeover: chips can still be
served with everything.

PAUL SMITH
**WESTBOURNE HOUSE
122 KENSINGTON PARK
ROAD, W11 2EP**
C 0171-727 3553
The designer's new
headquarters, with men's
and women's clothing,
accessories and shrewdly
chosen tempters, such as
vintage magazines and
watches.

THE SPICE SHOP
**1 BLENHEIM CRESCENT
W11 2EE**
C 0171-221 4448
Herbs and spices, nuts,
grains and pulses.

TOM'S
**226 WESTBOURNE GROVE
W11 2RH** *C* 0171-221 8818
Smart designer deli selling
ready-made sandwiches and
salads to eat in or take away,
alongside *de rigueur* raw
ingredients for smart West
London dinner parties.

VENT
**178A WESTBOURNE
GROVE, W11 2RH**
C 0171-938 2365
Simon Heath's Thirties
to Seventies women's
(and occasionally men's)
clothing and accessories
have a particularly gutsy
glamour.

WARRIS VIANNI
**85 GOLBORNE ROAD
W10 5NL**
C 0181-964 0069
Vianni's carefully edited
selection of contemporary
woven Indian fabrics is
among the best in London.
Visit for organzas, silk
wools, fine Paisleys or
punchy cotton stripes.

WILD AT HEART
**TURQUOISE ISLAND
222 WESTBOURNE GROVE
W11 2AA**
C 0171-727 3095
Part-Paris metro station,
part-submarine, this
extraordinary turquoise-
tiled building is home
to Portobello's best
flower stall (and the
nearest WC).

SPITALFIELDS BRICK LANE COLUMBIA ROAD

Petticoat Lane, the best known of the East End markets, takes its name from the secondhand clothes that have been sold there since the early 17th century. Though it continues to thrive, the market is now an anonymous mishmash of new leather jackets and tourist T-shirts. Better to head for Spitalfields Organic Market, which is housed in the grand wrought-iron shell of the famous fruit and vegetable market that was established in 1682. The current building was completed in the 1890s, modernized in the 1920s, and abandoned in 1991 when the market moved to larger premises. The present market has been on the site ever since and is now home to around fifteen organic food producers and forty bric-a-brac and clothes dealers. The atmosphere on Sundays feels refreshingly uncommercial.

The area reflects more vividly than any other London's constantly changing population. A Roman cemetery was discovered nearby in the 16th century and, from 1685, Protestant French Huguenots fleeing persecution from Catholic Louis XIV settled on the site. Many were silk weavers and they earned Spitalfields its reputation in the 18th century as the centre for fine-quality silks. Christ Church (1714–1729) in Commercial Street, opposite the market, was built by Nicholas Hawksmoor in response to the rise of local Nonconformity, to which the immigrants had contributed. Many houses survive from this period. The finest are in Fournier Street; their attic windows were designed to provide light for the weavers working at their looms.

Jewish immigrants settled in the area from the 1880s and shifted its economic mainstay from weaving to clothes manufacture. Spitalfields has since seen a huge influx of settlers from Bangladesh, so many of the street signs are now written in both Urdu and English. A building on the corner of Fournier Street and Brick Lane encapsulates these social changes: built as a Huguenot chapel in 1743, it later became a synagogue and is used today as a mosque. The Georgian houses are now greatly restored, but the gentrification of a handful of Spitalfields streets sits in uneasy juxtaposition with the surrounding deprivation.

Brick Lane was originally a mud track used for transporting bricks and tiles in the 16th century. It is now a glorious mixture of Indian

grocery shops, clothiers, haberdashers and curry houses. To the north, at no. 91, is the Black Eagle Brewery, which was started in 1660. Its Director's House (*c.* 1740) survives and is now linked to a modern glass-fronted structure by Ove Arup, while other parts of the brewery continue life as gallery spaces and recording studios. There has been a market here since the 1700s and the atmosphere is reminiscent of an earlier, more lawless age. Stalls sprawl into various streets, but bric-a-brac is concentrated in Cheshire Street. You are unlikely to come across anything other than broken plates, mattress foam or lone souls selling quantities of used zips, but there is an air of edgy excitement.

Further north are an enclave of unspoilt Victorian workers' cottages and Columbia Road Flower Market. It is the successor to Columbia Market (opened 1869), a vast cathedral-like structure, complete with Gothic hall, that was financed by the philanthropist Baroness Burdett-Coutts. Local costermongers preferred street trading and Columbia Market failed. It was demolished in 1958, but the model dwellings which Burdett-Coutts also funded in Columbia Road remain today.

Although Columbia Road specializes in plants and flowers, independent antique dealers, jewelry makers, milliners and designers have also established themselves here. Some have shops on the road itself, while others are hidden away in old commercial buildings, but all seem unspoilt by the heavy hand of consumerism.

SPITALFIELDS MARKET

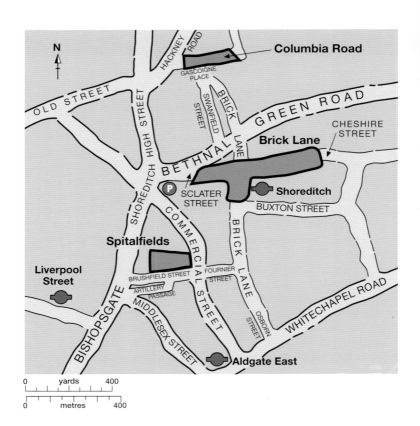

N

Columbia Road

HACKNEY ROAD

GASCOIGNE PLACE

OLD STREET

SHOREDITCH HIGH STREET

SWANFIELD STREET

BRICK LANE

BETHNAL GREEN ROAD

CHESHIRE STREET

Brick Lane

P SCLATER STREET

Shoreditch

BUXTON STREET

BRICK LANE

COMMERCIAL STREET

Spitalfields

Liverpool Street

BRUSHFIELD STREET

FOURNIER STREET

ARTILLERY PASSAGE

BISHOPSGATE

MIDDLESEX STREET

OSBORN STREET

WHITECHAPEL ROAD

Aldgate East

0   yards   400

0   metres   400

HOW & WHEN TO GO TO

SPITALFIELDS
BRICK LANE
COLUMBIA ROAD

SPITALFIELDS
COMMERCIAL STREET (LAMB STREET TO BRUSHFIELD STREET) E1 6BG
✆ 0171-247 6590

OPEN
Sunday, 11am–3.30pm (some stalls Monday to Friday also)

BRICK LANE
(NORTH OF RAILWAY BRIDGE), E2

OPEN
Sunday, 7am–1pm

COLUMBIA ROAD
(RAVENSCROFT STREET TO BARNET GROVE), E2

OPEN
Sunday, 7am–1pm

SPITALFIELDS & BRICK LANE

BY TUBE
Liverpool Street (Central, Circle and Metropolitan Lines) Aldgate East (Metropolitan and District Lines) Shoreditch (East London Line)

BY BUS
8, 26, 35, 47, 48, 55, 67, 78, 149, 242 and 243A; also 5 and 43 during Sunday market hours

PARKING
There is little parking in the area, the nearest car parks being off Primrose Street and at White's Row, off Commercial Street.

COLUMBIA ROAD

BY TUBE
Bethnal Green (Central Line), Liverpool Street (Central, Circle and Metropolitan Lines) Shoreditch (East London Line)

BY BUS
26, 35, 47, 48, 55, 67, 78, 149, 242 and 243A; also 5 and 43 during Sunday market hours

PARKING
Here, too, parking may be a problem, so it's best to leave the car at home and come by public transport. Most streets are restricted to residential parking, but there are a few parking meters on Columbia Road and Club Row.

SPITALFIELDS

LUCY EVERETT CENTRE MARKET
✆ 0181-675 7322
Lucy Everett has a passion for vintage plastic and sells shopping bags, cruet stands, 'Stay Fresh' food containers and other pastel-coloured plastic home essentials.

DIANA LAURIE OPPOSITE EAST ICE CREAM CO.
✆ 0171-831 6212
Laurie handmakes dressing-up jewelry for adults: beaded tiaras in boiled-sweet colours and wire rings emblazoned with camply cosy words such as 'pants' and 'fluff'. They are, she says, 'the kind of thing you wanted to wear when you were little… and still want to!'

MAGPIE BOOKSHOP 53 BRUSHFIELD STREET
✆ 0171-247 4263
A reliable secondhand bookshop, with a section devoted to the history of London, which always has stacks of useful free leaflets outside.

ONE EYE BOOKS CENTRE MARKET
✆ 0171-729 4997
For 'fifty-one weeks of the year', this stall sells books on architecture, anthropology, prehistory and tribal and fine art, including many standard works that are now hard to find. It also has pleasing oddities such as a 1920s catalogue of fitted furniture.

JARNAIL FOOD STORE   ROUGHNECK & THUG

ANDREAS SCHMID

ROUGHNECK & THUG 55 BRUSHFIELD STREET. ✆ 0958-409160

Selling at Spitalfields since 'there were only four stalls here', Roughneck & Thug now occupies one of the ring-side shops and several stalls. It offers a distinctive and well-chosen mixture of men's and women's clothes (particularly overcoats and, eccentrically, traditional Scottish Highland jackets 'to be worn with kilts'), blankets, quilts, carpets and curtains.

ANDREAS SCHMID CENTRE MARKET. ✆ 0171-375 1945

Schmid is a fashion designer who got sidetracked into selling Sixties and Seventies furniture and objects. He started buying at Brick Lane when he first came to London ten years ago and suddenly found he was addicted.

BRICK LANE

C.D. ARNOLD PITCH 33, CHESHIRE STREET, E2

Arnold has been selling army surplus clothing in this spot for forty years.

ATLANTIS ART SUPPLIES 146 BRICK LANE, EI 6RU
✆ 0171-377 8855

A vast art supply warehouse with paints, pigments, papers and canvas cut to order.

BEIGEL BAKE BAKERY 159 BRICK LANE, EI 6SB. ✆ 0171-729 0616

This 24-hour baker is one of Brick Lane's best-known haunts.

P.R.K. BLACKMANS SHOES 44 CHESHIRE STREET, E2 6EH
✆ 0850-883505

End-of-line and one-off pairs of men's shoes by traditional English makers sold very cheaply. If you're lucky enough to have narrow, size ten feet, you can buy a pair of chisel-toe slip-on brogues by Barkers for £15.

BRICK LANE   BRICK LANE

JARNAIL FOOD STORE 5 ARTILLERY PASSAGE, E1 7LJ

℡ 0171-247 7181

18th-century shop that continues life as an Indian grocer's. Food buying can't be any more aesthetically satisfying.

COLUMBIA ROAD

BERNSTOCK SPEIRS 10 COLUMBIA ROAD, E2 7NN

℡ 0171-729 7229

The hats and clothes of this fashion designer duo were *de rigueur* among London clubbers in the Eighties. Their latest collections continue to be just as innovative.

S & B EVANS & SONS 7A EZRA STREET, E2 7RH

℡ 0171-729 6635

A family business specializing in handmade terracotta pots and glazed garden wares.

JONES DAIRY 23 EZRA STREET, E2 7RH

℡ 0171-739 5372

Traditional dairy and bakery; walking in here is like stepping back in time.

LEE'S SEAFOODS 134 COLUMBIA ROAD, E2 7RG

℡ 0171-739 3685

A family-run business, established for over fifty years, that specializes in jellied eels and shellfish. 'Noted for all seafood in season', it announces proudly. Its deep-fried prawns and scampi make delicious lunch-time takeaways.

ODYSSEY FIRST FLOOR, THE COURTYARD, EZRA STREET, E2 7RH
℗ 0171-241 2803

'It's such a fab space', says Paul, when I ask why he started selling here. Now you can hardly see the walls of his shop for his mass of 20th-century accessories and camply collectable homewares: Sixties lamps, Whitefriars glass, ceramics, even a set of Fifties Melaware cups on a plastic stand.

ORGANICS 98 RAVENSCROFT STREET, E2 7QA
℗ 0171-739 7103

An enticing and well-stocked source for organic gardening paraphernalia, everything from fertilizers to plant-climbing frames made of coppiced willow.

PUTNAMS FIRST FLOOR, THE COURTYARD
EZRA STREET, E2 7RH

Antoinette Putnam has had shops in Covent Garden and Portobello Road, but this, she says, 'is the nicest'. She has a variety of countryish stock and old gardening books, plus her own range of printed cottons, which are decorated with motifs taken from the 19th-century blue-and-white china that she also stocks.

PUTNAMS   JONES DAIRY

Numerals refer to pages in the London end of the book.

Affinity, *Portobello* 76
After Noah,
 Camden Passage 45
Cheryl All, *Covent Garden* 50
Andy's Tin City,
 Portobello 80
Annie's Vintage Costume
 and Textiles,
 Camden Passage 42
A.P.C., *Portobello* 92
Appleby Antiques,
 Portobello 80
Aram Designs, *Covent
 Garden* 53
Raul Arantes, *Camden
 Passage* 42
Archive Bookstore,
 Alfies 23
C.D. Arnold,
 Brick Lane 101
Paul Arnold,
 Camden Lock 36
Atlam, *Portobello* 80
Atlantis Art Supplies,
 Brick Lane 101
At the Movies,
 Antiquarius 69
Ian Auld,
 Camden Passage 42
Aura Antiques, *Grays* 58
R.A. Barnes, *Portobello* 80
Viva Barnett, *Portobello* 76
Baroque 'n' Roll,
 Lillie Road 68
Don Bayney, *Grays* 58
Bazar Antiques &
 Decorative Items,
 Portobello 92
Bebe, *Alfies* 18
Linda Bee, *Grays* 58
Bill Bennett and Keith
 Thorogood, *Grays* 58
Chris Bennett,
 Bermondsey 28

Emma Bernhardt,
 Portobello 92
Bernstock Speirs,
 Columbia Road 102
Andrew Bewick and Jonathan
 Lee, *Lillie Road* 69
Bibliopola, *Alfies* 18
Susan Biltcliffe,
 Portobello 81
A. Binder, *Alfies* 23
P.R.K. Blackmans Shoes,
 Brick Lane 101
Heather and Clifford Bond,
 Portobello 81
Bonhams Lots Road,
 Antiquarius 71
Books for Cooks,
 Portobello 92
Bourbon-Hanby Antiques
 Centre, *Antiquarius* 71
Patrick Boyd-Carpenter,
 Grays 58
Britannia, *Grays* 58
Bill Brown, *Portobello* 81
Henry Brownrigg,
 Portobello 81
Browns, *Grays* 61
S. Brunswick, *Alfies* 18
David Burrows, *Alfies* 18
Peter Cameron,
 Portobello 81
Carol, *Covent Garden* 50
Aurea Carter, *Portobello* 81
Carter & Brady,
 Portobello 82
Christopher Cavey,
 Grays 58
Charlie,
 Bermondsey 28
Chelsea Gardener,
 Antiquarius 71
Ester Chighine,
 Portobello 82
Christie's, *Grays* 61
CO_2, *Camden Lock* 36
Sheila Cook Textiles,
 Portobello 92

The Corner Room,
 Camden Passage 42
Nic Costa,
 Camden Passage 42
Les Coussis du Chien,
 Portobello 76
Cranborne Antiques,
 Portobello 82
Madeline Crispin Antiques,
 Alfies 23
Cristobal, *Alfies* 18
Criterion Auction Rooms,
 Camden Passage 45
Charles Daggett Gallery,
 Portobello 82
Tony D'Almeida,
 Camden Passage 42
Gillian Danz, *Alfies* 18
N. Davalou Carpets,
 Bermondsey 28
Zal Davar, *Lillie Road* 69
Carlton Davidson Antiques,
 Camden Passage 42
Decodence,
 Camden Passage 43
Decorative Antiques,
 Lillie Road 69
Delehar, *Portobello* 82
Delfina Studios,
 Bermondsey 31
Jo De Sousa Macedo,
 Portobello 82
Nicholas Donn,
 Portobello 82
A. Douch, *Grays* 58
The Dover Bookshop,
 Covent Garden 53
Dudley and Genie, *Alfies* 19
The Duffer of St George,
 Covent Garden 53
Marc-Antoine Du Ry,
 Portobello 83
Eureka Antiques,
 Portobello 83
S & B Evans & Sons,
 Columbia Road 102
Lucy Everett, *Spitalfields* 100

Fantasticks, *Bermondsey* 28
Christopher Farr, *Portobello* 92
Liz Farrow, *Portobello* 83
Sandy Field, *Covent Garden* 50
J. First, *Grays* 59
Stephen Foster's Bookshop, *Alfies* 23
Agnes Fox, *Portobello* 83
Carlo Fuller, *Portobello* 84
Furniture + Designs 1870–1970, *Alfies* 19
Gallery of Antique Costume & Textiles, *Alfies* 23
Robin Gardiner, *Alfies* 19
Gardiner & Gardiner, *Alfies* 19
Garland Antiques, *Portobello* 84
Peter Gaunt, *Grays* 59
The Gilded Lily, *Grays* 59
John Goodison and Chris Paraskeva, *Camden Passage* 43
Brian Gordon, *Antiquarius* 69
Gordons Medals Ltd, *Grays* 59
Phyllis Gorlick-King, *Portobello* 84
Anne Gormley, *Alfies* 19
Graham and Dani, *Portobello* 76
Graham & Green, *Camden Lock* and *Portobello* 37, 93
Green & Stone, *Antiquarius* 71
Derek Greengrass, *Portobello* 84
Julie Gregory, *Portobello* 85
Gordon Gridley, *Camden Passage* 43
Colin Gross, *Portobello* 85
Guest & Gray, *Grays* 59
G Whizz, *Old Crowther* 68
H & C, *Covent Garden* 50
Mike Handford, *Portobello* 85
Owen Hargreaves, *Covent Garden* 51
Harrison's Books, *Grays* 60
Harry, *Portobello* 76
Hayman & Hayman, *Antiquarius* 69
Heather's Teddies, *Covent Garden* 51
Pam Hebbs, *Camden Passage* 43
Helios Gallery, *Portobello* 85
Helray Ltd, *Lillie Road* 69

Erna Hiscock and John Shepherd, *Portobello* 85
Historical Impressions, *Portobello* 85
Manuela Hofer, *Camden Passage* 45
Edward Holden *see* Greg Li
The Home Service, *Camden Lock* 36
David Huxtable, *Alfies* 19
Identity, *Portobello* 76
David Ireland, *Portobello* 85
Anthony Jack, *Portobello* 86
Jonathan's Belowstairs, *Camden Passage* 44
Jones and Campbell, *Alfies* 19
Hilary Kashden, *Covent Garden* 51
Kay Books, *Bermondsey* 29
Don Kelly, *Antiquarius* 70
John King, *Portobello* 86
Kitchen Bygones, *Alfies* 20
Lacy Gallery, *Portobello* 93
Barry Landsman, *Alfies* 20
Judith Lassalle, *Camden Passage* 44
Paul Lau, *Portobello* 77
Diana Laurie, *Spitalfields* 100
Peter Laurie, *Bermondsey* 29
Jonathan Lee *see* Andrew Bewick
David Levi Antiques, *Portobello* 86
David Lewin, *Portobello* 86
Sarah Lewis and June Victor, *Alfies* 20
Greg Li and Edward Holden, *Alfies* 20
Lisson Gallery, *Alfies* 23
Lots Road Galleries, *Antiquarius* 71
Magpie Bookshop, *Spitalfields* 100
Ian Mankin, *Camden Lock* 37
Margaret and Kim, *Portobello* 77
Connie Margrie, *Alfies* 20
Marie-Louise of Marylebone, *Alfies* 20
Francesca Martire, *Alfies* 20
Ben Maurice-Jones, *Portobello* 86

Shane Meredith, *Camden Passage* 44
Alan Milford, *Portobello* 86
Nigel Mills, *Covent Garden* 51
Susana Montiel, *Portobello* 87
Nadia, *Portobello* 87
The Nanking Porcelain Company, *Portobello* 87
Bruna Naufal, *Alfies* 21
B.A. Neal, *Portobello* 87
Rosslyn Neave, *Bermondsey* 29
Catherine Nimmo, *Lillie Road* 69
Sue Norman, *Antiquarius* 70
Pat Novissimo, *Portobello* 88
Odyssey, *Columbia Road* 103
The Old Father Time Clock Centre, *Portobello* 88
The Old Haberdasher, *Portobello* 88
The Old Tool Chest, *Camden Passage* 45
Michael Oliphant, *Bermondsey* 29
One Eye Books, *Spitalfields* 100
Jacqueline Oosthuizen, *Portobello* 88
Organics, *Columbia Road* 103
Stephen Osborn, *Portobello* 77
Paola and Iaia, *Alfies* 21
Chris Paraskeva *see* John Goodison
Past Time Wristwatches, *Portobello* 89
Paul Smith, *Portobello* 93
Paul Smith Sale Shop, *Grays* 61
Christopher Pearce, *Camden Passage* 44
Sue Perks, *Bermondsey* 29
Richard Perry, *Bermondsey* 29
Persiflage, *Alfies* 21
Phillips, *Grays* 61
Neil Phillips, *Portobello* 89
The Photographers' Gallery, *Covent Garden* 53
Planet Bazaar, *Camden Lock* 36
PL-B, *Bermondsey* 29
Laraine Plummer, *Alfies* 21
Katherine Pole, *Alfies* 21
Judith Pollitt, *Portobello* 89
Posters for Collectors, *Grays* 60

Noel and Elizabeth Pullman,
    Portobello 89
Putnams,
    Columbia Road 103
Radford-Muir, *Grays* 60
Geoffrey Robinson,
    Alfies 22
Gerald Robinson *see*
    Colin Smith
Dale Rogers, *Portobello* 89
Rojeh Antiques, *Alfies* 22
Roughneck & Thug,
    Spitalfields 101
Keith Roughton,
    Camden Lock 36
Chad Sansean,
    Bermondsey 30
Sarah and Jo, *Portobello* 77
Andreas Schmid,
    Spitalfields 101
Shapiro & Co., *Grays* 60
John Shepherd *see*
    Erna Hiscock
Shiraz Antiques, *Grays* 60
Kim Sinclair, *Portobello* 89
Colin Smith and Gerald
    Robinson, *Portobello* 89
Kit Smith,
    Covent Garden 52
Moya Smith,
    Bermondsey 30
Sotheby's, *Grays* 61
Sparkle Moore, *Alfies* 22
Barbara Springall,
    Bermondsey 30
Stable Five, *Camden Lock* 36
Martyn Stamp,
    Portobello 89
Steinberg & Tolkein,
    Antiquarius 71
Rita Stephenson,
    Portobello 90
Jane Stewart, *Grays* 60

Sultani Antiques,
    Grays 60
Susie Cooper Ceramics,
    Alfies 22
Swift Antique Lace,
    Portobello 90
Michael Telfer-Smollett,
    Portobello 90
Templar Antiques,
    Camden Passage 44
Tetragon Antiquities,
    Portobello 90
Textilean, *Alfies* 22
The Thimble Society,
    Grays 60
Alastair Thomas,
    Portobello 90
Bryony Thomasson,
    Portobello 90
Keith Thorogood *see*
    Bill Bennett
Titanic, *Old Crowther* 68
TNT, *Old Crowther* 68
Paul Treadaway,
    Portobello 90
Turning Worms,
    Portobello 91
twentytwentyone,
    Camden Passage 45
Unit 78, *Camden Lock* 36
Vent, *Portobello* 93
Warris Vianni,
    Portobello 93
June Victor *see*
    Sarah Lewis
Victory Motorcycles,
    Camden Lock 37
Emerich Vidich,
    Antiquarius 70
Vinci Antiques,
    Grays 61
Vintage Piscatoriana,
    Portobello 91

M. Von Taubenheim,
    Bermondsey 30
Catherine Wallis, *Alfies* 22
Jessica Ward, *Alfies* 22
Geoffrey Waters,
    Antiquarius 70
Wheatley Antiques,
    Grays 60
Steven Wheeler,
    Covent Garden 52
Linda Wigglesworth, *Grays* 61
Wynward R.T. Wilkinson,
    Portobello 91
Betty and Len Wiltshire,
    Portobello 91
World, *Covent Garden* 53
X.S. Baggage Co.,
    Antiquarius 70
Yesterday Child,
    Camden Passage 44
Zwemmers,
    Covent Garden 53

RESTORERS

Jones and Campbell,
    Alfies 19
Textilean, *Alfies* 22
Yesterday Child,
    Camden Passage 44
Charles Daggett Gallery,
    Portobello 82
The Old Father Time Clock
    Centre, *Portobello* 88
Paul Treadaway,
    Portobello 90
Julie Gregory,
    Portobello 85

ENGRAVERS

Bill Bennett and Keith
    Thorogood, *Grays* 58

WHAT TO BUY INDEX

When a category lists dealers in both cities, London stalls precede the Paris ones, separated by a rule. Numerals refer to page numbers in their respective ends of the book. Since some categories are more typically English, while others are more French, not every category lists stalls in both cities.

ADVERTISING ART
David Huxtable, *Alfies* 19
Paul Arnold, *Camden Lock* 36
Nic Costa, *Camden Passage* 42
Posters for Collectors,
    Grays 60
Andy's Tin City, *Portobello* 80
Liz Farrow, *Portobello* 83

Françoise Chappuy,
    Vernaison, St-O 17
Philippe, *Vernaison, St-O* 20
Galerie V., *Vernaison, St-O* 20
Email et Puces,
    Malassis, St-O 62
Rétro Pub, *Dauphine, St-O* 68

AFRICA see **TRIBAL ART**

AMERICANA
Sparkle Moore, *Alfies* 22

La Tranchée Militaire,
    Malik, St-O 25
Stall 52, *Jules Vallès, St-O* 36
As Time Goes By… and Spirit,
    Malassis, St-O 62

ANTIQUITIES
Hilary Kashden,
    Covent Garden 51
Nigel Mills, *Covent Garden* 51
Jane Stewart, *Grays* 60
Helios Gallery, *Portobello* 85
Tetragon Antiquities,
    Portobello 90

Poisson, *Vanves* 90

ARCHITECTURAL SALVAGE
see **FIREPLACES**

ART DECO see also
CERAMICS
Geoffrey Robinson, *Alfies* 22
Rojeh Antiques, *Alfies* 22
Alexia Say, *Biron, St-O* 30
Stall 402, *Paul Bert, St-O* 45
Walfredo Barth,
    Cambo, St-O 47
Art et Design,
    Serpette, St-O 54
Sycomore, *Malassis, St-O* 62
D.W. Antiquités,
    Malassis, St-O 62
P.B., *Dauphine, St-O* 70
Antilope,
    rue Paul Bert, St-O 76

ARTISTS' MATERIALS
Michael Oliphant,
    Bermondsey 29
Green & Stone, *Antiquarius* 71
Atlantis Art Supplies,
    Brick Lane 101

ART NOUVEAU
Raul Arantes,
    Camden Passage 42
R. Toupenet, *Biron, St-O* 27
Jean Doutrepont,
    Biron, St-O 28
Stall 72, *Biron, St-O* 29
Alexia Say, *Biron, St-O* 30
Stall 402, *Paul Bert, St-O* 45
Walfredo Barth,
    Cambo, St-O 47
Claude Boyer,
    Rosiers, St-O 49
Bernard Liagre,
    Rosiers, St-O 49
Michel Giraud,
    Rosiers, St-O 49
Christian Serres,
    Rosiers, St-O 49
J.-P. Richard, *Rosiers, St-O* 49
A. Gauthier, *Rosiers, St-O* 49

ARTS AND CRAFTS
Furniture + Designs
    1870–1970, *Alfies* 19
Keith Roughton,
    Camden Lock 36
Christian Sapet,
    Paul Bert, St-O 44

BARBOTINE WARE see
CERAMICS

BAR ACCESSORIES
Galerie V., *Vernaison, St-O* 20
Déco Bistro,
    Paul Bert, St-O 45
Jean-Paul Costey,
    Serpette, St-O 53
Du Billard au Comptoir,
    Serpette, St-O 54
Normand,
    Dauphine, St-O 68
Jane de Livron,
    Dauphine, St-O 71
Flao, *Vanves* 86

BASKETS
H&C, *Covent Garden* 50
Putnams, *Columbia Road* 103

Bachelier Antiquités,
    Paul Bert, St-O 40
Michel Morin,
    Paul Bert, St-O 40
Stall 236, *Dauphine, St-O* 71

BATHROOM ACCESSORIES
Dudley and Genie, *Alfies* 19

Brigitte Perruchot,
    Paul Bert, St-O 43
J-P. Jankovsky,
    Serpette, St-O 55

Stalls 19–20,
    Malassis, St-O 60
Rebière Antiquités,
    Malassis, St-O 63
Mazeaux, Aux Vieux Métaux,
    rue Jules Vallès, St-O 77

BEADS AND BEADWORK
Kit Smith, *Covent Garden* 52
Sultani Antiques, *Grays* 60
Nicholas Donn, *Portobello* 82
David Lewin, *Portobello* 86
Michael Telfer-Smollett,
    Portobello 90

Maison Jacques,
    Vernaison, St-O 13

BICYCLES
G Whizz, *Old Crowther* 68

BILLIARDS see **SPORT**

BOOKS
Bibliopola, *Alfies* 18
Gardiner & Gardiner, *Alfies* 19
Archive Bookstore, *Alfies* 23
Stephen Foster's Bookshop,
    Alfies 23
Kay Books, *Bermondsey* 29
Sandy Field,
    Covent Garden 50
The Dover Bookshop,
    Covent Garden 53
Zwemmers,
    Covent Garden 53
Harrison's Books, *Grays* 60
Don Kelly, *Antiquarius* 70
Susan Biltcliffe, *Portobello* 81
Historical Impressions,
    Portobello 85
Books for Cooks,
    Portobello 90
Magpie Bookshop,
    Spitalfields 100
One Eye Books,
    Spitalfields 100

Nicolas Rémon,
    Vernaison, St-O 19
Stall 181, *Vernaison, St-O* 21
Violette Morel,
    Vernaison, St-O 21
Monsieur Harry,
    Malik, St-O 25
Librairie Boulouiz-Ferez,
    Malassis, St-O 65
Habib Arfaoui,
    Dauphine, St-O 70
Françoise Rémy,
    Dauphine, St-O 70
Au Pied de la Lettre,
    Dauphine, St-O 70
Papiers Anciens,
    Dauphine, St-O 70

Anthare de Schuyter,
    Dauphine, St-O 70
Stall 3,
    Lécuyer-Vallès, St-O 73
Stall 15,
    Lécuyer-Vallès, St-O 73
temporary stalls,
    Marché d'Aligre 93
temporary stalls,
    Marché du Livre Ancien 101
    TRADE CATALOGUES
    Don Kelly, *Antiquarius* 70
    Susan Biltcliffe,
        Portobello 81

BOTTLES
Clara Eliane,
    Vernaison, St-O 16
Denise Balbon,
    Vernaison, St-O 21
Françoise Renoult,
    Serpette, St-O 53
Danièle Bouillot,
    Antica, St-O 57
K.F.J., *Malassis, St-O* 62
Marie-Thérèse Nays-Favre,
    Malassis, St-O 63
Circé, *Malassis, St-O* 64
Christian Arnoux,
    Dauphine, St-O 69

BOUTIQUES DE CHARME
Sylvie et Pierre-Gilles,
    Vernaison, St-O 15
Stall 105bis, *Vernaison, St-O* 17
Irma, *Vernaison, St-O* 22
Maïté Poupées,
    Vernaison, St-O 23
Le Curieux, *Biron, St-O* 30
Blandine Lefèvre,
    Biron, St-O 31
Philippe Lachaux,
    Biron, St-O 32
Dominique, *Biron, St-O* 33
Michel Peraches et Eric Miel,
    Paul Bert, St-O 40
Potron Minet,
    Paul Bert, St-O 42
Floris Houwinck,
    Paul Bert, St-O 42
Catherine Millant,
    Paul Bert, St-O 42
Martine Reynaud,
    Paul Bert, St-O 43
Christian Sapet,
    Paul Bert, St-O 44
Hervé Choningbaum,
    Cambo, St-O 47
Daniel Delétrain,
    Serpette, St-O 51
Françoise Renoult,
    Serpette, St-O 53
Anne-Marie Despas,
    Serpette, St-O 53
Stall 12, *Serpette, St-O* 54
Arte, *Serpette, St-O* 54
Stall 18, *Serpette, St-O* 55
Alice, *Malassis, St-O* 60
Sylviane Cristobal,
    Malassis, St-O 61
Aux Libellules,
    Malassis, St-O 62
Zerline, *Malassis, St-O* 62
Jadis à Malassis,
    Malassis, St-O 64

Attitudes, *Malassis, St-O* 65
Humeurs, *Malassis, St-O* 65
Stalls 229–30,
    Malassis, St-O 65
Couespel & Gallot,
    Dauphine, St-O 67
Isabelle Feugère,
    Dauphine, St-O 69
Ambiance, *Dauphine, St-O* 69
Gérard Leprêtre,
    Dauphine, St-O 70
La Petite Maison aux Puces,
    rue Paul Bert, St-O 76
L'Atelier N'O,
    Viaduc des Arts 96
Pascal Maingourd,
    Viaduc des Arts 97
Astier de Villatte,
    Viaduc des Arts 98
Matières Premières,
    Viaduc des Arts 98
Artefact, *Viaduc des Arts* 98

BRASS *see* **METALWARE**

BRIC-A-BRAC
Chris Bennett,
    Bermondsey 28
Richard Perry,
    Bermondsey 29
print dealer,
    Bermondsey 30
Chad Sansean,
    Bermondsey 30
M. Von Taubenheim,
    Bermondsey 30

La Guimandie,
    Vernaison, St-O 15
Stall 69, *Vernaison, St-O* 15
Guy-Laurent Setruk,
    Vernaison, St-O 20
Stall 220, *Vernaison, St-O* 22
Stall 7, *Biron, St-O* 27
Dominique, *Biron, St-O* 33
Stall 31, *Jules Vallès, St-O* 36
Choisi pour Vous,
    Jules Vallès, St-O 37
Thomas Bonzom et Pierre
    Nicolas, *Serpette, St-O* 51
Stall 5, *Serpette, St-O* 53
Veyret, *Malassis, St-O* 61
Maya Antiquités,
    Dauphine, St-O 67
Célestin-Henri Devot,
    Dauphine, St-O 68
Stalls 128–29,
    Dauphine, St-O 69
temporary stalls,
    Lécuyer-Vallès, St-O 73
Albert, *Lécuyer-Vallès, St-O* 73
Muriel,
    rue des Rosiers, St-O 76
31 *rue Jules Vallès, St-O* 77
Le Marché des Antiquaires,
    rue Jules Vallès, St-O 78
F. Magistry, *Vanves* 86
temporary stalls,
    Marché d'Aligre 93

BRIDAL HEADDRESSES
Stall 105bis,
    Vernaison, St-O 17
Jadis à Malassis,
    Malassis, St-O 64
Danièle Engliz-Bey, *Vanves* 87

BUTTONS
Moya Smith, *Bermondsey* 30
H&C, *Covent Garden* 50
Judith Pollitt, *Portobello* 89
Rita Stephenson, *Portobello* 90

Galerie ABC,
    Vernaison, St-O 15
Irma, *Vernaison, St-O* 22
Stall 250, *Vernaison, St-O* 22
Chantal Dagommer,
    Paul Bert, St-O 41

**CARPETS, RUGS
AND TAPESTRIES**
N. Davalou Carpets,
    Bermondsey 28
Christopher Farr,
    Portobello 92
Roughneck & Thug,
    Spitalfields 101

Stall 29, *Vernaison, St-O* 14
Stany Hoffmann,
    Biron, St-O 29
Stall 27, *Serpette, St-O* 51
Trésors de Perse,
    Malassis, St-O 61
Prestige-Art du Textile,
    Malassis, St-O 64
Parissa, *Malassis, St-O* 64
Ghislain Antiques,
    Malassis, St-O 65
Prestige, *Dauphine, St-O* 68
Luc Bouveret,
    Dauphine, St-O 69
Exotic Kalagas,
    Dauphine, St-O 70

CERAMICS
print dealer, *Bermondsey* 30
M. Von Taubenheim,
    Bermondsey 30
The Home Service,
    Camden Lock 36
Vinci Antiques, *Grays* 61
Green & Stone, *Antiquarius* 71
R.A. Barnes, *Portobello* 80

Stall 27, *Vernaison, St-O* 14
Morel-Zysset,
    Vernaison, St-O 14
Stall 110, *Vernaison, St-O* 17
Nicolas Giovannoni, *Vernaison*
    and *Serpette, St-O* 19, 55
Alain Cical, *Biron, St-O* 30
Frédérique Couque,
    Jules Vallès, St-O 37
Stall 58, *Paul Bert, St-O* 41
J-P. Richard, *Rosiers, St-O* 49
Stall 18, *Serpette, St-O* 55
Hier… Encore, *Antica, St-O* 57
Trace de Chine,
    Antica, St-O 57
Jean-Pierre Caietta,
    Malassis, St-O 60
Stéphane Bardot et Patricia
    Attwood, *Malassis, St-O* 61
L'Escalier de Cristal,
    Malassis, St-O 61
Rondeur des Jours,
    Malassis, St-O 61
Franck Bergé,
    Malassis, St-O 63
Stall 121, *Dauphine, St-O* 69
Exotic Kalagas,
    Dauphine, St-O 70

109

Stall 236, *Dauphine, St-O* 71
Stall 3,
  Lécuyer-Vallès, St-O 73
Jellal Kesraoui,
  Lécuyer-Vallès, St-O 73
Jean-Pierre Beaujean,
  Vanves 86
Boulin, *Vanves* 86
Gabrielle, *Vanves* 87
Marie Moulis, *Vanves* 88
René Marie, *Vanves* 88
Daniel Sanz, *Vanves* 89
Gribouille, *Vanves* 89
A & G. Roy, *Vanves* 89
Parisot, *Vanves* 89
Françoise Chatelain, *Vanves* 89
L'Atelier Le Tallec,
  Viaduc des Arts 97
Astier de Villatte,
  Viaduc des Arts 98
ART DECO
Susie Cooper Ceramics,
  Alfies 22
Radford-Muir, *Grays* 60
BARBOTINE WARE
Claude Boyer,
  Biron, St-O 30
Catherine Dian-Dumond,
  Malassis, St-O 62
Monique Germano,
  Dauphine, St-O 71
L'Aidjolate Antiquités,
  rue des Rosiers, St-O 76
BLUE AND WHITE
Sue Norman,
  Antiquarius 70
**EARLY (DELFT, CREAMWARE,
JACKFIELD, ETC.)**
Gardiner & Gardiner,
  Alfies 19
Gordon Gridley,
  Camden Passage 43
Patrick Boyd-Carpenter,
  Grays 58
Guest and Gray, *Grays* 59
Appleby Antiques,
  Portobello 80
Aurea Carter, *Portobello* 81
Jo De Sousa Macedo,
  Portobello 81
Agnes Fox, *Portobello* 83
Garland Antiques,
  Portobello 84
Mike Handford,
  Portobello 85
Erna Hiscock and John
  Shepherd, *Portobello* 85
Alan Milford,
  Portobello 86
Susana Montiel,
  Portobello 87
MAJOLICA
Britannia, *Grays* 58
ORIENTAL see **ORIENTAL ART**
STAFFORDSHIRE
Jacqueline Oosthuizen,
  Portobello 88

CHAIRS see **FURNITURE**

CHANDELIERS see
LIGHTING

CHINA see **CERAMICS
AND TABLEWARE**

CHROME see **METALWARE**

CHROMOLITHOGRAPHS
see **PRINTS**

**CIRCUS AND FAIRGROUND
DECORATION**
Henri Emberger, *Biron, St-O* 28

CLOCKS
The Old Father Time Clock
  Centre, *Portobello* 88
Stall 238, *Vernaison, St-O* 22
Jacqueline Edouard,
  Biron, St-O 28
La Grosse Horloge,
  Jules Vallès, St-O 35
Stall 16,
  Lécuyer-Vallès, St-O 73

CLOTHES see also
**FASHION ACCESSORIES,
HATS AND HANDBAGS**
Victory Motorcycles,
  Camden Lock 37
Annie's Vintage Costume
  and Textiles,
  Camden Passage 42
Browns, *Grays* 61
TNT, *Old Crowther* 68
Graham and Dani,
  Portobello 76
A.P.C., *Portobello* 92
Graham & Green,
  Portobello 93
Paul Smith, *Portobello* 93
Vent, *Portobello* 93
Roughneck & Thug,
  Spitalfields 101

Françoise, *Vernaison, St-O* 14
Francine, *Vernaison, St-O* 18
Béatrice Cuvelier,
  Vernaison, St-O 22
Chantal Dagommer,
  Paul Bert, St-O 41
Artémise et Cunégonde,
  Serpette, St-O 51
Schwartz, *Dauphine, St-O* 67
Boutique Lydia,
  Dauphine, St-O 69
Stall 10,
  Lécuyer-Vallès, St-O 73
Dominique Bory,
  rue Jules Vallès, St-O 78
141 *rue des Rosiers, St-O* 76
156 *rue des Rosiers, St-O* 76
Violette et Sarah,
  rue Paul Bert, St-O 77
Irma et André, *Montreuil* 83
Nadine Buy, *Montreuil* 83
Nordine, *Montreuil* 83
Kimono-Dô, *Montreuil* 83
Scarlett, *Vanves* 89
  COSTUME
  Gallery of Antique Costume
    & Textiles, *Alfies* 23
  Linda Wigglesworth,
    Grays 61
  David Ireland, *Portobello* 85
  Sheila Cook Textiles,
    Portobello 92
  Anne-Marie Despas,
    Serpette, St-O 53
  Nordine, *Montreuil* 83

Métier Costumier,
  Viaduc des Arts 96
**COUTURE AND
DESIGNER LABELS**
Linda Bee, *Grays* 58
Paul Smith Sale Shop,
  Grays 61
Steinberg & Tolkein,
  Antiquarius 71
Identity, *Portobello* 76
Paul Smith, *Portobello* 93

Chantal Dagommer,
  Paul Bert, St-O 41
Boutique Lydia,
  Dauphine, St-O 69
Scarlett, *Vanves* 89
MENSWEAR ONLY
The Duffer of St George,
  Covent Garden 53
Paul Smith Sale Shop,
  Grays 61
C.D. Arnold, *Brick Lane* 101
WOMENSWEAR ONLY
Bebe, *Alfies* 18
Persiflage, *Alfies* 21
Sparkle Moore, *Alfies* 22
Linda Bee, *Grays* 58
Steinberg & Tolkein,
  Antiquarius 71
Affinity, *Portobello* 76
Viva Barnett, *Portobello* 76
Sheila Cook Textiles,
  Portobello 92
Bernstock Speirs,
  Columbia Road 102
VIVIENNE WESTWOOD
Identity, *Portobello* 76

COINS
Nigel Mills, *Covent Garden* 51
Sultani Antiques, *Grays* 60
Helios Gallery, *Portobello* 85

COMMEMORATIVE WARES
Britannia, *Grays* 58
Titanic, *Old Crowther* 68

COPPER see **METALWARE**

CORKSCREWS
Turning Worms, *Portobello* 91

COSTUME see **CLOTHES**

COUNTRY ANTIQUES
see also **FOLK ART**
Anne Gormley, *Alfies* 19
Laraine Plummer, *Alfies* 21
Katherine Pole, *Alfies* 21
Garland Antiques,
  Portobello 84
David Lewin, *Portobello* 86

COUTURE see **CLOTHES**

CRYSTALS see **SHELLS**

CURIOS see **WORKS OF ART**

CUTLERY see **TABLEWARE**

DECORATIVE ACCESSORIES
Gillian Danz, *Alfies* 18
Francesca Martire, *Alfies* 20
Jessica Ward, *Alfies* 22

M. Von Taubenheim,
  Bermondsey 30
Graham & Green,
  Camden Lock 37
The Corner Room,
  Camden Passage 42
John Goodison and
  Chris Paraskeva,
  Camden Passage 43
Shane Meredith,
  Camden Passage 44
World, *Covent Garden* 53
Helray Ltd, *Lillie Road* 69
Colin Smith and Gerald
  Robinson, *Portobello* 89
Bazar Antiques & Decorative
  Items, *Portobello* 92
Emma Bernhardt,
  Portobello 92
Graham & Green, *Camden
  Lock* and *Portobello* 37, 93
Roughneck & Thug,
  Spitalfields 101
Putnams, *Columbia Road* 103

DECORATIVE ANTIQUES
Gardiner & Gardiner, *Alfies* 19
Anne Gormley, *Alfies* 19
Laraine Plummer, *Alfies* 21
Katherine Pole, *Alfies* 21
Catherine Wallis, *Alfies* 22
Madeline Crispin Antiques,
  Alfies 23
The Corner Room,
  Camden Passage 42
Tony D'Almeida,
  Camden Passage 42
John Goodison and
  Chris Paraskeva,
  Camden Passage 43
Gordon Gridley,
  Camden Passage 43
Shane Meredith,
  Camden Passage 44
Baroque 'n' Roll, *Lillie Road* 68
Andrew Bewick and Jonathan
  Lee, *Lillie Road* 69
Zal Davar, *Lillie Road* 69
Decorative Antiques,
  Lillie Road 69
Helray Ltd, *Lillie Road* 69
Catherine Nimmo,
  Lillie Road 69
Bourbon-Hanby Antiques
  Centre, *Antiquarius* 71
Green & Stone, *Antiquarius* 71
Garland Antiques,
  Portobello 84
Bazar Antiques & Decorative
  Items, *Portobello* 92

DESKS AND PENS
Phyllis Gorlick-King,
  Portobello 84

Marie, *Vernaison, St-O* 21
Stall 171, *Biron, St-O* 32
Stall 180, *Biron, St-O* 32
Stall 194ter, *Biron, St-O* 33
Michel Musson, *Biron, St-O* 33
Christophe Gaignon,
  Paul Bert, St-O 42
L'Homme de Plume,
  Malassis, St-O 65
Couespel & Gallot,
  Dauphine, St-O 67

Stall 180,
  Dauphine, St-O 70
Monique Germano,
  Dauphine, St-O 71
L'Atelier Michel Fey,
  Viaduc des Arts 96

DOLLS see TOYS

DRAWINGS
Charlie, *Bermondsey* 28
Phyllis Gorlick-King,
  Portobello 84

Patrice Salet,
  Vernaison, St-O 17
Pierre Jonchères,
  Vernaison, St-O 18

EIGHTIES
CO_2, *Camden Lock* 36

ENAMEL
Kitchen Bygones, *Alfies* 20
Jonathan's Belowstairs,
  Camden Passage 44
Kim Sinclair, *Portobello* 89

Olga Horde,
  Vernaison, St-O 17
Nicole Aker,
  Malassis, St-O 63
Stall 179, *Dauphine, St-O* 69
Stall 236, *Dauphine, St-O* 71
Monique Germano,
  Dauphine, St-O 71
Louise Royer, *Vanves* 88

ENGRAVINGS see PRINTS

EROTICA
Béatrice Cuvelier,
  Vernaison, St-O 22
Au Bonheur du Jour,
  Dauphine, St-O 67

FABRICS see TEXTILES

FANS
Barbara Springall,
  Bermondsey 30

Françoise, *Vernaison, St-O* 14
Le Curieux, *Biron, St-O* 30

FASHION see CLOTHES

**FASHION ACCESSORIES
see also HATS, HANDBAGS**
Bebe, *Alfies* 18
Cristobal, *Alfies* 18
Francesca Martire, *Alfies* 20
Persiflage, *Alfies* 21
Sparkle Moore, *Alfies* 22
Annie's Vintage
  Costume and Textiles,
  Camden Passage 42
Kit Smith, *Covent Garden* 52
World, *Covent Garden* 53
Linda Bee, *Grays* 58
Affinity, *Portobello* 76
Viva Barnett, *Portobello* 76
Graham and Dani,
  Portobello 76
Margaret and Kim,
  Portobello 77
Sarah and Jo, *Portobello* 77

Emma Bernhardt,
  Portobello 92
Sheila Cook Textiles,
  Portobello 92
Paul Smith, *Portobello* 93
Vent, *Portobello* 93
P.R.K. Blackmans Shoes,
  Brick Lane 101
Bernstock Speirs,
  Columbia Road 102

Francine, *Vernaison, St-O* 18
Janine Giovannoni,
  Vernaison, St-O 18
Béatrice Cuvelier,
  Vernaison, St-O 22
Brudasz, *Biron, St-O* 30
Chantal Dagommer,
  Paul Bert, St-O 41
Danièle Bouillot,
  Antica, St-O 57
Boutique Lydia,
  Dauphine, St-O 69
Stall 10, *Lécuyer-Vallès, St-O* 73
141 *rue des Rosiers, St-O* 76
156 *rue des Rosiers, St-O* 76
Violette et Sarah,
  rue Paul Bert, St-O 77
Scarlett, *Vanves* 89

FIFTIES
Bruna Naufal, *Alfies* 21
Paola and Iaia, *Alfies* 21
Geoffrey Robinson, *Alfies* 22
Sparkle Moore, *Alfies* 22
Susie Cooper Ceramics,
  Alfies 22
The Home Service,
  Camden Lock 36
Planet Bazaar,
  Camden Lock 36
Stable Five,
  Camden Lock 36
Annie's Vintage Costume
  and Textiles,
  Camden Passage 42
Linda Bee, *Grays* 58
TNT, *Old Crowther* 68
Betty and Len Wiltshire,
  Portobello 91
Vent, *Portobello* 93

Cyril et Marie Grizot,
  Paul Bert, St-O 42
Eric Lentz, *Paul Bert, St-O* 43
Vingtième Siècle,
  Paul Bert, St-O 45
As Time Goes By… and Spirit,
  Malassis, St-O 62
Giraud, *Dauphine, St-O* 70

**FIREGUARDS see
METALWARE**

**FIREPLACES, PILLARS,
ARCHITECTURAL SALVAGE**
Les Coussis du Chien,
  Portobello 76

Stall 163, *Vernaison, St-O* 21
Stall 176, *Vernaison, St-O* 21
Stall 253, *Vernaison, St-O* 23
Stall 263, *Vernaison, St-O* 23
Stall 48, *Jules Vallès, St-O* 36
Stall 59, *Paul Bert, St-O* 41
Jean Beaumarié,
  Paul Bert, St-O 41

Marc Maison,
    Paul Bert, St-O 44
Marc Deligny,
    Paul Bert, St-O 45
Le Savoir Fer,
    Serpette, St-O 51
Carmina Antiquités,
    Serpette, St-O 52
Pierrette et Pierre Quitard,
    Serpette, St-O 54
Dominique Heidenger,
    Serpette, St-O 54
ABJ, Dauphine, St-O 69
L'Entrepôt,
    rue des Rosiers, St-O 75
La Boutique 75,
    rue des Rosiers, St-O 75
Les Vieilles Pierres du Mellois,
    rue des Rosiers, St-O 76
SEMA, rue Paul Bert, St-O 76
Lorenove, Viaduc des Arts 96
Ripamonti, Viaduc des Arts 96
Matières Premières,
    Viaduc des Arts 98

FISHING see **SPORT**

FLATWARE see
TABLEWARE

FLOORING see **TILES**

FOLK ART see also
COUNTRY ANTIQUES
Edwige Lelouch,
    Biron, St-O 33
Michel, Jules Vallès, St-O 37
Frédérique Couque,
    Jules Vallès, St-O 37
Bachelier Antiquités,
    Paul Bert, St-O 40
Michel Morin,
    Paul Bert, St-O 40
Paul Khormaïan,
    Paul Bert, St-O 41
Potron Minet,
    Paul Bert, St-O 42
Théorême, Cambo, St-O 47
Jean-Pierre Caietta,
    Malassis, St-O 60
Stall 236, Dauphine, St-O 71
Josette et Gilbert Antoine,
    Vanves 88
L'Atelier Guigue Locca,
    Viaduc des Arts 97

FORTIES
Bebe, Alfies 18
Bruna Naufal, Alfies 21
Paola and Iaia, Alfies 21
Susie Cooper Ceramics,
    Alfies 22
The Home Service,
    Camden Lock 36
Stable Five, Camden Lock 36
Annie's Vintage Costume
    and Textiles,
    Camden Passage 42
Linda Bee, Grays 58
Affinity, Portobello 76
Betty and Len Wiltshire,
    Portobello 91
Vent, Portobello 93

Cyril et Marie Grizot,
    Paul Bert, St-O 42

Eric Lentz, Paul Bert, St-O 43
Cervantès, Paul Bert, St-O 44
Patrick Fourtin,
    Paul Bert, St-O 44
Arte, Serpette, St-O 54
Gilda Saiman,
    Malassis, St-O 63
Giraud, Dauphine, St-O 70

FOSSILS
Dale Rogers, Portobello 89

Mireille Favre,
    Vernaison, St-O 20

FRAMES
Jones and Campbell, Alfies 19
Hayman & Hayman,
    Antiquarius 69
Emerich Vidich, Antiquarius 70
Green & Stone, Antiquarius 71
Charles Daggett Gallery,
    Portobello 82
David Levi Antiques,
    Portobello 86
Paul Treadaway, Portobello 90
Lacy Gallery, Portobello 93

Stall 29, Vernaison, St-O 14
Stall 95, Vernaison, St-O 17
Stall 99bis, Vernaison, St-O 17
Stall 163, Vernaison, St-O 21
Violette Morel,
    Vernaison, St-O 21
Stall 195, Vernaison, St-O 22
Christophe Reynal,
    Paul Bert, St-O 45
Stall 30, Malassis, St-O 61
Jean-Louis Heitzmann,
    Vanves 86
Daniel Sanz, Vanves 89
Le Cadre d'Or,
    Viaduc des Arts 96
L'Atelier Lebeau,
    Viaduc des Arts 98

FURNITURE see also
SHOP FITTINGS
Furniture + Designs
    1870–1970, Alfies 19
Gardiner & Gardiner, Alfies 19
Anne Gormley, Alfies 19
Connie Margrie, Alfies 20
Laraine Plummer, Alfies 21
Katherine Pole, Alfies 21
Rojeh Antiques, Alfies 22
Catherine Wallis, Alfies 22
Madeline Crispin Antiques,
    Alfies 23
Keith Roughton,
    Camden Lock 36
Graham & Green, Camden
    Lock and Portobello 37, 93
The Corner Room,
    Camden Passage 42
Tony D'Almeida,
    Camden Passage 42
Carlton Davidson Antiques,
    Camden Passage 42
John Goodison and
    Chris Paraskeva,
    Camden Passage 43
Gordon Gridley,
    Camden Passage 43
After Noah,
    Camden Passage 45

Baroque 'n' Roll,
    Lillie Road 68
Andrew Bewick and Jonathan
    Lee, Lillie Road 69
Zal Davar, Lillie Road 69
Decorative Antiques,
    Lillie Road 69
Catherine Nimmo,
    Lillie Road 69
Bourbon-Hanby Antiques
    Centre, Antiquarius 71
Bazar Antiques & Decorative
    Items, Portobello 92
Stall 27, Vernaison, St-O 14
Stall 29, Vernaison, St-O 14
Sylvie et Pierre-Gilles,
    Vernaison, St-O 15
Stall 95, Vernaison, St-O 17
Catan, Vernaison, St-O 22
Stall 253, Vernaison, St-O 23
Stall 255, Vernaison, St-O 23
Stall 263, Vernaison, St-O 23
Natlyne, Biron, St-O 29
Gisèle, Biron, St-O 29
Tradition, Biron, St-O 29
Stall 60, Biron, St-O 29
Stany Hoffmann,
    Biron, St-O 29
Hélène Jordan, Biron, St-O 30
Stall 125, Biron, St-O 30
Stall 136, Biron, St-O 31
Stall 142, Biron, St-O 31
Stall 155, Biron, St-O 32
Philippe Lachaux,
    Biron, St-O 32
Stall 160, Biron, St-O 32
Au Fil du Temps,
    Biron, St-O 32
Stalls 164–65, Biron, St-O 32
Stalls 167–68, Biron, St-O 32
Stall 171, Biron, St-O 32
Stall 190, Biron, St-O 32
Stall 194ter, Biron, St-O 33
Edwige Lelouch,
    Biron, St-O 33
Stall 200, Biron, St-O 33
Stall 202, Biron, St-O 33
Choisi pour Vous,
    Jules Vallès, St-O 37
Bachelier Antiquités,
    Paul Bert, St-O 40
Michel Morin,
    Paul Bert, St-O 40
Michel Peraches et Eric Miel,
    Paul Bert, St-O 40
Paul Khormaïan,
    Paul Bert, St-O 41
Stall 41, Paul Bert, St-O 41
La Martinière,
    Paul Bert, St-O 41
Stall 59, Paul Bert, St-O 42
Potron Minet,
    Paul Bert, St-O 42
Christophe Gaignon,
    Paul Bert, St-O 42
Cyril et Marie Grizot,
    Paul Bert, St-O 42
Catherine Millant,
    Paul Bert, St-O 42
Marc Bouchetard,
    Paul Bert, St-O 43
Martine Reynaud,
    Paul Bert, St-O 43
Patrice Mayer,
    Paul Bert, St-O 44

112

Patrick Fourtin,
Paul Bert, St-O 44
Christian Sapet,
Paul Bert, St-O 44
Vingtième Siècle,
Paul Bert, St-O 45
Lits et Lampes,
Paul Bert, St-O 45
Stalls 403–5,
Paul Bert, St-O 45
Daniel et Claudine Bour,
Cambo, St-O 47
Patrick Garanjoud,
Cambo, St-O 47
Antiquités Camille,
Cambo, St-O 47
Le Camphrier,
Cambo, St-O 47
La Maison du Roy,
Cambo, St-O 47
Corinne Tonelli,
Cambo, St-O 47
Bernard Liagre,
Rosiers, St-O 49
Christian Serres,
Rosiers, St-O 49
Mahé, *Serpette, St-O* 52
Stall 41, *Serpette, St-O* 53
Renaud Vuaillat et Xavier
Chollet, *Serpette, St-O* 53
Pierrette et Pierre Quitard,
Serpette, St-O 54
Arte, *Serpette, St-O* 54
Stall 17,*Serpette, St-O* 55
Trace de Chine, *Antica, St-O* 57
Stalls 19-20, *Malassis, St-O* 60
Carte Blanche,
Malassis, St-O 61
Stéphane Bardot et Patricia
Attwood, *Malassis, St-O* 61
Zerline, *Malassis, St-O* 62
Christian Leclerc,
Malassis, St-O 64
L'Homme de Plume,
Malassis, St-O 65
Shanaz, *Dauphine, St-O* 67
Daniel Longueville,
Dauphine, St-O 68
Michel Klein,
Dauphine, St-O 69
Gérard Leprêtre,
Dauphine, St-O 70
Exotic Kalagas,
Dauphine, St-O 70
Mammoth Antiek,
Dauphine, St-O 71
L'Entrepôt,
rue des Rosiers, St-O 75
Maison Beys,
rue des Rosiers, St-O 75
Meubles Anciens de
nos Grand-mères,
rue des Rosiers, St-O 76
La Petite Maison aux Puces,
rue Paul Bert, St-O 76
Eric Heitzmann,
rue Paul Bert, St-O 77
Galerie Cailleux,
rue Paul Bert, St-O 77
Espinosa, *Vanves* 89
Poisson, *Vanves* 90
Le Via, *Viaduc des Arts* 96
Yamakado, *Viaduc des Arts* 96
Astier de Villatte,
Viaduc des Arts 98

Dix Heures Dix,
Viaduc des Arts 98
CHAIRS
Connie Margrie, *Alfies* 20
Keith Roughton,
Camden Lock 36
John Goodison and
Chris Paraskeva,
Camden Passage 43
twentytwentyone,
Camden Passage 45

Blandine Lefèvre,
Biron, St-O 31
Stalls 164–65,
Biron, St-O 32
Edwige Lelouch,
Biron, St-O 33
Renaud Vuaillat et
Xavier Chollet,
Serpette, St-O 53
Hier… Encore,
Antica, St-O 57
Rebière Antiquités,
Malassis, St-O 63
Le Club, *Malassis, St-O* 61
Ghislain Antiques,
Malassis, St-O 65
Stall 121, *Dauphine, St-O* 69
Michel Klein,
Dauphine, St-O 69
Le Via, *Viaduc des Arts* 96
Yamakado,
Viaduc des Arts 96
GARDEN
S. Brunswick, *Alfies* 18
Chelsea Gardener,
Antiquarius 71
MODERN
Bruna Naufal, *Alfies* 21
CO_2, *Camden Lock* 36
The Home Service,
Camden Lock 36
Planet Bazaar,
Camden Lock 36
Unit 78, *Camden Lock* 36
After Noah,
Camden Passage 45
twentytwentyone,
Camden Passage 45
Aram Designs,
Covent Garden 53
Helray Ltd, *Lillie Road* 69
Les Coussis du Chien,
Portobello 76
Christopher Farr,
Portobello 92
Graham & Green,
Portobello 93
Andreas Schmid,
Spitalfields 101
PAINTED
Anne Gormley, *Alfies* 19
Laraine Plummer, *Alfies* 21
Katherine Pole, *Alfies* 21
Gordon Gridley,
Camden Passage 43
Baroque 'n' Roll,
Lillie Road 68
Andrew Bewick and
Jonathan Lee,
Lillie Road 69
Decorative Antiques,
Lillie Road 69
Catherine Nimmo,
Lillie Road 69

David Lewin,
Portobello 86
Bazar Antiques &
Decorative Items,
Portobello 92

Patrice Mayer,
Paul Bert, St-O 44
L'Escalier de Cristal,
Malassis, St-O 61
Exotic Kalagas,
Dauphine, St-O 70
Mammoth Antiek,
Dauphine, St-O 71
L'Atelier Guigue Locca,
Viaduc des Arts 97
TABLES
Furniture + Designs
1870–1970, *Alfies* 19
Keith Roughton,
Camden Lock 36
twentytwentyone,
Camden Passage 45

Stall 27, *Vernaison, St-O* 14
Olga Horde,
Vernaison, St-O 17
Catan, *Vernaison, St-O* 22
Stall 255, *Vernaison, St-O* 23
Gisèle, *Biron, St-O* 29
Stall 171, *Biron, St-O* 32
Michel Peraches et Eric
Miel, *Paul Bert, St-O* 40
Stall 35, *Serpette, St-O* 52
Carmina Antiquités,
Serpette, St-O 52
Mammoth Antiek,
Dauphine, St-O 71
L'Entrepôt,
rue des Rosiers, St-O 75
Le Via, *Viaduc des Arts* 96
Yamakado,
Viaduc des Arts 96
UPHOLSTERED
Textilean, *Alfies* 22
Connie Margrie, *Alfies* 20

GAMES *see* **TOYS**

GARDEN WARES
S. Brunswick, *Alfies* 18
Chelsea Gardener,
Antiquarius 71
Cranborne Antiques,
Portobello 82
Mike Handford, *Portobello* 85
S & B Evans & Sons,
Columbia Road 102
Organics, *Columbia Road* 103
Putnams, *Columbia Road* 103
　　GARDEN FURNITURE
　　see **FURNITURE**
　　GARDEN ORNAMENTS
John Goodison and
Chris Paraskeva,
Camden Passage 43
Baroque 'n' Roll,
Lillie Road 68
Helray Ltd, *Lillie Road* 69

Stall 163,
Vernaison, St-O 21
Stall 176,
Vernaison, St-O 21
Stall 122, *Paul Bert, St-O* 41
Jean Beaumarié,
Paul Bert, St-O 41

113

Marc Maison,
  Paul Bert, St-O 44
Marc Deligny,
  Paul Bert, St-O 45
Stall 11, *Serpette, St-O* 54
Stéphane Bardot
  et Patricia Attwood,
  Malassis, St-O 61
Ripamonti,
  Viaduc des Arts 96

GEM STONES see **SHELLS**

GILT WOOD see **WOOD**

GLASS AND CRYSTALWARE
Geoffrey Robinson, *Alfies* 22
print dealer, *Bermondsey* 30
Planet Bazaar, *Camden Lock* 36
Christopher Pearce,
  Camden Passage 44
Templar Antiques,
  Camden Passage 44
Green & Stone, *Antiquarius* 71
Mike Handford, *Portobello* 85
Alan Milford, *Portobello* 86

Robert et Fils,
  Vernaison, St-O 14
Sylvie et Pierre-Gilles,
  Vernaison, St-O 15
Stall 110, *Vernaison, St-O* 17
Nicolas Giovannoni, *Vernaison*
  and *Serpette, St-O* 19, 55
Denise Balbon,
  Vernaison, St-O 21
Violette Morel,
  Vernaison, St-O 21
Irma, *Vernaison, St-O* 22
Les Verres de nos Grand-
  mères, *Biron, St-O* 27
Stall 135, *Paul Bert, St-O* 41
L'Escalier de Cristal,
  Malassis, St-O 61
G.L.B., *Malassis, St-O* 62
Franck Bergé,
  Malassis, St-O 63
Jane de Livron,
  Dauphine, St-O 71
Gabrielle, *Vanves* 87
Claire Lavoine, *Vanves* 87
Françoise Chatelain,
  Vanves 89
  DOMES
  The Old Father Time Clock
    Centre, *Portobello* 88
  LALIQUE
  Susie Cooper Ceramics,
    Alfies 22
  Raul Arantes,
    Camden Passage 42

Stall 94, *Biron, St-O* 30
Alexia Say, *Biron, St-O* 30
G.L.B., *Malassis, St-O* 62
  PÂTE DE VERRE
  Stalls 241–43,
    Vernaison, St-O 22
  Jean Doutrepont,
    Biron, St-O 28
  Elisabeth, *Biron, St-O* 29
  Benoît, *Biron, St-O* 29
  Stall 94, *Biron, St-O* 30
  Alexia Say, *Biron, St-O* 30
  Largeault, *Biron, St-O* 30
  Claude Boyer, *Biron* and
    Rosiers, St-O 30, 49

Le Camphrier,
  Cambo, St-O 47
Bernard Liagre,
  Rosiers, St-O 49
Michel Giraud,
  Rosiers, St-O 49
Christian Serres,
  Rosiers, St-O 49
J-P. Richard,
  Rosiers, St-O 49
A. Gauthier,
  Rosiers, St-O 49
Christian Arnoux,
  Dauphine, St-O 69
  STAINED GLASS
  Neil Phillips, *Portobello* 89

Largeault,
  Biron, St-O 30
Stall 48,
  Jules Vallès, St-O 36
Dominique Heidenger,
  Serpette, St-O 54
Cariatides,
  Serpette, St-O 55

HANDBAGS
Bebe, *Alfies* 18
Kit Smith, *Covent Garden* 52
Linda Bee, *Grays* 58
X.S. Baggage Co.,
  Antiquarius 70
Viva Barnett, *Portobello* 76

Brudasz, *Biron, St-O* 30
Le Monde du Voyage,
  Serpette, St-O 53
Danièle Bouillot,
  Antica, St-O 57
Thierry Amblard,
  Dauphine, St-O 68
156 *rue des Rosiers, St-O* 76
Scarlett, *Vanves* 89

HARDWARE
Dudley and Genie, *Alfies* 19
Richard Perry, *Bermondsey* 29

Stall 5, *Vernaison, St-O* 13
Art et Cristal,
  Vernaison, St-O 13
Stall 12, *Vernaison, St-O* 14
Stall 46, *Vernaison, St-O* 15
Stall 74, *Vernaison, St-O* 16
Stall 168, *Vernaison, St-O* 21
Le Marché des Antiquaires,
  rue Jules Vallès, St-O 78
  CURTAIN POLES
  Gillian Danz, *Alfies* 18

HATS
Bebe, *Alfies* 18
Marie-Louise of Marylebone,
  Alfies 20
Sarah and Jo, *Portobello* 77

Un Parfum d'Aventure,
  Vernaison, St-O 15
Stall 78, *Vernaison, St-O* 16
Francine,
  Vernaison, St-O 18
Stall 40, *Jules Vallès, St-O* 36
Chantal Dagommer,
  Paul Bert, St-O 41
Danièle Bouillot,
  Antica, St-O 57
Boutique Lydia,
  Dauphine, St-O 69

Stall 10,
  Lécuyer-Vallès, St-O 73
156 *rue des Rosiers, St-O* 76
Violette et Sarah,
  rue Paul Bert, St-O 77
Métier Costumier,
  Viaduc des Arts 96
Jean-Charles Brosseau,
  Viaduc des Arts 98

HORSERIDING see **SPORT**

HUNTING see **SPORT**

ICONS
Garry, *Biron, St-O* 28

IRONWORK see
METALWARE

ISLAMIC ART
Shiraz Antiques, *Grays* 60
Sultani Antiques, *Grays* 60
Henry Brownrigg, *Portobello* 81

JEWELRY
Raul Arantes,
  Camden Passage 42
Kit Smith, *Covent Garden* 52
Aura Antiques, *Grays* 58
A. Douch, *Grays* 58
Shapiro & Co., *Grays* 60
Vinci Antiques, *Grays* 61
Delehar, *Portobello* 82
Carlo Fuller, *Portobello* 84
Nadia, *Portobello* 87
Pat Novissimo, *Portobello* 88

Stall 83, *Vernaison, St-O* 15
Au Grenier de Lucie,
  Vernaison, St-O 18
Stall 153, *Vernaison, St-O* 20
Mireille Favre,
  Vernaison, St-O 20
Garry, *Biron, St-O* 28
Biron 28, *Biron, St-O* 28
Hélène Jordan, *Biron, St-O* 30
Stall 202, *Biron, St-O* 33
Sylvie Corbelin,
  Paul Bert, St-O 45
Patricia Timsit,
  Serpette, St-O 52
Saint-Ouen Antiquités,
  Serpette, St-O 52
Diamantina, *Dauphine, St-O* 69
Yves Baruchel, *Vanves* 86
Claire Lavoine, *Vanves* 87
Abec, *Vanves* 89
Patrice Bodzen, *Vanves* 89
Catherine Manoci, *Vanves* 89
  COSTUME JEWELRY
  Cristobal, *Alfies* 18
  Francesca Martire, *Alfies* 20
  Linda Bee, *Grays* 58
  The Gilded Lily, *Grays* 59
  Steinberg & Tolkein,
    Antiquarius 71
  Betty and Len Wiltshire,
    Portobello 91
  Diana Laurie,
    Spitalfields 100

  Galerie ABC,
    Vernaison, St-O 15
  Au Grenier de Lucie,
    Vernaison, St-O 16, 18
  Brudasz, *Biron, St-O* 30

114

Olwen Forest,
    Serpette, St-O 53
Boutique Lydia,
    Dauphine, St-O 69
Robert Jonard et Brigitte
    Olivier, *Vanves* 88
Patrice Bodzen, *Vanves* 89
Cécile et Jeanne,
    Viaduc des Arts 96
TRIBAL JEWELRY
Owen Hargeaves,
    Covent Garden 51
Henry Brownrigg,
    Portobello 81
Nicholas Donn,
    Portobello 82

Les Chevaux du Vent,
    Vanves 89

KEYRINGS
Françoise Chappuy,
    Vernaison, St-O 17

KITCHENALIA
Kitchen Bygones, *Alfies* 20
Paola and Iaia, *Alfies* 21
Jonathan's Belowstairs,
    Camden Passage 44
H&C, *Covent Garden* 50
Kim Sinclair, *Portobello* 89
Emma Bernhardt, *Portobello* 92
Lucy Everett, *Spitalfields* 100
Odyssey, Columbia Road 103

Olga Horde, *Vernaison, St-O* 17
Stall 25, *Jules Vallès, St-O* 36
Nicole Aker, *Malassis, St-O* 63
Stall 179, *Dauphine, St-O* 69
Au Roi des Antiquaires,
    rue Jules Vallès, St-O 77
Monnier, *Vanves* 87
Josette et Gilbert Antoine,
    Vanves 88
Louise Royer, *Vanves* 88
L'Atelier du Cuivre et de
    l'Argent, *Viaduc des Arts* 98
    BREADBOARDS
    Rosslyn Neave,
        Bermondsey 29

KITSCH
Jessica Ward, *Alfies* 22
Emma Bernhardt, *Portobello* 92
Diana Laurie, Spitalfields 100

Françoise Chappuy,
    Vernaison, St-O 17
Béatrice Cuvelier,
    Vernaison, St-O 22
Au Bonheur du Jour,
    Dauphine, St-O 67

LACE see **TEXTILES**

LIGHTING
    CHANDELIERS
    Carlton Davidson Antiques,
        Camden Passage 42
    Baroque 'n' Roll,
        Lillie Road 68

    Art et Cristal,
        Vernaison, St-O 13
    Stall 12, *Vernaison, St-O* 14
    Robert et Fils,
        Vernaison, St-O 14

Stall 27, *Vernaison, St-O* 14
Stall 46, *Vernaison, St-O* 15
Stall 105bis,
    Vernaison, St-O 17
Stalls 241–43,
    Vernaison, St-O 22
F. Bruyneel, *Biron, St-O* 28
Yvette Robert,
    Biron, St-O 28
Stany Hoffmann,
    Biron, St-O 29
Philippe Lachaux,
    Biron, St-O 32
Stall 54,
    Jules Vallès, St-O 36
Carpentier,
    Paul Bert, St-O 40
La Martinière,
    Paul Bert, St-O 41
Stall 239, *Paul Bert, St-O* 43
Lits et Lampes,
    Paul Bert, St-O 45
Stall 27, *Serpette, St-O* 51
Carmina Antiquités,
    Serpette, St-O 52
Stall 41, *Serpette, St-O* 53
Jean-Yves Barczyk,
    Serpette, St-O 53
Renaud Vuaillat et
    Xavier Chollet,
    Serpette, St-O 53
Stall 17, *Serpette, St-O* 55
Stall 18, *Serpette, St-O* 55
Attitudes, *Malassis, St-O* 65
ABJ, *Dauphine, St-O* 69
Stall 16,
    Lécuyer-Vallès, St-O 73
L'Entrepôt,
    rue des Rosiers, St-O 75
Baguès,
    Viaduc des Arts 96
    LAMPS AND WALL BRACKETS
    David Burrows, *Alfies* 18
    Dudley and Genie, *Alfies* 19
    Francesca Martire, *Alfies* 20
    Geoffrey Robinson, *Alfies* 22
    Rojeh Antiques, *Alfies* 22
    Susie Cooper Ceramics,
        Alfies 22
    CO_2, *Camden Lock* 36
    The Corner Room,
        Camden Passage 42
    Carlton Davidson Antiques,
        Camden Passage 42
    Decodence,
        Camden Passage 43
    John Goodison and
        Chris Paraskeva,
        Camden Passage 43
    Shane Meredith,
        Camden Passage 44
    After Noah,
        Camden Passage 45
    twentytwentyone,
        Camden Passage 45
    Aram Designs,
        Covent Garden 53
    Decorative Antiques,
        Lillie Road 69
    Catherine Nimmo,
        Lillie Road 69
    Chelsea Gardener,
        Antiquarius 71
    Les Coussis du Chien,
        Portobello 76

Stephen Osborn,
    Portobello 77
Bazar Antiques &
    Decorative Items,
    Portobello 92
Roughneck & Thug,
    Spitalfields 101
Odyssey,
    Columbia Road 103

Stall 95,
    Vernaison, St-O 17
Stalls 241–43,
    Vernaison, St-O 22
Yvette Robert,
    Biron, St-O 28
Stall 190, *Biron, St-O* 32
Stall 78,
    Jules Vallès, St-O 37
Stall 41, *Paul Bert, St-O* 41
Stall 59, *Paul Bert, St-O* 41
Attitudes,
    Malassis, St-O 65
P.B., *Dauphine, St-O* 70
Au Roi des Antiquaires,
    rue Jules Vallès, St-O 77
Les Templiers, *Vanves* 87
Le Via, *Viaduc des Arts* 96
Baguès, *Viaduc des Arts* 96
Dix Heures Dix,
    Viaduc des Arts 98

LINEN see **TEXTILES**

LUGGAGE
X.S. Baggage Co.,
    Antiquarius 70

Luggage, *Vernaison, St-O* 18
Stall 194ter, *Biron, St-O* 33
Voyages, *Serpette, St-O* 53
Le Monde du Voyage,
    Serpette, St-O 53
Thierry Amblard,
    Dauphine, St-O 68

MEDIEVAL ART
Nigel Mills, *Covent Garden* 51
Jane Stewart, *Grays* 60
Marc-Antoine Du Ry,
    Portobello 83

METALWARE
Richard Perry, *Bermondsey* 29
Shane Meredith,
    Camden Passage 44
David Levi Antiques,
    Portobello 86

L'Entrepôt,
    rue des Rosiers, St-O 75
Mazeaux, Aux Vieux Métaux,
    rue Jules Vallès, St-O 77
René Marie, *Vanves* 88
    BRASS AND COPPER
    Dudley and Genie, *Alfies* 19
    R.A. Barnes, *Portobello* 80
    Noel and Elizabeth Pullman,
        Portobello 89
    CHROME
    Stable Five,
        Camden Lock 36
    FIREGUARDS
    Noel and Elizabeth Pullman,
        Portobello 89

Stall 59, *Paul Bert, St-O* 41

Marc Bouchetard,
    Paul Bert, St-O 43
Le Savoir Fer,
    Serpette, St-O 51
L'Entrepôt,
    rue des Rosiers, St-O 75
Mazeaux, Aux
    Vieux Métaux,
    rue Jules Vallès, St-O 77
IRONWORK
Stall 163, *Vernaison, St-O* 21
Stall 176,
    Vernaison, St-O 21
Philippe Lachaux,
    Biron, St-O 32
Jean Beaumarié,
    Paul Bert, St-O 41
Christophe Gaignon,
    Paul Bert, St-O 42
Marc Bouchetard,
    Paul Bert, St-O 43
Le Savoir Fer,
    Serpette, St-O 51
Jean-Yves Barczyk,
    Serpette, St-O 53
L'Entrepôt,
    rue des Rosiers, St-O 75
La Boutique 75,
    rue des Rosiers, St-O 75
SEMA,
    rue Paul Bert, St-O 76
Mazeaux, Aux
    Vieux Métaux,
    rue Jules Vallès, St-O 77
René Marie, *Vanves* 88
PEWTER
Hilary Kashden,
    Covent Garden 51
Jane Stewart, *Grays* 60
ZINC
Stall 74, *Vernaison, St-O* 16

MILITARIA
Richard Perry,
    Bermondsey 29
London Military Market,
    Camden Passage 41
Steven Wheeler,
    Covent Garden 52
Don Bayney, *Grays* 58
Gordons Metals Ltd,
    Grays 59
Anthony Jack, *Portobello* 86
David Lewin, *Portobello* 86
Novella, *Vernaison, St-O* 13
Un Parfum d'Aventure,
    Vernaison, St-O 15
Stall 74bis,
    Vernaison, St-O 16
Stall 78, *Vernaison, St-O* 16
La Tranchée Militaire,
    Malik, St-O 25
Stall 40, *Jules Vallès, St-O* 36
Stall 52, *Jules Vallès, St-O* 36
Choisi pour Vous,
    Jules Vallès, St-O 37
Stall 80, *Jules Vallès, St-O* 37
Renaud Tessier,
    Paul Bert, St-O 45
Stall 4, *Serpette, St-O* 51
La Garde, *Serpette, St-O* 51
Surplus Militaire Garba,
    rue Jules Vallès, St-O 78
Surplus Simon,
    rue Jules Vallès, St-O 78

Métier Costumier,
    Viaduc des Arts 96

MIRRORS
David Burrows, *Alfies* 18
Rojeh Antiques, *Alfies* 22
Carlton Davidson Antiques,
    Camden Passage 42
Shane Meredith,
    Camden Passage 44
Andrew Bewick and Jonathan
    Lee, *Lillie Road* 69
Decorative Antiques,
    Lillie Road 69
Catherine Nimmo,
    Lillie Road 69
Stalls 241–43,
    Vernaison, St-O 22
Blandine Lefèvre, *Biron, St-O* 31
Stall 150, *Biron, St-O* 31
Philippe Lachaux, *Biron, St-O* 32
Carpentier, *Paul Bert, St-O* 40
H.P., *Paul Bert, St-O* 41
Stall 239, *Paul Bert, St-O* 43
Laurence Lenglare,
    Paul Bert, St-O 43
Patrice Mayer,
    Paul Bert, St-O 44
Christophe Reynal,
    Paul Bert, St-O 45
Stall 26, *Serpette, St-O* 51
Stall 27, *Serpette, St-O* 51
Mahé, *Serpette, St-O* 52
Dominique Heidenger,
    Serpette, St-O 54
Marie-Eve Rosenthal,
    Serpette, St-O 54
Michèle Perceval,
    Serpette, St-O 55
Stall 30, *Malassis, St-O* 61
ABJ, *Dauphine, St-O* 69
P.B., *Dauphine, St-O* 70
La Galerie des Glaces,
    rue des Rosiers, St-O 75
Miroirs,
    rue des Rosiers, St-O 75
Eric Heitzmann,
    rue Paul Bert, St-O 77

MODERN DESIGN *see also*
FURNITURE
Francesca Martire, *Alfies* 20
Bruna Naufal, *Alfies* 21
CO₂, *Camden Lock* 36
The Home Service,
    Camden Lock 36
Planet Bazaar, *Camden Lock* 36
Stable Five, *Camden Lock* 36
Unit 78, *Camden Lock* 36
Decodence,
    Camden Passage 43
After Noah,
    Camden Passage 45
twentytwentyone,
    Camden Passage 45
Aram Designs,
    Covent Garden 53
Les Coussis du Chien,
    Portobello 76
Paul Lau, *Portobello* 77
Andreas Schmid,
    Spitalfields 101
Odyssey, *Columbia Road* 103

Eric Lentz, *Paul Bert, St-O* 43

Vingtième Siècle,
    Paul Bert, St-O 45
Fantazio, *Vanves* 87
    FORNASETTI
    Francesca Martire, *Alfies* 20

MOTORCYCLES
Victory Motorcycles,
    Camden Lock 37

MUSICAL INSTRUMENTS
Novella, *Vernaison, St-O* 13
Allain Cadinot,
    Viaduc des Arts 97
Roger Lanne,
    Viaduc des Arts 97

NATURAL HISTORY
Cranborne Antiques,
    Portobello 82
Michael Telfer-Smollett,
    Portobello 90

**NAUTICAL OBJECTS
AND ANTIQUES**
Peter Laurie, *Bermondsey* 29
Titanic, *Old Crowther* 68
B.A. Neal, *Portobello* 87
Brophy, *Biron, St-O* 30
Stall 173, *Biron, St-O* 32
Brick à Barc, *Malassis, St-O* 62
L'Armada, *Dauphine, St-O* 70
Monnier, *Vanves* 87

NEWSPAPERS
Stall 47, *Vernaison, St-O* 15
Nicolas Rémon,
    Vernaison, St-O 19
Stall 181, *Vernaison, St-O* 21
temporary stalls,
    Marché du Livre Ancien 101

NINETIES
CO₂, *Camden Lock* 36

**ORIENTAL ART
AND CERAMICS**
Don Bayney, *Grays* 58
Guest and Gray, *Grays* 59
Wheatley Antiques, *Grays* 60
Linda Wigglesworth, *Grays* 61
Geoffrey Waters, *Antiquarius* 70
R.A. Barnes, *Portobello* 80
Henry Brownrigg, *Portobello* 81
Jo De Sousa Macedo,
    Portobello 82
The Nanking Porcelain
    Company, *Portobello* 87
Alastair Thomas, *Portobello* 90
Annie Minet, *Biron, St-O* 29
Stall 179, *Biron, St-O* 32
Lucien Pineau,
    Serpette, St-O 54
Trace de Chine,
    Antica, St-O 57
Trésors de Perse,
    Malassis, St-O 61
Stéphane Bardot et Patricia
    Attwood, *Malassis, St-O* 61
Exotic Kalagas,
    Dauphine, St-O 70
Kimono-Dô, *Montreuil* 83
Les Chevaux du Vent,
    Vanves 89

BUDDHISM
Aura Antiques, *Grays* 58

PAINTINGS
Greg Li and Edward Holden,
Alfies 20
Madeline Crispin Antiques,
Alfies 23
Gordon Gridley,
Camden Passage 43
Carter & Brady, *Portobello* 82
Charles Daggett Gallery,
Portobello 82
Colin Gross, *Portobello* 85
Susana Montiel, *Portobello* 87

Stall 29, *Vernaison, St-O* 14
Au Grenier de Lucie,
Vernaison, St-O 16
Stall 193, *Vernaison, St-O* 21
Garry, *Biron, St-O* 28
Paul Milgen, *Biron, St-O* 29
Gilbert Fischer, *Biron, St-O* 29
Hélène Jordan, *Biron, St-O* 30
Stall 125, *Biron, St-O* 30
Stall 54, *Jules Vallès, St-O* 36
Stall 215, *Paul Bert, St-O* 42
Transparences,
Rosiers, St-O 49
Mahé, *Serpette, St-O* 52
Stall 12, *Serpette, St-O* 54
Lucien Pineau,
Serpette, St-O 54
Hier... Encore, *Antica, St-O* 57
Carte Blanche,
Malassis, St-O 61
Marie-Thérèse Nays-Favre,
Malassis, St-O 63
Daniel Longueville,
Dauphine, St-O 68
Maison Beys,
rue des Rosiers, St-O 75
La Boutique 75,
rue des Rosiers, St-O 75
La Petite Maison aux Puces,
rue Paul Bert, St-O 76
Danièle Engliz-Bey, *Vanves* 87
René Marie, *Vanves* 88
Philippe Lambert, *Vanves* 89
Poisson, *Vanves* 90
TAPESTRY CARTOONS
Lhomond,
Vernaison, St-O 13
Stalls 167–68,
Biron, St-O 32
Sylviane Cristobal,
Malassis, St-O 61
WATERCOLOURS
Barry Landsman, *Alfies* 20
Charlie, *Bermondsey* 28
Carter & Brady,
Portobello 82
Ester Chigine, *Portobello* 82

Patrice Salet,
Vernaison, St-O 17
Pierre Jonchères,
Vernaison, St-O 18
Françoise Renoult,
Serpette, St-O 53
Isabelle Feugère,
Dauphine, St-O 69
La Petite Maison aux Puces,
rue Paul Bert, St-O 76
Danièle Engliz-Bey,
Vanves 87

Philippe Lambert,
Vanves 89

PANELLING *see* **WOOD**

PENS *see* **DESKS**

PEWTER *see* **METALWARE**

**PHOTOGRAPHS AND
PHOTOGRAPHIC
EQUIPMENT**
Kay Books, *Bermondsey* 29
Manuela Hofer,
Camden Passage 45
The Photographers' Gallery,
Covent Garden 53
Historical Impressions,
Portobello 85

Mourad Amezal,
Malassis, St-O 60
Au Bonheur du Jour,
Dauphine, St-O 67
Au Passé Simple,
Dauphine, St-O 70
Stall 12,
Lécuyer-Vallès, St-O 73

PIPES
Stall 195, *Vernaison, St-O* 22
Gérard Leprêtre,
Dauphine, St-O 70

PLASTIC
Emma Bernhardt,
Portobello 92
Lucy Everett, *Spitalfields* 100
Odyssey,
Columbia Road 103

Stall 41, *Paul Bert, St-O* 41
Stall 180, *Paul Bert, St-O* 42
Vingtième Siècle,
Paul Bert, St-O 45
BAKELITE
Paola and Iaia, *Alfies* 21
Decodence,
Camden Passage 43

POSTCARDS
Cheryl All, *Covent Garden* 50

Stall 188, *Vernaison, St-O* 21
Stall 195, *Vernaison, St-O* 22
D'Autreppe,
Vernaison, St-O 22
Renaud Tessier,
Paul Bert, St-O 45
Aire du Temps,
Malassis, St-O 62
Normand, *Dauphine, St-O* 68
Alpha Collections,
rue des Rosiers, St-O 76
Sylvie Cablat, *Vanves* 90

POSTERS
Posters for Collectors,
Grays 60
At the Movies,
Antiquarius 69
Liz Farrow, *Portobello* 83

Stall 47, *Vernaison, St-O* 15
Stall 148, *Vernaison, St-O* 19
Philippe, *Vernaison, St-O* 20
Jane Moufflet, *Biron, St-O* 27

Stall 140, *Biron, St-O* 31
Rétro Pub,
Dauphine, St-O 68
Au Passé Simple,
Dauphine, St-O 70
L'Atelier Robin Tourenne,
Viaduc des Arts 96

POTTERY *see* **CERAMICS**

PRINTS AND ENGRAVINGS
Robin Gardiner, *Alfies* 19
Kay Books,
Bermondsey 29
print dealer,
Bermondsey 30
Sandy Field,
Covent Garden 50
Patrick Boyd-Carpenter,
Grays 58
Emerich Vidich,
Antiquarius 70
Ester Chigine, *Portobello* 82
Cranborne Antiques,
Portobello 82
Julie Gregory, *Portobello* 85

Stall 65, *Biron, St-O* 29
Stall 83, *Biron, St-O* 29
Olivier Deboscker,
Paul Bert, St-O 43
M.L.V., *Paul Bert, St-O* 44
Walfredo Barth,
Cambo, St-O 47
Anne-Marie Despas,
Serpette, St-O 53
Librairie du Louvre,
Malassis, St-O 64
Au Réverbère,
Dauphine, St-O 67
Luc Bouveret,
Dauphine, St-O 69
Papiers Anciens,
Dauphine, St-O 70
Anthare de Schuyter,
Dauphine, St-O 70
Jean-Louis Heitzmann,
Vanves 86
temporary stalls,
Marché du Livre Ancien 101
CHROMOLITHOGRAPHS
Stalls 128–29,
Dauphine, St-O 69
Marie Moulis, *Vanves* 88

RADIOS AND HI-FI
Decodence,
Camden Passage 43

Antik Art, *Vernaison, St-O* 15
Stall 12,
Lécuyer-Vallès, St-O 73
Docks de la Radio,
rue Jules Vallès, St-O 78

RECORDS
Au Passé Simple,
Dauphine, St-O 70
Discophilie,
rue des Rosiers, St-O 76
Alpha Collections,
rue des Rosiers, St-O 76
Docks de la Radio,
rue Jules Vallès, St-O 78
Copa Music,
rue Jules Vallès, St-O 78

117

RIBBONS see **SEWING**

**ROOF RIDGE
DECORATIONS**
Michel, *Jules Vallès, St-O* 37
Michel Morin,
  Paul Bert, St-O 40
Michel Peraches et Eric Miel,
  Paul Bert, St-O 40
Marc Maison,
  Paul Bert, St-O 44
L'Entrepôt,
  rue des Rosiers, St-O 75
Maison Beys,
  rue des Rosiers, St-O 75

RUGS see **CARPETS**

SAMPLERS see **TEXTILES**

SCIENTIFIC EQUIPMENT
Delehar, *Portobello* 82
Colin Gross, *Portobello* 85
B.A. Neal, *Portobello* 87

F.G. Richard,
  Vernaison, St-O 17
Brophy, *Biron, St-O* 30
Stall 173, *Biron, St-O* 32
L'Armada, *Dauphine, St-O* 70

SCULPTURE
Sultani Antiques, *Grays* 60
Helray Ltd, *Lillie Road* 69
Marc-Antoine Du Ry,
  Portobello 83

SEVENTIES
Bruna Naufal, *Alfies* 21
CO_2, *Camden Lock* 36
The Home Service,
  Camden Lock 36
Planet Bazaar, *Camden Lock* 36
TNT, *Old Crowther* 68
Affinity, *Portobello* 76
Viva Barnett,
  Portobello 76
Betty and Len Wiltshire,
  Portobello 91
Vent, *Portobello* 93
Andreas Schmid,
  Spitalfields 101
Odyssey,
  Columbia Road 103

Eric Lentz, *Paul Bert, St-O* 43
Vingtième Siècle,
  Paul Bert, St-O 45
Fantazio, *Vanves* 87

SEWING
Judith Pollitt, *Portobello* 89
Swift Antique Lace,
  Portobello 90
  RIBBONS
  The Old Haberdasher,
    Portobello 88

  Maison Jacques,
    Vernaison, St-O 13
  Francine,
    Vernaison, St-O 18
  THIMBLES
  Nigel Mills,
    Covent Garden 51
  The Thimble Society,
    Grays 60

TRIMMINGS
Sarah Lewis and June
  Victor, *Alfies* 20
PL-B, *Bermondsey* 29
Margaret and Kim,
  Portobello 77
Sarah and Jo,
  Portobello 77
The Old Haberdasher,
  Portobello 88

Françoise,
  Vernaison, St-O 14
Houlès, *Viaduc des Arts* 96

**SHELLS, CRYSTALS
AND GEM STONES**
Christopher Cavey, *Grays* 58

Mireille Favre,
  Vernaison, St-O 20

SHOP FITTINGS
A. Binder, *Alfies* 23

Stall 168, *Vernaison, St-O* 21
Philippe Lachaux,
  Biron, St-O 32
Stall 171, *Biron, St-O* 32
Michel Peraches et Eric Miel,
  Paul Bert, St-O 40
Martine Reynaud,
  Paul Bert, St-O 43
Patrice Mayer,
  Paul Bert, St-O 44
L'Entrepôt,
  rue des Rosiers, St-O 75

SILVER
Sue Perks, *Bermondsey* 29
Moya Smith, *Bermondsey* 30
A. Douch, *Grays* 58
J. First, *Grays* 59
Peter Gaunt, *Grays* 59
Shapiro & Co., *Grays* 60
Brian Gordon, *Antiquarius* 69
Peter Cameron, *Portobello* 81
Wynyard R.T. Wilkinson,
  Portobello 91

Françoise, *Vernaison, St-O* 13
Chauvet, *Vernaison, St-O* 14
Stall 83, *Vernaison, St-O* 15
Stall 187, *Vernaison, St-O* 21
Garry, *Biron, St-O* 28
Biron 28, *Biron, St-O* 28
Jacqueline Edouard,
  Biron, St-O 28
Stall 40, *Serpette, St-O* 52
Nicolas Giovannoni
  et Francis Toussaint,
  Serpette, St-O 55
G.L.B., *Malassis, St-O* 62
Daniel Longueville,
  Dauphine, St-O 68
Jane de Livron,
  Dauphine, St-O 71
Jellal Kesraoui,
  Lécuyer-Vallès, St-O 73
Simone Fabre,
  Vanves 86
Zerrouki, *Vanves* 87
Claire Lavoine, *Vanves* 87
Gribouille, *Vanves* 89
Françoise Chatelain,
  Vanves 89
M-T. Colinet, *Vanves* 90

L'Atelier du Cuivre
  et de L'Argent,
  Viaduc des Arts 98

SIXTIES
Bruna Naufal, *Alfies* 21
CO_2, *Camden Lock* 36
The Home Service,
  Camden Lock 36
Planet Bazaar,
  Camden Lock 36
Linda Bee, *Grays* 58
TNT, *Old Crowther* 68
Affinity, *Portobello* 76
Viva Barnett, *Portobello* 76
Betty and Len Wiltshire,
  Portobello 91
Vent, *Portobello* 93
Andreas Schmid,
  Spitalfields 101
Odyssey, *Columbia Road* 103

Stall 180, *Paul Bert, St-O* 42
Eric Lentz, *Paul Bert, St-O* 43
Vingtième Siècle,
  Paul Bert, St-O 45
Fantazio, *Vanves* 87

SPORT
Luggage, *Vernaison, St-O* 18
  BILLIARDS
  Du Billard au Comptoir,
    Serpette, St-O 54
  FISHING
  Ben Maurice-Jones,
    Portobello 86
  Vintage Piscatoriana,
    Portobello 91
  HORSERIDING
  Cheval Collection,
    Vernaison, St-O 20
  HUNTING
  Michel Peraches et Eric
    Miel, *Paul Bert, St-O* 40
  Eric Lentz,
    Paul Bert, St-O 43

STAINED GLASS
see **GLASS**

STAIRCASES
Philippe Lachaux,
  Biron, St-O 32
L'Entrepôt,
  rue des Rosiers, St-O 75

SUITCASES see **LUGGAGE**

TABLES see **FURNITURE**

TABLEWARE see also
CERAMICS
Kitchen Bygones, *Alfies* 20
M. Von Taubenheim,
  Bermondsey 30
Jonathan's Belowstairs,
  Camden Passage 44
Bazar Antiques & Decorative
  Items, *Portobello* 92
Odyssey, *Columbia Road* 103
Putnams, *Columbia Road* 103
  CUTLERY AND FLATWARE
  Sue Perks, *Bermondsey* 29
  Moya Smith,
    Bermondsey 30
  A. Douch, *Grays* 58

Bill Brown, *Portobello* 81
Peter Cameron,
   Portobello 81
Aurea Carter, *Portobello* 81
Wynyard R.T. Wilkinson,
   Portobello 91

Françoise,
   Vernaison, St-O 13
Chauvet, *Vernaison, St-O* 14
Stall 187,
   Vernaison, St-O 21
Stall 40, *Serpette, St-O* 52
Françoise Renoult,
   Serpette, St-O 53
Nicolas Giovannoni et
   Francis Toussaint,
   Serpette, St-O 55
G.L.B., *Malassis, St-O* 62
Marie-Thérèse Nays-Favre,
   Malassis, St-O 63
Jane de Livron,
   Dauphine, St-O 71
Muriel,
   rue des Rosiers, St-O 76
Simone Fabre, *Vanves* 86
Zerrouki, *Vanves* 87
Françoise Chatelain,
   Vanves 89
GLASSES see **GLASS AND
CRYSTALWARE**

TAPESTRIES see **CARPETS**

TAPESTRY CARTOONS
see **PAINTINGS**

TARTANWARE
Eureka Antiques, *Portobello* 83

TEDDY BEARS see **TOYS**

TELEPHONES
Dudley and Genie, *Alfies* 19
Decodence,
   Camden Passage 43

TEXTILES
Gardiner & Gardiner, *Alfies* 19
Sarah Lewis and June Victor,
   Alfies 20
Bruna Naufal, *Alfies* 21
Katherine Pole, *Alfies* 21
Gallery of Antique Costume
   & Textiles, *Alfies* 23
PL-B, *Bermondsey* 29
Ian Mankin, *Camden Lock* 37
The Corner Room,
   Camden Passage 42
Tony D'Almeida,
   Camden Passage 42
Carol, *Covent Garden* 45
Baroque 'n' Roll,
   Lillie Road 68
Catherine Nimmo, *Lillie Road* 69
Margaret and Kim,
   Portobello 77
Sarah and Jo, *Portobello* 77
Delehar, *Portobello* 82
David Ireland, *Portobello* 85
David Lewin, *Portobello* 86
Michael Telfer-Smollett,
   Portobello 90
Sheila Cook Textiles,
   Portobello 92
Warris Vianni, *Portobello* 93

Roughneck & Thug,
   Spitalfields 101
Putnams, *Columbia Road* 103

Françoise, *Vernaison, St-O* 14
Sylvie et Pierre-Gilles,
   Vernaison, St-O 15
Stall 40, *Vernaison, St-O* 15
Francine, *Vernaison, St-O* 18
Stall 220, *Vernaison, St-O* 22
Stall 123, *Biron, St-O* 30
Chantal Dagommer,
   Paul Bert, St-O 41
Perle Jallot, *Paul Bert, St-O* 41
Brigitte Perruchot,
   Paul Bert, St-O 43
Prestige-Art du Textile,
   Malassis, St-O 64
Parissa, *Malassis, St-O* 64
Prestige, *Dauphine, St-O* 68
Exotic Kalagas,
   Dauphine, St-O 70
Micheline Rolland, *Vanves* 89
Marie Lavande,
   Viaduc des Arts 97
LACE
PL-B, *Bermondsey* 29
Carol, *Covent Garden* 45
The Old Haberdasher,
   Portobello 88
Swift Antique Lace,
   Portobello 90

Francine,
   Vernaison, St-O 18
Janine Giovannoni,
   Vernaison, St-O 18
Irma, *Vernaison, St-O* 22
Schwartz,
   Dauphine, St-O 67
Micheline Rolland,
   Vanves 89
LINEN
Bryony Thomasson,
   Portobello 90

Françoise,
   Vernaison, St-O 14
Sylvie et Pierre-Gilles,
   Vernaison, St-O 15
Francine,
   Vernaison, St-O 18
Janine Giovannoni,
   Vernaison, St-O 18
Irma, *Vernaison, St-O* 22
Stall 34,
   Jules Vallès, St-O 36
Daniel et Claudine Bour,
   Cambo, St-O 47
Artémise et Cunégonde,
   Serpette, St-O 51
Schwartz, *Dauphine, St-O* 67
Stall 236, *Dauphine, St-O* 71
Irma et André, *Montreuil* 83
Nadine Buy, *Montreuil* 83
Nordine, *Montreuil* 83
Marie Moulis, *Vanves* 88
Micheline Rolland, *Vanves* 89
Christian Jacquot,
   Vanves 89
Jacqueline Scaccia,
   Vanves 90
Gremion, *Vanves* 90
temporary stalls,
   Marché d'Aligre 93
Marie Lavande,
   Viaduc des Arts 97

SAMPLERS
Erna Hiscock and John
   Shepherd, *Portobello* 85

Francine, *Vernaison, St-O* 18
Le Bonheur des Dames,
   Viaduc des Arts 96

THIMBLES see **SEWING**

THIRTIES
Bebe, *Alfies* 18
Bruna Naufal, *Alfies* 21
Paola and Iaia, *Alfies* 21
The Home Service,
   Camden Lock 36
Stable Five, *Camden Lock* 36
Annie's Vintage Costume
   and Textiles,
   Camden Passage 42
Carol, *Covent Garden* 45
H&C, *Covent Garden* 50
Linda Bee, *Grays* 58
Affinity, *Portobello* 76
Sarah and Jo, *Portobello* 77
Betty and Len Wiltshire,
   Portobello 91

Stall 81, *Biron, St-O* 29
Cyril et Marie Grizot,
   Paul Bert, St-O 42
Eric Lentz, *Paul Bert, St-O* 43
Stall 402, *Paul Bert, St-O* 45
Cabotse, *Serpette, St-O* 51
Jean-Paul Costey,
   Serpette, St-O 53
Gilda Saiman,
   Malassis, St-O 63
Stall 6,
   Lécuyer-Vallès, St-O 73

**TILES, PAVING AND
FLOORING**
N.V.M. Nadine Cottinet,
   Malassis, St-O 60

TOOLS
The Old Tool Chest,
   Camden Passage 45
Harry, *Portobello* 76
John King, *Portobello* 86

Stall 168, *Vernaison, St-O* 21
Stall 25, *Jules Vallès, St-O* 36
Michel, *Jules Vallès, St-O* 37
Michel Morin,
   Paul Bert, St-O 40
Paul Khormaïan,
   Paul Bert, St-O 41
Présents Passés,
   Dauphine, St-O 67

TOYS AND GAMES
Rosslyn Neave,
   Bermondsey 29
Nic Costa,
   Camden Passage 42
Judith Lassalle,
   Camden Passage 44
Heather's Teddies,
   Covent Garden 51

Zoé, *Vernaison, St-O* 18
Stall 142, *Vernaison, St-O* 19
Stall 199, *Vernaison, St-O* 22
Henri Emberger, *Biron, St-O* 28
Stall 21, *Jules Vallès, St-O* 35

Michel, *Jules Vallès, St-O* 37
Paul Khormaïan,
  Paul Bert, St-O 41
Papillon, *Paul Bert, St-O* 42
L'Insolite, l'Autre Pas,
  Serpette, St-O 54
La Collectionnite,
  Malassis, St-O 60
Automates et Poupées,
  Viaduc des Arts 97

DOLLS
Yesterday Child,
  Camden Passage 44
Heather and Clifford Bond,
  Portobello 81

Ursula M. Dieterich,
  Vernaison, St-O 17
Zoé, *Vernaison, St-O* 18
Stall 195,
  Vernaison, St-O 22
Maïté Poupées,
  Vernaison, St-O 23
Chantal Dagommer,
  Paul Bert, St-O 41
Papillon, *Paul Bert, St-O* 42
Automates et Poupées,
  Viaduc des Arts 97

TEDDY BEARS
Pam Hebbs,
  Camden Passage 43
Heather's Teddies,
  Covent Garden 51

TREEN *see* **WOOD**

TRIBAL ART *see also*
JEWELRY
Ian Auld, *Camden Passage* 42
Owen Hargeaves,
  Covent Garden 51
Aura Antiques, *Grays* 58
Nicholas Donn, *Portobello* 82
Anthony Jack, *Portobello* 86
David Lewin, *Portobello* 86
Susana Montiel, *Portobello* 87
Michael Telfer-Smollett,
  Portobello 90

AFRICA
Ian Auld,
  Camden Passage 42
Owen Hargeaves,
  Covent Garden 51
Anthony Jack,
  Portobello 86
David Lewin, *Portobello* 86

Annie Minet, *Biron, St-O* 29

TRIMMINGS *see* **SEWING**

TRINKETS *see* **WORKS OF ART**

TRUNKS *see* **LUGGAGE**

TWELFTH-CAKE BEANS
Papillon, *Paul Bert, St-O* 42

TWENTIES
Bebe, *Alfies* 18
Paola and Iaia, *Alfies* 21
Stable Five, *Camden Lock* 36
Annie's Vintage
  Costume and Textiles,
  Camden Passage 42

Carol, *Covent Garden* 45
H&C, *Covent Garden* 50
Sarah and Jo,
  Portobello 77
Betty and Len Wiltshire,
  Portobello 91

Stall 81, *Biron, St-O* 29
Eric Lentz, *Paul Bert, St-O* 43
Stall 402, *Paul Bert, St-O* 45

UNIFORMS *see* **MILITARIA**

VERTU
Peter Gaunt, *Grays* 59
Delehar, *Portobello* 82
Colin Smith and Gerald
  Robinson, *Portobello* 89

WALKING STICKS
Fantasticks,
  Bermondsey 28
Derek Greengrass,
  Portobello 84

Garry, *Biron, St-O* 28
Stall 202, *Biron, St-O* 33
Gisèle Vaury-Sourmais,
  Antica, St-O 57
Abec, *Vanves* 89

WATCHES
Unit 78, *Camden Lock* 36
Atlam, *Portobello* 80
Nadia, *Portobello* 87
Past Time Wristwatches,
  Portobello 89
Martyn Stamp,
  Portobello 89

Novella, *Vernaison, St-O* 13
Au Grenier de Lucie,
  Vernaison, St-O 18
Biron 28, *Biron, St-O* 28
Rondeur des Jours,
  Malassis, St-O 61
Diamantina,
  Dauphine, St-O 69

WATERCOLOURS *see*
PAINTINGS

WEAPONS *see* **MILITARIA**

WOOD
CARVINGS
Catherine Wallis,
  Alfies 22
Delehar, *Portobello* 82
Mike Handford,
  Portobello 85

GILT WOOD
Stany Hoffmann,
  Biron, St-O 29
Stall 150, *Biron, St-O* 31
H.P., *Paul Bert, St-O* 41
Marie-Eve Rosenthal,
  Serpette, St-O 54
Michèle Perceval,
  Serpette, St-O 55
L'Atelier Lebeau,
  Viaduc des Arts 98

PANELLING
Stall 253,
  Vernaison, St-O 23
Philippe Lachaux,
  Biron, St-O 32

Olivier Deboscker,
  Paul Bert, St-O 43
Pierrette et Pierre Quitard,
  Serpette, St-O 54
Michèle Perceval,
  Serpette, St-O 55
L'Entrepôt,
  rue des Rosiers, St-O 75
TREEN
David Levi Antiques,
  Portobello 86

WORKS OF ART *see also*
PAINTINGS, DRAWINGS,
PRINTS AND SCULPTURE
Patrick Boyd-Carpenter,
  Grays 58
Guest and Gray, *Grays* 59
Shapiro & Co., *Grays* 60
Delehar, *Portobello* 82
Agnes Fox, *Portobello* 83
Derek Greengrass, *Portobello* 84
Colin Gross, *Portobello* 85
Susana Montiel, *Portobello* 87

Françoise, *Vernaison, St-O* 14
Stall 153, *Vernaison, St-O* 20
Jean-Luc Balleur,
  Vernaison, St-O 21
Stall 193, *Vernaison, St-O* 21
Irma, *Vernaison, St-O* 22
Stall 250, *Vernaison, St-O* 22
Jacques Bitoun, *Biron, St-O* 27
F. Bruyneel, *Biron, St-O* 28
Alain Cical, *Biron, St-O* 30
Le Curieux, *Biron, St-O* 30
Stall 78, *Jules Vallès, St-O* 37
Michel, *Jules Vallès, St-O* 37
Frédérique Couque,
  Jules Vallès, St-O 37
Stall 58, *Paul Bert, St-O* 41
Laurence Lenglare,
  Paul Bert, St-O 43
Patrick Garanjoud,
  Cambo, St-O 47
Saint-Ouen Antiquités,
  Serpette, St-O 52
Gisèle Vaury-Sourmais,
  Antica, St-O 57
Jean-Pierre Caietta,
  Malassis, St-O 60
Collection's, *Malassis, St-O* 62
Marie-Thérèse Nays-Favre,
  Malassis, St-O 63
Daniel Longueville,
  Dauphine, St-O 68
Maison Beys,
  rue des Rosiers, St-O 75
L'Aidjolate Antiquités,
  rue des Rosiers, St-O 76
La Petite Maison aux Puces,
  rue Paul Bert, St-O 76
Galerie Cailleux,
  rue Paul Bert, St-O 77
Simone Fabre, *Vanves* 86
Les Templiers, *Vanves* 87
Robert Jonard et Brigitte
  Olivier, *Vanves* 88
Barbeau, *Vanves* 88
Abec, *Vanves* 89
Gribouille, *Vanves* 89
Catherine Manoci,
  Vanves 89
Parisot, *Vanves* 89

ZINC *see* **METALWARE**

Automates et Poupées,
Viaduc des Arts 97

Rosslyn Neave,
Bermondsey 29
Nic Costa,
Camden Passage 42
Judith Lassalle,
Camden Passage 44
Heather's Teddies,
Covent Garden 51
DOLLS
Ursula M. Dieterich,
Vernaison, St-O 17
Zoé, Vernaison, St-O 18
Stall 195,
Vernaison, St-O 22
Maïté Poupées,
Vernaison, St-O 23
Chantal Dagommer,
Paul Bert, St-O 41
Papillon, Paul Bert, St-O 42
Automates et Poupées,
Viaduc des Arts 97

Yesterday Child,
Camden Passage 44
Heather and Clifford Bond,
Portobello 81
TEDDY BEARS
Pam Hebbs,
Camden Passage 43
Heather's Teddies,
Covent Garden 51

TREEN see WOOD

**TRIBAL ART see also
JEWELRY**
Ian Auld, Camden Passage 42
Owen Hargeaves,
Covent Garden 51
Aura Antiques, Grays 58
Nicholas Donn, Portobello 82
Anthony Jack, Portobello 86
David Lewin, Portobello 86
Susana Montiel, Portobello 87
Michael Telfer-Smollett,
Portobello 90
AFRICA
Annie Minet, Biron, St-O 29

Ian Auld,
Camden Passage 42
Owen Hargeaves,
Covent Garden 51
Anthony Jack,
Portobello 86
David Lewin,
Portobello 86

TRIMMINGS see SEWING

**TRINKETS see
WORKS OF ART**

TRUNKS see LUGGAGE

TWELFTH-CAKE BEANS
Papillon, Paul Bert, St-O 42

TWENTIES
Stall 81, Biron, St-O 29
Eric Lentz, Paul Bert, St-O 43
Stall 402, Paul Bert, St-O 45

Bebe, Alfies 18

Paola and Iaia, Alfies 21
Stable Five, Camden Lock 36
Annie's Vintage
Costume and Textiles,
Camden Passage 42
Carol, Covent Garden 45
H&C, Covent Garden 50
Sarah and Jo, Portobello 77
Betty and Len Wiltshire,
Portobello 91

UNIFORMS see MILITARIA

VERTU
Peter Gaunt, Grays 59
Delehar, Portobello 82
Colin Smith and Gerald
Robinson, Portobello 89

WALKING STICKS
Garry, Biron, St-O 28
Stall 202, Biron, St-O 33
Gisèle Vaury-Sourmais,
Antica, St-O 57
Abec, Vanves 89

Fantasticks,
Bermondsey 28
Derek Greengrass,
Portobello 84

WATCHES
Novella, Vernaison, St-O 13
Au Grenier de Lucie,
Vernaison, St-O 18
Biron 28, Biron, St-O 28
Rondeur des Jours,
Malassis, St-O 61
Diamantina,
Dauphine, St-O 69

Unit 78, Camden Lock 36
Atlam, Portobello 80
Nadia, Portobello 87
Past Time Wristwatches,
Portobello 89
Martyn Stamp,
Portobello 89

**WATERCOLOURS
see PAINTINGS**

WEAPONS see MILITARIA

WOOD
CARVINGS
Catherine Wallis, Alfies 22
Delehar, Portobello 82
Mike Handford,
Portobello 85
GILT WOOD
Stany Hoffmann,
Biron, St-O 29
Stall 150, Biron, St-O 31
H.P., Paul Bert, St-O 41
Marie-Eve Rosenthal,
Serpette, St-O 54
Michèle Perceval,
Serpette, St-O 55
L'Atelier Lebeau,
Viaduc des Arts 98
PANELLING
Stall 253,
Vernaison, St-O 23
Philippe Lachaux,
Biron, St-O 32

Olivier Deboscker,
Paul Bert, St-O 43
Pierrette et Pierre Quitard,
Serpette, St-O 54
Michèle Perceval,
Serpette, St-O 55
L'Entrepôt,
rue des Rosiers, St-O 75
TREEN
David Levi Antiques,
Portobello 86

**WORKS OF ART see also
PAINTINGS, DRAWINGS,
PRINTS AND SCULPTURE**
Françoise, Vernaison, St-O 14
Stall 153, Vernaison, St-O 20
Jean-Luc Balleur,
Vernaison, St-O 21
Stall 193, Vernaison, St-O 21
Irma, Vernaison, St-O 22
Stall 250, Vernaison, St-O 22
Jacques Bitoun, Biron, St-O 27
F. Bruyneel, Biron, St-O 28
Alain Cical, Biron, St-O 30
Le Curieux, Biron, St-O 30
Stall 78, Jules Vallès, St-O 37
Michel, Jules Vallès, St-O 37
Frédérique Couque,
Jules Vallès, St-O 37
Stall 58, Paul Bert, St-O 41
Laurence Lenglare,
Paul Bert, St-O 43
Patrick Garanjoud,
Cambo, St-O 47
Saint-Ouen Antiquités,
Serpette, St-O 52
Gisèle Vaury-Sourmais,
Antica, St-O 57
Jean-Pierre Caietta,
Malassis, St-O 60
Collection's, Malassis, St-O 62
Marie-Thérèse Nays-Favre,
Malassis, St-O 63
Daniel Longueville,
Dauphine, St-O 68
Maison Beys,
rue des Rosiers, St-O 75
L'Aidjolate Antiquités,
rue des Rosiers, St-O 76
La Petite Maison aux Puces,
rue Paul Bert, St-O 76
Galerie Cailleux,
rue Paul Bert, St-O 77
Simone Fabre, Vanves 86
Les Templiers, Vanves 87
Robert Jonard et Brigitte
Olivier, Vanves 88
Barbeau, Vanves 88
Abec, Vanves 89
Gribouille, Vanves 89
Catherine Manoci,
Vanves 89
Parisot, Vanves 89

Patrick Boyd-Carpenter,
Grays 58
Guest and Gray, Grays 59
Shapiro & Co., Grays 60
Delehar, Portobello 82
Agnes Fox, Portobello 83
Derek Greengrass, Portobello 84
Colin Gross, Portobello 85
Susana Montiel, Portobello 87

ZINC see METALWARE

120

Stall 40, *Serpette, St-O* 52
Françoise Renoult,
  Serpette, St-O 53
Nicolas Giovannoni et
  Francis Toussaint,
  Serpette, St-O 55
G.L.B., *Malassis, St-O* 62
Marie-Thérèse Nays-Favre,
  Malassis, St-O 63
Jane de Livron,
  Dauphine, St-O 71
Muriel,
  rue des Rosiers, St-O 76
Simone Fabre, *Vanves* 86
Zerrouki, *Vanves* 87
Françoise Chatelain,
  Vanves 89

Sue Perks, *Bermondsey* 29
Moya Smith,
  Bermondsey 30
A. Douch, *Grays* 58
Bill Brown, *Portobello* 81
Peter Cameron,
  Portobello 81
Aurea Carter, *Portobello* 81
Wynyard R.T. Wilkinson,
  Portobello 91
GLASSES see **GLASS AND
CRYSTALWARE**

TAPESTRIES see **CARPETS**

TAPESTRY CARTOONS
see **PAINTINGS**

TARTANWARE
Eureka Antiques, *Portobello* 83

TEDDY BEARS see **TOYS**

TELEPHONES
Dudley and Genie, *Alfies* 19
Decodence,
  Camden Passage 43

TEXTILES
Françoise, *Vernaison, St-O* 14
Sylvie et Pierre-Gilles,
  Vernaison, St-O 15
Stall 40, *Vernaison, St-O* 15
Francine, *Vernaison, St-O* 18
Stall 220, *Vernaison, St-O* 22
Stall 123, *Biron, St-O* 30
Chantal Dagommer,
  Paul Bert, St-O 41
Perle Jallot, *Paul Bert, St-O* 41
Brigitte Perruchot,
  Paul Bert, St-O 43
Prestige-Art du Textile,
  Malassis, St-O 64
Parissa, *Malassis, St-O* 64
Prestige, *Dauphine, St-O* 68
Exotic Kalagas,
  Dauphine, St-O 70
Micheline Rolland, *Vanves* 89
Marie Lavande,
  Viaduc des Arts 97

Gardiner & Gardiner, *Alfies* 19
Sarah Lewis and June Victor,
  Alfies 20
Bruna Naufal, *Alfies* 21
Katherine Pole, *Alfies* 21
Gallery of Antique Costume &
  Textiles, *Alfies* 23

PL-B, *Bermondsey* 29
Ian Mankin, *Camden Lock* 37
The Corner Room,
  Camden Passage 42
Tony D'Almeida,
  Camden Passage 42
Carol, *Covent Garden* 45
Baroque 'n' Roll, *Lillie Road* 68
Catherine Nimmo, *Lillie Road* 69
Margaret and Kim,
  Portobello 77
Sarah and Jo, *Portobello* 77
Delehar, *Portobello* 82
David Ireland, *Portobello* 85
David Lewin, *Portobello* 86
Michael Telfer-Smollett,
  Portobello 90
Sheila Cook Textiles,
  Portobello 92
Warris Vianni, *Portobello* 93
Roughneck & Thug,
  Spitalfields 101
Putnams, *Columbia Road* 103
  LACE
  Francine,
    Vernaison, St-O 18
  Janine Giovannoni,
    Vernaison, St-O 18
  Irma, *Vernaison, St-O* 22
  Schwartz,
    Dauphine, St-O 67
  Micheline Rolland,
    Vanves 89

  PL-B, *Bermondsey* 29
  Carol, *Covent Garden* 45
  The Old Haberdasher,
    Portobello 88
  Swift Antique Lace,
    Portobello 90
  LINEN
  Françoise,
    Vernaison, St-O 14
  Sylvie et Pierre-Gilles,
    Vernaison, St-O 15
  Francine,
    Vernaison, St-O 18
  Janine Giovannoni,
    Vernaison, St-O 18
  Irma, *Vernaison, St-O* 22
  Stall 34,
    Jules Vallès, St-O 36
  Daniel et Claudine Bour,
    Cambo, St-O 47
  Artémise et Cunégonde,
    Serpette, St-O 51
  Schwartz, *Dauphine, St-O* 67
  Stall 236, *Dauphine, St-O* 71
  Irma et André, *Montreuil* 83
  Nadine Buy, *Montreuil* 83
  Nordine, *Montreuil* 83
  Marie Moulis, *Vanves* 88
  Micheline Rolland,
    Vanves 89
  Christian Jacquot,
    Vanves 89
  Jacqueline Scaccia,
    Vanves 90
  Gremion, *Vanves* 90
  temporary stalls,
    Marché d'Aligre 93
  Marie Lavande,
    Viaduc des Arts 97

  Bryony Thomasson,
    Portobello 90

SAMPLERS
Francine, *Vernaison, St-O* 18
Le Bonheur des Dames,
  Viaduc des Arts 96

Erna Hiscock and John
  Shepherd, *Portobello* 85

THIMBLES see **SEWING**

THIRTIES
Stall 81, *Biron, St-O* 29
Cyril et Marie Grizot,
  Paul Bert, St-O 42
Eric Lentz, *Paul Bert, St-O* 43
Stall 402, *Paul Bert, St-O* 45
Cabotse, *Serpette, St-O* 51
Jean-Paul Costey,
  Serpette, St-O 53
Gilda Saiman,
  Malassis, St-O 63
Stall 6,
  Lécuyer-Vallès, St-O 73

Bebe, *Alfies* 18
Bruna Naufal, *Alfies* 21
Paola and Iaia, *Alfies* 21
The Home Service,
  Camden Lock 36
Stable Five, *Camden Lock* 36
Annie's Vintage Costume
  and Textiles,
  Camden Passage 42
Carol, *Covent Garden* 45
H&C, *Covent Garden* 50
Linda Bee, *Grays* 58
Affinity, *Portobello* 76
Sarah and Jo, *Portobello* 77
Betty and Len Wiltshire,
  Portobello 91

**TILES, PAVING AND
FLOORING**
N.V.M. Nadine Cottinet,
  Malassis, St-O 60

TOOLS
Stall 168, *Vernaison, St-O* 21
Stall 25, *Jules Vallès, St-O* 36
Michel, *Jules Vallès, St-O* 37
Michel Morin,
  Paul Bert, St-O 40
Paul Khormaïan,
  Paul Bert, St-O 41
Présents Passés,
  Dauphine, St-O 67

The Old Tool Chest,
  Camden Passage 45
Harry, *Portobello* 76
John King, *Portobello* 86

TOYS AND GAMES
Zoé, *Vernaison, St-O* 18
Stall 142, *Vernaison, St-O* 19
Stall 199, *Vernaison, St-O* 22
Henri Emberger,
  Biron, St-O 28
Stall 21, *Jules Vallès, St-O* 35
Michel, *Jules Vallès, St-O* 37
Paul Khormaïan,
  Paul Bert, St-O 41
Papillon, *Paul Bert, St-O* 42
L'Insolite, l'Autre Pas,
  Serpette, St-O 54
La Collectionnite,
  Malassis, St-O 60

119

RIBBONS see **SEWING**

ROOF RIDGE DECORATIONS
Michel, *Jules Vallès, St-O* 37
Michel Morin,
Paul Bert, St-O 40
Michel Peraches et Eric Miel,
Paul Bert, St-O 40
Marc Maison,
Paul Bert, St-O 44
L'Entrepôt,
rue des Rosiers, St-O 75
Maison Beys,
rue des Rosiers, St-O 75

RUGS see **CARPETS**

SAMPLERS see **TEXTILES**

SCIENTIFIC EQUIPMENT
F.G. Richard,
Vernaison, St-O 17
Brophy, *Biron, St-O* 30
Stall 173, *Biron, St-O* 32
L'Armada, *Dauphine, St-O* 70
Delehar, *Portobello* 82
Colin Gross, *Portobello* 85
B.A. Neal, *Portobello* 87

SCULPTURE
Sultani Antiques, *Grays* 60
Helray Ltd, *Lillie Road* 69
Marc-Antoine Du Ry,
Portobello 83

SEVENTIES
Eric Lentz, *Paul Bert, St-O* 43
Vingtième Siècle,
Paul Bert, St-O 45
Fantazio, *Vanves* 87
Bruna Naufal, *Alfies* 21
CO_2, *Camden Lock* 36
The Home Service,
Camden Lock 36
Planet Bazaar, *Camden Lock* 36
TNT, *Old Crowther* 68
Affinity, *Portobello* 76
Viva Barnett,
Portobello 76
Betty and Len Wiltshire,
Portobello 91
Vent, *Portobello* 93
Andreas Schmid,
Spitalfields 101
Odyssey,
Columbia Road 103

SEWING
Judith Pollitt, *Portobello* 89
Swift Antique Lace,
Portobello 90
RIBBONS
Maison Jacques,
Vernaison, St-O 13
Francine,
Vernaison, St-O 18
The Old Haberdasher,
Portobello 88
THIMBLES
Nigel Mills,
Covent Garden 51
The Thimble Society,
Grays 60

TRIMMINGS
Françoise,
Vernaison, St-O 14
Houlès, *Viaduc des Arts* 96
Sarah Lewis and June
Victor, *Alfies* 20
PL-B, *Bermondsey* 29
Margaret and Kim,
Portobello 77
Sarah and Jo,
Portobello 77
The Old Haberdasher,
Portobello 88

SHELLS, CRYSTALS AND GEM STONES
Mireille Favre,
Vernaison, St-O 20
Christopher Cavey, *Grays* 58

SHOP FITTINGS
Stall 168, *Vernaison, St-O* 21
Philippe Lachaux,
Biron, St-O 32
Stall 171, *Biron, St-O* 32
Michel Peraches et Eric Miel,
Paul Bert, St-O 40
Martine Reynaud,
Paul Bert, St-O 43
Patrice Mayer,
Paul Bert, St-O 44
L'Entrepôt,
rue des Rosiers, St-O 75
A. Binder, *Alfies* 23

SILVER
Françoise, *Vernaison, St-O* 13
Chauvet, *Vernaison, St-O* 14
Stall 83, *Vernaison, St-O* 15
Stall 187, *Vernaison, St-O* 21
Garry, *Biron, St-O* 28
Biron 28, *Biron, St-O* 28
Jacqueline Edouard,
Biron, St-O 28
Stall 40, *Serpette, St-O* 52
Nicolas Giovannoni
et Francis Toussaint,
Serpette, St-O 55
G.L.B., *Malassis, St-O* 62
Daniel Longueville,
Dauphine, St-O 68
Jane de Livron,
Dauphine, St-O 71
Jellal Kesraoui,
Lécuyer-Vallès, St-O 73
Simone Fabre, *Vanves* 86
Zerrouki, *Vanves* 87
Claire Lavoine, *Vanves* 87
Gribouille, *Vanves* 89
Françoise Chatelain,
Vanves 89
M-T. Colinet, *Vanves* 90
L'Atelier du Cuivre
et de L'Argent,
Viaduc des Arts 98
Sue Perks, *Bermondsey* 29
Moya Smith, *Bermondsey* 30
A. Douch, *Grays* 58
J. First, *Grays* 59
Peter Gaunt, *Grays* 59
Shapiro & Co., *Grays* 60
Brian Gordon, *Antiquarius* 69
Peter Cameron, *Portobello* 81

Wynyard R.T. Wilkinson,
Portobello 91

SIXTIES
Stall 180, *Paul Bert, St-O* 42
Eric Lentz, *Paul Bert, St-O* 43
Vingtième Siècle,
Paul Bert, St-O 45
Fantazio, *Vanves* 87
Bruna Naufal, *Alfies* 21
CO_2, *Camden Lock* 36
The Home Service,
Camden Lock 36
Planet Bazaar,
Camden Lock 36
Linda Bee, *Grays* 58
TNT, *Old Crowther* 68
Affinity, *Portobello* 76
Viva Barnett, *Portobello* 76
Betty and Len Wiltshire,
Portobello 91
Vent, *Portobello* 93
Andreas Schmid,
Spitalfields 101
Odyssey, *Columbia Road* 103

SPORT
Luggage, *Vernaison, St-O* 18
BILLIARDS
Du Billard au Comptoir,
Serpette, St-O 54
FISHING
Ben Maurice-Jones,
Portobello 86
Vintage Piscatoriana,
Portobello 91
HORSERIDING
Cheval Collection,
Vernaison, St-O 20
HUNTING
Michel Peraches et Eric
Miel, *Paul Bert, St-O* 40
Eric Lentz,
Paul Bert, St-O 43

STAINED GLASS
see **GLASS**

STAIRCASES
Philippe Lachaux,
Biron, St-O 32
L'Entrepôt,
rue des Rosiers, St-O 75

SUITCASES see **LUGGAGE**

TABLES see **FURNITURE**

TABLEWARE see also **CERAMICS**
Kitchen Bygones, *Alfies* 20
M. Von Taubenheim,
Bermondsey 30
Jonathan's Belowstairs,
Camden Passage 44
Bazar Antiques & Decorative
Items, *Portobello* 92
Odyssey, *Columbia Road* 103
Putnams, *Columbia Road* 103
CUTLERY AND FLATWARE
Françoise,
Vernaison, St-O 13
Chauvet, *Vernaison, St-O* 14
Stall 187,
Vernaison, St-O 21

118

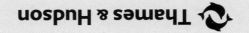
Thames & Hudson

with 332 color illustrations

Photographs by Rupert Thomas

ANTIQUE & FLEA MARKETS OF LONDON & PARIS

RUPERT THOMAS · ÉGLÉ SALVY

To Marie-Aimée, my lovely daughter,
in memory of a hardworking year 1997–1998.

Acknowledgments
With many thanks to Patrick Mauriès, who sent me out to cover
the Paris flea markets, to my editors on either side of the
Channel and to the inventor of the fax.

FRONTISPIECE: Puces de Vanves

All the information in this book relates to the period January–October 1998,
when it was compiled. Guidelines on stock and dealer specialities are subject
to change, as are locations and ownership of stalls.

Translated from the French by Lorna Dale

© 1999 Thames & Hudson Ltd, London

First published in paperback in the United States of America in 1999 by Thames & Hudson Inc.,
500 Fifth Avenue, New York, New York 10110
Reprinted 2001

Library of Congress Catalog Card Number 98-61510
ISBN 0-500-28112-2

Printed and bound in Italy

PARIS CONTENTS

Using Your Guide   7

Author's Perspective   8

A History of Paris Flea Markets   8

PUCES DE SAINT-OUEN   10
  Marché Vernaison   12
  Marché Malik   24
  Marché Biron   26
  Marché Jules Vallès   34
  Marché Paul Bert   38
  Marché Cambo   46
  Marché des Rosiers   48
  Marché Serpette   50
  Marché Antica   56
  Marché Malassis   58
  Marché Dauphine   66
  Marché Lécuyer-Vallès   72
  Shops in Saint-Ouen   74

PUCES DE MONTREUIL   80

PUCES DE VANVES   84

MARCHÉ D'ALIGRE/VIADUC DES ARTS   92

MARCHÉ DU LIVRE ANCIEN   100

Where to Buy Index   105

What to Buy Index   108

Where possible, we have provided telephone numbers for the stalls themselves (in which case, you will only get a reply on trading days). In other instances, the number listed is either the mobile or the home telephone number of the dealer. Readers telephoning from abroad should remember to replace the initial 'o' of the telephone number with the country code for either England or France.

Where illustrations are not captioned, the stall photographed is not mentioned in the book.

Maps by Hardlines

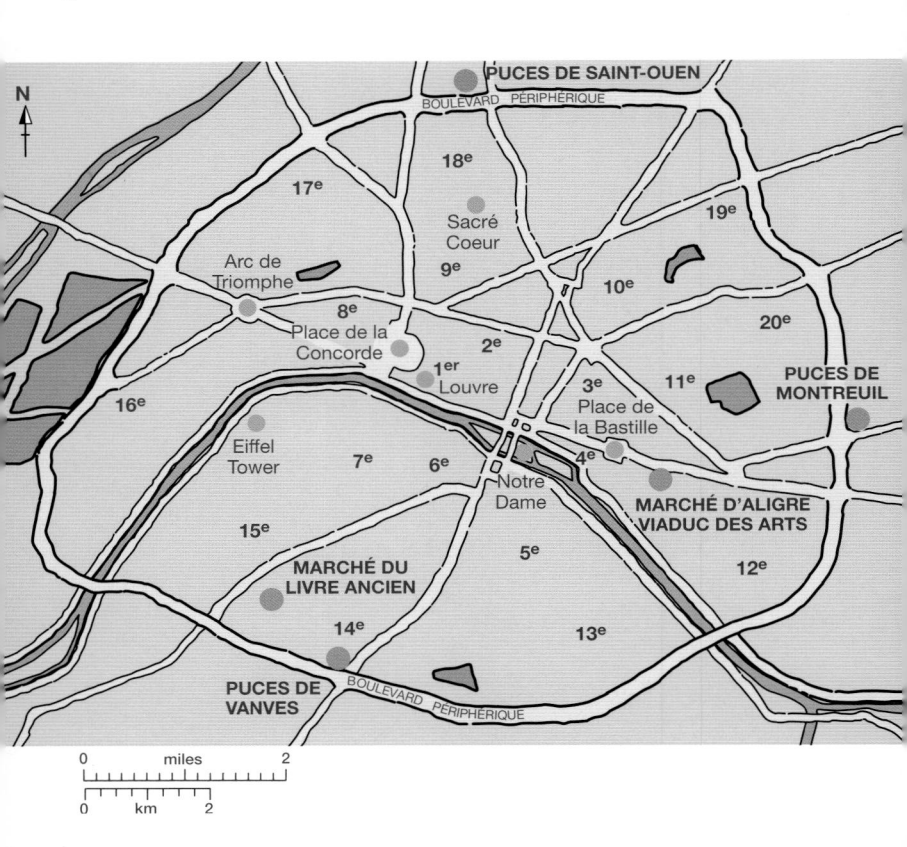

USING **YOUR GUIDE**

- Firstly, get your bearings. Look at the Contents Page for Paris (the one for London is at the other end of the book) to find a full list of the markets covered. The map opposite shows where the markets are situated in the city.

- If you know what you want, go straight to the Indexes. They will direct you both to dealers you may have heard of (Where to Buy Index, see p. 105) and to stands that specialize in the kind of stock you're looking for (What to Buy Index, see p. 108).

- If you simply want to explore, use the Contents Page to direct you to a particular market. Turn to the market in question to discover how it came into being, when trading takes place and what are the best ways of getting there; the maps are designed to make it as easy as possible.

- The following pages give you the facts, as well as anecdotes, about some of the stallholders you will encounter. ● indicates a stall that is a particular favourite of the author.

- When you get there, be sure to hunt around, to talk to the dealers and perhaps try a spot of bargaining. If you're tired and need a break, turn to your guide's Nearbuys for advice on local cafés.

AUTHOR'S **PERSPECTIVE**

Going to secondhand markets, especially the Paris flea markets, is an endless source of pleasure. You begin by browsing and rummaging among the stock, taking a good look at the motley collection of objects (although it's not always clear what some of them are). You might get into conversation with the stallholders who love the things they sell and certainly don't mind talking about them; in fact, they actively enjoy it. There are times when you fall for an object straight away and decide to buy it. You know exactly where you're going to put it or hang it or who you'll give it to. This can lead on to another pleasurable activity: bargaining. You hesitate, walk away, come back, make another offer. In some cases the object you want is completely beyond your means. The stallholder knows that only a serious antique dealer, a major interior decorator or even a museum curator is likely to buy it, but for as long as it is on their stall, it belongs to them; they love and admire it too and take pleasure in talking about it. Wandering around the Paris flea markets every weekend, I came across all kinds of wonderful things. I had to resist temptation on many occasions and only succumbed once – after all you have to be strict with yourself, either you're working or you're antique-hunting. But I was fortunate enough to see a Régence mirror that was absolutely exceptional (more about that later).

Obviously this book is intended as a guide and not a directory and I have written about the stalls where the stock appealed to me and where I found the people friendly. I lay no claim to being impartial.

Each market is described in turn, with stalls listed numerically, by aisle or by floor. Where stalls are not numbered, they have been listed in the order that you encounter them once you have entered the market. Collectors or anyone who knows what they are looking for should refer to the What to Buy Index (see p. 108) to find out which stalls stock their chosen category.

A HISTORY OF **PARIS FLEA MARKETS**

When I was a little girl in the Fifties and Sixties, it was still quite common to hear the hoarse cry of the rag-and-bone man and the ringing of his bell in the streets of Paris. Rag-and-bone merchants in every city have always collected and resold the things people throw away. From the 14th century onwards, efforts were made to regulate the trade, with sites set aside for displaying the goods, fixed hours and descriptions of the stock. Before long, traders even had to have a licensed numbered plate. By about 1860 the rag-and-bone merchants were becoming increasingly unpopular in Paris and were only allowed to sell between midnight and five o'clock in the morning. They moved

out beyond the fortifications, which at the time surrounded the city, to outlying villages such as Bicêtre, Montreuil, Vanves and Saint-Ouen, trading on wasteland beneath the fortifications, near fields that were still cultivated as small market gardens. In *Les Puces ont cent ans* (The Flea Markets are a Hundred Years Old), Jean Bedel estimates that the merchants numbered about thirty thousand at that time.

In the following twenty years, more and more rag-and-bone men flocked to the Malassis plain, beyond the Porte de Clignancourt. As they sifted through their wares on Sundays, on the ground naturally, curious bystanders came from Paris to look at the grubby but picturesque display of goods and they started buying. The shrewdest traders soon began organizing themselves and setting up trestle tables; then they built makeshift shelters and even rented sites (highly illegally) to newcomers. The local council in Saint-Ouen realized it could turn this situation to its advantage and started to regulate the market, especially after a metro line to the Porte de Clignancourt was completed in 1908. In hot weather, traders, onlookers and customers get thirsty; when it is cold, they want to warm up, so cafés opened. Some years later and before they became famous, Django Reinhardt and Edith Piaf appeared there. The affectionate term '*marché aux puces*' or 'flea markets' was first coined in the early 20th century and appears on postcards of Saint-Ouen dating from that period. Although 'the weekend' was an unknown concept at the time, customers and curious onlookers started coming to the flea markets on Saturdays. When the old fortifications were demolished and cheap housing started to be built around Paris after World War I, the Saint-Ouen dealers, the largest group of traders, began to organize themselves properly and permanent market structures gradually developed.

Nowadays there are several flea markets (at the Porte de Vanves, the Porte de Montreuil and the place d'Aligre), but the Saint-Ouen markets are the most famous. Over 2,500 secondhand and junk stalls, spread over fifteen acres, display quality goods along more than nine miles of aisles. The Saint-Ouen flea markets are one of Paris's most popular tourist sights. According to the Observatoire du Tourisme (which collects statistics on tourism in France), eleven million people visited them in 1996, which puts them on a par with Notre-Dame and makes the Puces de Saint-Ouen more popular than the Eiffel Tower! Eighty per cent of the turnover is export and you hear people bargaining in every language under the sun. But listen carefully and you'll realize that the stallholders have their own jargon. When you hear someone talk about '*drouille*' (rubbish) or say something '*n'est pas un château*' (is not all that interesting), watch out. But if it is '*de la grande musique*' (high quality), get in quickly. And pay special attention when they talk about their '*chines*' (finds).

PERLE JALLOT, PAUL BERT   PERLE JALLOT, PAUL BERT

IO

SAINT-OUEN

N

Paul Bert

Jules Vallès

Cambo

Serpette

Lécuyer-Vallès

RUE DES

RUE PIERRE CURIE

RUE MARIE CURIE

P

P

RUE JULES VALLÈS

RUE LÉCUYER

RUE PAUL BERT

RUE

ROSIERS

RUE BIRON

RUE VOLTAIRE

AVENUE MICHELET

Biron

Antica

Vernaison

Rosiers Dauphine

P

Malik

Malassis

RUE JEAN - HENRI FABRE

BOULEVARD PÉRIPHÉRIQUE

PARIS

Porte de Clignancourt

M

0   yards   200

0   metres   200

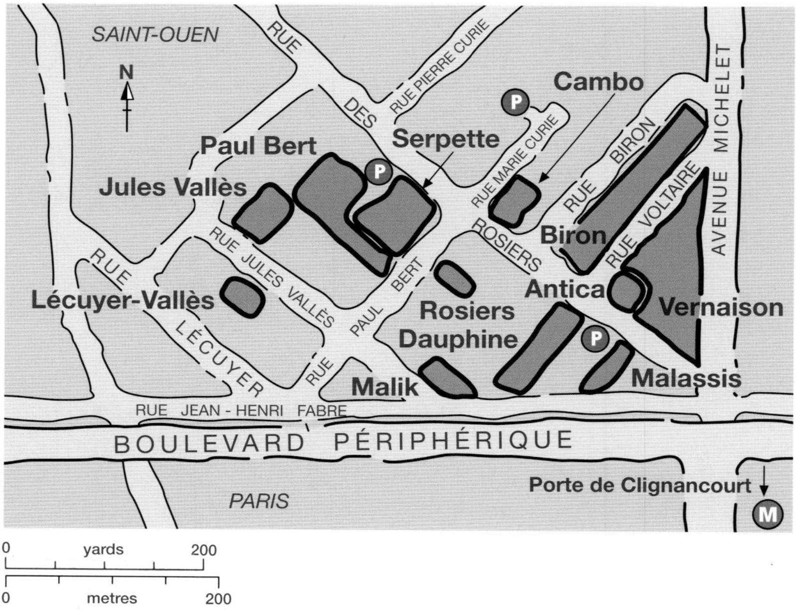

PUCES DE SAINT-OUEN

HOW & WHEN TO GO TO THE
PUCES DE SAINT-OUEN

PUCES DE SAINT-OUEN
SAINT-OUEN, 93400

OPEN
Saturday to Monday, 9/9.30am–6.30/7pm (although many of the stalls are closed on Mondays). At one time, the markets opened very early in the morning but nowadays opening hours can be unpredictable. When the weather is bad, the stalls obviously take longer to open up.

BY METRO
Porte de Clignancourt (line 4 Porte d'Orléans–Porte de Clignancourt) or **Garibaldi** (line 13 Châtillon Montrouge–Saint Denis Basilique)

BY BUS
Route 85 (Jardin du Luxembourg–Mairie Saint-Ouen) goes down the rue des Rosiers. Get off at the Marchés aux Puces stop. On the PC, the stop is Porte de Clignancourt. No. 56 (Porte de Clignancourt–Château de Vincennes) runs on Sundays.

PARKING
Take the Porte de Clignancourt exit from the ring road (the *boulevard périphérique*). There are three paying car parks in the centre of the Saint-Ouen flea markets: at 142 rue de Rosiers (under the Marché Malassis), at 110 rue des Rosiers (at the Marché Serpette) and at the end of the rue Marie Curie. There is also a car park on the Paris side of the Porte de Clignancourt.

MINIMUM
UN
GOBELET
120

MARCHÉ VERNAISON

The story goes that in 1885 a market gardener by the name of Romain Vernaison had the idea of renting his land to rag-and-bone merchants. Others claim that it was in 1920 that Romain Vernaison built small booths on his land and rented them out to traders. Whichever is true, the Marché Vernaison was the first of the Saint-Ouen flea markets to be professionally organized and registered, and it can therefore claim with some justification to be the oldest. The orange sign marking the two entrances at 99 rue des Rosiers and 136 avenue Michelet depicts its mascot, an automated figure of a little man in a tailcoat and 18th-century wig. He is holding a fishing rod, presumably symbolizing the variety of goods to be found in the market. With its ten narrow winding aisles of stalls that are sometimes so tiny that they are crammed to overflowing, the Marché Vernaison is the most picturesque of the markets.

AISLE 1

FRANÇOISE STALL 4. ℂ 01 40 11 26 95
Antique and modern silverware with lots of attractive timbale moulds, place settings in various styles and fine dinner services. Also chocolate pots, boxes, frames, snuffboxes and rattles.

STALL 5 ℂ 01 40 12 16 49
Hardware specialists. As well as having lamps and chandeliers repaired here, you can also unearth engraved-glass door plates, Bakelite switches and curtain rings, in all sizes. Take along anything that needs mending; then dive in to find replacement parts.

MAISON JACQUES STALL 6 (CORNER OF AISLES 1 AND 2)
Braid, ribbons and a vast selection of beads – in every colour, shape and size – which are temptingly arranged in boxes and sold by the cupful. To the greedy, they look just like sweets or spices.

ART ET CRISTAL STALL 7
Chandeliers and useful bits and pieces for repairing them.

NOVELLA STALL 8
Weapons, watches and violins. A peculiar mixture, but why not? Also on offer is a repair service for watches and clocks.

LHOMOND STALL 11. ℂ 01 40 12 73 84
All sizes and styles of tapestry cartoons, some of which are framed. Patterns were painted on to the canvas and then used by tapestry weavers as templates.

FRANÇOISE

STALL 12
Everything you need to repair an old chandelier: sockets, pendants and so on.

ROBERT ET FILS STALL 14. ℂ 01 40 10 13 76
A huge range of crockery, glass chemists' jars and a few attractive glass pendant chandeliers.

STALL 27
An enormous stall that looks like a restaurant, with plates laid out on half a dozen large polished tables. The rest of the china is displayed in the surrounding cabinets and chandeliers hang from the ceiling. Of course, everything is for sale.

STALL 29
Frames, tapestries and pictures hang above a few fine pieces of inlaid furniture.

MOREL-ZYSSET STALL 32. ℂ 01 40 12 63 66
Wonderful stacks of crockery.

FRANÇOISE STALL 33. ℂ 01 40 12 56 65
Françoise specializes in Art Nouveau clothes, underwear and fabrics, which she piles up on an enormous draper's table. Although the stall is huge, you need to ask for what you want because she has a very large reserve stock. In order to protect them, many of the most delicate pieces are not put on show. Lots of pelmets and bed canopies (which are back in fashion at the moment), plus trimmings, trinkets and fans. Damaged goods are specially labelled. A friendly atmosphere.

CHAUVET STALL 34. ℂ 01 40 11 64 95
19th- and 20th-century silver plate, with plenty of large dishes, place settings and even whole canteens of cutlery in their presentation boxes. Attractive engraved cake servers, grape scissors, dredgers and egg cups.

UN PARFUM D'AVENTURE STALL 36. ℂ 06 80 81 49 94

Serge-Antoine Legrand sells to the kind of fashion designers who borrow ideas and cuts from military tailors. In fact, he claims that Gianni Versace's 'gorgon' logo was copied from one of his French army belts. Kepis, sabres and sola topis are all arranged under the stern gaze of the officers in his selected portraits, some of whom wear the decorations that can be seen in the display cases.

SYLVIE ET PIERRE-GILLES STALL 39. ℂ 01 40 12 66 44

A friendly couple, each with a different speciality. Sylvie hunts for fabrics and household linen and has built up a good selection of embroidered and lace pillowcases, exquisite damask table napkins (some monogrammed) and all kinds of curtains. Pierre-Gilles's field is furniture and he is particularly fond of the Empire and Restoration styles. The whole stall is a harmonious blend of the things they have chosen. Also worth noting are the sets of Baccarat and Saint-Louis glasses.

STALL 40

Wonderful hangings and fabrics – damask and Jacquard weaves, embroideries, and even quilted pieces – are displayed on the walls of this stand or stacked in heaps around it. The overall effect is a bit like being in an Oriental *diwan*, where mountains of cushions, often covered in all sorts of different fabrics, are arranged on piles of mattresses.

LA GUIMANDIE STALL 43. ℂ 01 40 11 32 02

A real odds-and-ends stall, with fabrics, trinkets and crockery.

STALL 46

Sells glass-bead and pendant chandeliers, and also the individual parts for you to do your own repairs.

STALL 47 ℂ 01 40 12 68 69

Posters, newspapers and books, arranged according to subject.

AISLE 2

STALL 69

This bric-a-brac stall plays music while you browse.

STALL 83

Elegant silverware and lots of small objects, like pepper pots and salt cellars with blue-glass liners. A few pieces of jewelry and even rosaries.

GALERIE ABC STALL 156

A varied range of costume jewelry, buttons and hatpins to wear as brooches. They all go together, so why not wear several at once?

ANTIK ART STALL 157. ℂ 01 49 45 96 88

Radios from the Twenties to the Seventies, ornamental of course, but some in working order. Plus vinyl records. Listening to the tunes of our past always induces nostalgia; what's surprising is when some of the songs are popular with the young.

AISLE 3

CLARA ELIANE STALL 144
Large flacons and small sample bottles of old-fashioned perfumes, such as Habanita, Le Mouchoir de Monsieur and Amour-Amour.

AISLE 4

STALL 74
'We buy anything', announces the haphazardly placed slate to one side. The stall is run by a scrap-metal dealer who also sells door handles, enamel number plates, coal buckets, cisterns and zinc buckets (the ultimate in chic for stylish flower displays).

STALL 74BIS ✆ 06 08 74 04 44
Weapons, uniforms and medals for those who want to play at soldiers. Be careful, though, it's illegal to wear them if you're not entitled to!

AU GRENIER DE LUCIE STALL 77. ✆ 01 40 12 24 42
(ALSO AT STALL 139, AISLE 7.)
Pictures and well-made costume jewelry. Her much larger stall bearing the same name in aisle 7 is also worth a visit.

STALL 78 ✆ 01 40 11 36 98
Specializing in World War II uniforms, this stand stocks 1940s caps, cartridge belts and uniforms, including those worn by the Arab units in the North African shock troops.

AISLE 5

URSULA M. DIETERICH STALL 84. ℭ 01 40 10 93 09

Visiting this stand is like walking into a doll's house. Miniature furniture – a piano, a cart, armchairs and so on – and dolls' clothes surround the array of toy houses. Ursula repairs old dolls and also has wonderful babies' and children's clothes.

FRANÇOISE CHAPPUY STALL 88. ℭ 01 40 10 91 10

Every inch of the stall is covered with keyrings and Françoise claims that she has over five thousand on display. She started as an enthusiastic collector in 1965 and went on to write a book on the subject, with a preface by Paul-Loup Sulitzer. In the summer of 1997 she turned her hobby into a job, opening her stall at Vernaison. The keyrings are carefully arranged according to shape or subject: air, sea, animals, journalism, bottles, drinks, advertising, politics, agriculture, etc.

AISLE 6

STALL 95

Small pieces of furniture and library steps, shelves, frames and lamps from the Thirties.

STALL 99BIS ℭ 01 40 11 55 80

Frames in gilded wood and plaster, in every shape and style.

STALL 105BIS ℭ 01 40 11 82 50

Against a background of cashmere-patterned fabric, exquisite bridal head-dresses are displayed under glass. Opaline lampshades and chandeliers are also for sale.

F.-G. RICHARD STALL 107BIS. ℭ 01 40 11 29 13

Globes, telescopes, a large still, barometers and a whole range of objects that look strange and unfamiliar to anyone who is not a scientific expert. The notice at the back of the stall explains: 'We buy anything old and curious.'

PATRICE SALET STALL 108. ℭ 01 40 10 99 15

There are only two people in the Saint-Ouen flea markets who deal in old drawings and both have stalls in Vernaison. They are good friends and extremely knowledgeable. This interesting selection, helpfully annotated, attracts an impressive clientele.

STALL 110

Plates, glasses and cups of all kinds are stacked precariously on this stall – you wouldn't want to take a bull, or even someone a bit on the clumsy side, anywhere near it.

OLGA HORDE STALL 111 ℭ 01 69 09 51 60

Traditional kitchenware: salt or match boxes, flat irons that you heat on the stove, coffee mills that give off a delicious smell as you turn the handle, enamel or pottery spice jars and a few drop-leaf tables.

AISLE 7

PIERRE JONCHÈRES STALL 65. ✆ 01 40 11 94 59
A former history teacher-cum-journalist, who now specializes in drawings from the 16th century to 1870, explains that drawing is an intellectual pursuit, 'because it involves both intellect and knowledge'. Once you have chosen what you want, ask his advice on the best way to display it. Theoretically his frames are not for sale, but you might be able to persuade him…. It's not impossible that you will come across an eminent curator from a major French museum at this little stall.

FRANCINE STALLS 121–23. ✆ 01 40 10 93 36
(ALSO AT STALL 140BIS, AISLE 7.)
White is the predominant colour here, with embroidered fabrics, lace, christening robes, bonnets, traditional regional headdresses and net curtains on display. Lots of tablecloths, bed linen, cushions and tablemats with Richelieu embroidery, etc., all of which are in good condition. Also linen shirts, exquisitely embroidered waistcoats and a few canes for dandies. Some curios too, and even the occasional piece of silverware.

ZOÉ STALL 127BIS. ✆ 01 40 10 85 24
Plenty of rewards for well-behaved children: dolls, boats, trains, Pope Joan card games and cut-outs.

AU GRENIER DE LUCIE STALL 139. ✆ 01 40 12 24 42
(ALSO AT STALL 77, AISLE 4.)
The 1950s were noted for costume jewelry, especially the work of Myriam Haskell and Stanley Hagler in the United States. A wide range of pieces – and prices – are available on this large stall, which also sells jewelry in gold and precious stones, watches (from 18th-century to modern) and fountain pens.

FRANCINE STALL 140BIS. ✆ 01 40 12 05 58
(ALSO AT STALLS 121–23, AISLE 7.)
An Aladdin's cave of fabrics and ribbons from the 18th century to the 1940s and 1950s. Old-fashioned toile de Jouy prints, piqués, embroidered samplers and braid. A few antique dresses and hats turn up too. Everything is beautifully arranged and grouped by colour.

JANINE GIOVANNONI STALL 141. ✆ 01 40 12 39 13
As she opens drawers and reverently takes out exquisite pieces of embroidery and quilting, you can see that this delightful lady is passionate about her work. In the centre of her enormous shop-cum-stall is a large table displaying linen in perfect condition, freshly washed and ironed: quilts, pillowcases, sheets, bridal handkerchiefs edged with several rows of lace and piles of big white napkins (currently fashionable paired with a coloured tablecloth). Also traycloths, table runners – recently rediscovered by designers – and cashmere shawls. A few Hermès bags and lambskin gloves in the display cabinet.

LUGGAGE STALL 141BIS. ✆ 01 40 10 01 18
Seasoned globe-trotters may travel light but they carry good strong luggage. The pieces on this stall are made of leather, with either a wooden frame or leather

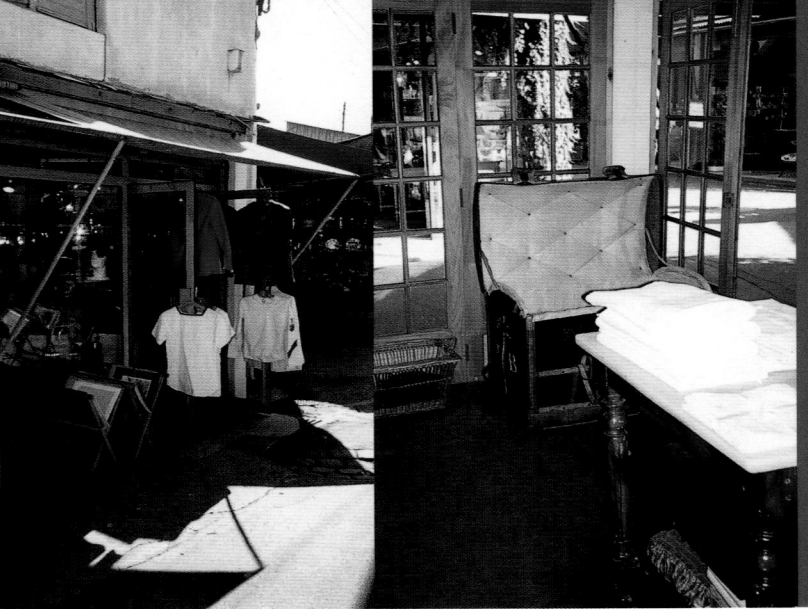

JANINE GIOVANNONI

19

straps. Claude Duperrier says he is a great traveller and when he opens the drawers of a camphor-wood trunk, the evocative smell transports you miles away. Travel, leisure and sport often go together, so it is only logical that Duperrier should also sell, among other things, some 1930s Davis Cup wooden tennis racquets; some skis from before the days of bindings that were attached instead with leather straps; and early versions of the type of ice skates that Olympic champions now wear.

STALL 142
Visit for wonderful metal toys: cars, trains and lead soldiers.

NICOLAS GIOVANNONI STALL 146. ℰ 01 40 10 17 91
(ALSO AT MARCHÉ SERPETTE, STALLS 8 AND 10, AISLE 6.)
Nicolas has followed his mother Janine (see Stall 141, Aisle 7) into the trade, but he specializes in tableware – a mixture of Sarreguemines, Lunéville, Vieux Paris, Saint-Louis and Baccarat. The formal pieces are magnificent and he sells individual items as well as complete services.

STALL 148 ℰ 06 80 13 14 04
More posters.

NICOLAS RÉMON STALL 148BIS. ℰ 01 40 10 29 32
An eclectic range of books, magazines and newspapers. A history of the Bible sits side by side with the classic French strip cartoon featuring the *Famille Fenouillard*; the satirical French newspaper *Crapouillot* is housed alongside Hansi's late 19th-century illustrated works (which set French hearts beating again after they had lost Alsace and Lorraine to Germany in 1870); and rows of the daily *Petit Journal* alternate with those of the rival *Petit Parisien*. Long live the press and publishing!

STALL 168

20

PHILIPPE STALL 149. ✆ 06 07 24 27 96

1940s publicity posters and other advertising paraphernalia, such as Martell, Byrrh and Perrier boxes and ashtrays, arranged by brand name.

GALERIE V. STALL 150BIS. ✆ 01 40 11 39 94

Plenty of bar accessories on sale here: ashtrays, dishes, glasses and enamel advertising plates for famous aperitifs. Also the kind of pin-ups you often see on garage walls.

CHEVAL COLLECTION STALL 151. ✆ 01 40 10 27 76

Everything on Geneviève Roger's stall is connected with horses: a polo stick, signed Cecil Aldin prints of hunting scenes, a martingale and a side saddle. Guaranteed to appeal to anyone who rides.

GUY-LAURENT SETRUK STALL 152. ✆ 01 40 12 38 09

The delightful chairman of the Vernaison stallholders' association has a fascinating range of bric-a-brac: from leather suitcases and Remington typewriters to stringless violins, candlesticks, mirrors, wooden pushchairs.... A feast for the imagination.

STALL 153

Lots of attractive carved jade, ivory and coral jewelry, and ornaments for display cabinets.

AISLE 8

MIREILLE FAVRE STALL 159 (CORNER OF AISLES 2 AND 8)
✆ 01 40 12 42 65

Attractive jewelry, surrounded by blocks of semi-precious stone and fossilized shells.

STALL 163 ℭ 01 40 12 42 65

This selection of stone and marble fireplaces and fountains, wrought-iron latticework and frames, made of intertwined branches, are arranged against a background of wooden walls and large polished flagstones.

STALL 168 ℭ 01 40 11 23 81

The back of this stall is crammed with old and beautiful tools. It also has keys and locks and a few beautiful pieces of handcrafted furniture with plentiful drawers.

STALL 176 ℭ 01 40 12 42 65

Stone benches, terracotta pots and scrolling ironwork for spacious gardens. Also fireplaces, which constitute the central focus of any home.

MARIE STALL 179. ℭ 01 40 10 97 03

In the age of the computer, journalists and writers are still fascinated by writing implements and, of course, there are many technophobes who could not get by without them. This stall sells fountain pens, penholders and all kinds of nibs for different styles of handwriting, laid out on cards. Attractive lithographed boxes too.

STALL 181 ℭ 01 40 10 81 16

A large stock of leather-bound books and newspapers, including fine collections of illustrations.

DENISE BALBON STALL 185. ℭ 01 40 12 75 35

Denise, a glass expert at the auction house Hôtel Drouot, came to Vernaison twenty-five years ago. She offers a high-quality selection of stemmed glasses, decanters and interesting objects (all made of glass, naturally) from the 17th, 18th and 19th centuries, right up to the 1920s.

VIOLETTE MOREL STALL 186. ℭ 01 40 10 89 01

On the right of the stall are bookshelves piled with English books (in fact, there is a discreet sign at the entrance advertising 'English books'). She also sells glasses and frames.

JEAN-LUC BALLEUR STALL 186BIS

Balleur says he buys trinkets that appeal to him and that he thinks are reasonably priced. His stall is one of the smallest at Vernaison, but everything is high quality. A boat-shaped blue-and-white porcelain opium-smoker's pillow is a sophisticated example of the stock he sells.

STALL 187

Silverware, particularly good for knives.

STALL 188 ℭ 01 49 45 06 18

More postcards to send or frame, plus a few books.

STALL 193 ℭ 01 40 10 04 48

Small pictures, large ceramic vases, a few pieces of silverware and lots of trinkets displayed against a dark-brown hessian background.

STALL 195

A real odds-and-ends stall, with a fascinating mixture of bric-a-brac: postcards, lace, silver-gilt spoons, pipes, dolls and frames.

BÉATRICE CUVELIER STALL 197

Béatrice, an outspoken blonde, sells erotica. Her customers, ranging from the couturier Azzedine Alaïa to leading interior designers, sculptors, painters, photographers and highly discerning collectors, flock to buy the basques, mannequins, feather headdresses, studded underpants and lacy slips she stocks. Béatrice says, 'I'm the only person who does this', and you can well believe it. The bundles of magazines with photos of nude women are, of course, for sale. These men and their fantasies!

AISLE 9

STALL 199 ✆ 01 40 11 93 97

Although these days boys prefer computer games, their fathers and grandfathers are still fascinated by the Dinky Toy (and bigger) model cars and scale models (of rear-platform Parisian buses, of Air France coaches, of propeller aircraft and of transatlantic liners like the *France*) that can be found on this stall.

IRMA STALL 200. ✆ 01 40 10 08 57

'Lace, old linen and trinkets' are advertised on her card. She also has wonderful old clothes, curtains and hangings (it's well worth bringing window measurements with you) and a large range of stemmed glasses, 19th- and 20th-century decanters and gorgeous buttons.

STALL 220

Piles of embroidered, damask and tapestry cushions, fabrics and crockery, plus a few pictures.

CATAN STALLS 223–29. ✆ 01 40 10 29 41

Massive carved armoires and enormous tables for convivial meals. You'll need high ceilings and plenty of space.

D'AUTREPPE STALL 234. ✆ 01 40 11 70 92

Thousands of postcards, carefully arranged by subject.

STALL 238

The ticking is deafening. With clocks in every conceivable style, it's just like being in Switzerland.

AISLE 10

STALLS 241–43

Original Gallé lamps and pâte de verre examples inspired by them. Also chandeliers, china and mirrors.

STALL 250 ✆ 06 11 65 58 01

A small stall with attractive buttons and curios (a lot of porcelain), displayed in glass cases.

STALL 253 ☎ 01 40 12 88 36

This stand has an extremely high ceiling, so there's plenty of room to accommodate splendid pillars, and a parquet floor that shows the range of furniture here to its best advantage.

STALL 255 ☎ 01 40 11 95 63

An enormous stall with a mixture of sideboards, china cabinets and large rustic-style tables.

MAÏTÉ POUPÉES STALL 259

The exquisite dolls (from 1860 to 1920) and their glass-fronted wardrobes, crammed with pretty lace-edged dresses, dainty strap shoes and elegant button boots, are protected against the elements at this covered corner stall at the end of the Marché Vernaison. Everything – corsets, pantalets, jewelry and handbags – is beautifully presented. Maïté has been selling dolls for longer than anyone else at Vernaison and she now works with her daughter Julie. She also repairs broken dolls in her workshop at 8 rue Brochant, 75017 Paris ☎ 01 42 63 23 93.

STALL 263 ☎ 01 40 11 95 63

Fireplaces in wood and stone alongside large comfortable furniture with a rustic edge.

MARCHÉ MALIK

Marché Malik, covered by a glass roof with a red-painted metal frame, was set up by an Albanian called Malik Hajrullac after World War I. Its entrance is at the beginning of the rue Jules Vallès, near the ring road. Cassettes play at full blast, the air is heavy with incense and exotic smells and the temporary stalls are crammed with cheap junk and souvenirs. Crowds gather around the card sharps and there is a constant stream of people entering the body-piercing booth. The market used to specialize in secondhand clothes, but these days, it sells nothing but jeans, T-shirts with slogans, sexy crop-tops and fluorescent platform-soled trainers for Spice Girl 'wannabes', plus a few Chinese jackets and South American ponchos. Most of the clothes are new. Strictly for teenagers.

MIKAEL
Mikael is a tattoo artist here and although tattoos are currently in vogue, they are permanent. The transfer tattoos that were all the rage in the summer of 1998 are probably a better idea.

MONSIEUR HARRY STALL 56
This stall is run by an enormous man with a moustache and an appealing sense of humour. His bookstall (selling mainly paperbacks) seems totally incongruous in this setting. He says jokingly that he should have been selling books on the banks of the River Seine but he got lost. He has a particularly good selection of Pléïade books, in excellent condition.

LA TRANCHÉE MILITAIRE ℂ 01 40 12 47 87
This army-surplus stall with entrances from both the Marché Malik and the rue Jules Vallès is ideal for youngsters and particularly for girls who go for the tomboy look. Jackets, trousers, boots, combat dress and American car number plates, posters and flags.

MARCHÉ BIRON

In 1925, seventy secondhand dealers set up the market on the place du champ des Rosiers, which at the time was still a market garden. At the instigation of Saint-Ouen council, it was built as a permanent structure from the very beginning to make it more comfortable both for the stallholders and for their customers. Two aisles run the whole length of the market, which you enter via 85 rue des Rosiers or 118 avenue Michelet. Aisle 1 (the Grande Allée) is open to the elements and lined with large stalls on both sides. Aisle 2 is an extremely narrow covered aisle with all the stalls laid out on the same side. Although the stands are small, two or three have sometimes been knocked together. In this aisle the lights are on all day and the atmosphere is cosy and intimate.

AISLE 1

JANE MOUFFLET STALL I. ✆ 01 40 10 84 09
Jane Moufflet sells wonderful large posters in good condition. Many of the best examples are film posters (some of which were banned in certain countries), but you shouldn't miss the advertising posters. People tend to collect by subject.

LES VERRES DE NOS GRAND-MÈRES STALLS 2–3
✆ 01 40 12 72 19
Christiane Tassin is the daughter and granddaughter of flea market stallholders and it was her father's idea to specialize in antique glass and in finding matches for odd pieces. She is not sure how many glasses and decanters she has on her enormous stall or in stock. She sells glasses in every style and from every period, individually or in sets of six: stemmed or goblet, clear or coloured, engraved or moulded, Baccarat, Saint-Louis or Daum – the choice is bewildering. To find a matching one, take your glass to Christiane or send her a good photo with the necessary details and she will look through her books. With any luck she will have what you want; if not, she will seek it out patiently, but it could take a while.

R. TOUPENET STALL 6. ✆ 01 40 12 71 77
Art Nouveau furniture and lighting. The sinuous lines were inspired by plants.

STALL 7 ✆ 01 40 10 86 81
A real 'junk' stall that is completely out of place here, but its untidiness and its heaps of small furniture and pewter jugs, chandeliers and assorted pots are certainly appealing.

JACQUES BITOUN STALL 8. ✆ 01 40 11 96 54
Porcelain shepherdesses and females statuettes to put on your mantelpiece.

These figurines were popular in the 18th century and manufactured throughout Europe, at Nymphenburg in Germany, among other places.

GARRY STALL 10. ✆ 01 40 10 09 87
This large stall is full of spectacular Russian icons, plus pictures, jewelry, silverware and walking sticks. 'All are pre-Revolution', explains its owner.

JEAN DOUTREPONT STALL 17
Visit for Art Nouveau-style wooden seats, pâte de verre chandeliers and lighting.

F. BRUYNEEL STALL 22. ✆ 01 40 12 93 27
A good selection of assorted bibelots, but mainly chandeliers. The gilt-bronze ones are said to be Flemish, the blown-glass ones may be Venetian.

HENRI EMBERGER STALL 25. ✆ 01 40 10 99 26
Emberger's wooden roundabout horses take you back to your childhood and his toys – metal trains and lorries – are likely to appeal to little boys. He also finds bits and pieces of circus decoration.

BIRON 28 STALL 28. ✆ 01 40 12 43 28
Some fine silverware but mainly jewelry, much of it late 19th-century or Napoleon III: brooch and earring sets, sometimes with matching bracelets, lots of turnip watches and unmounted hard-stone intaglios.

JACQUELINE EDOUARD STALL 29. ✆ 01 40 10 23 00
Exquisite pieces of silverware – trays, dishes, teapots, samovars…. Also clocks.

YVETTE ROBERT STALL 48. ✆ 01 40 11 26 72
She sells all kinds of lighting: chandeliers, lamps, wall lights, etc.

STALL 65   STALL 83

NATLYNE STALL 49. ✆ 01 40 11 04 64
Rounded commodes with ornamental hinges are a speciality here. Check to make sure that both are in the same style. Also pier glasses and screens.

GISÈLE STALL 53. ✆ 01 40 11 74 97
A real specialist in mahogany tables of all shapes and sizes. The grainier the mahogany, the more valuable the piece is.

TRADITION STALL 56. ✆ 01 40 12 66 91
All the furniture on this stand has been stripped, so its cabinets and game tables are now light-coloured. Some pieces, however, are made from naturally blond wood.

STALL 60
Magnificent carved wooden furniture. Look for the curving cornices and follow the sinuous lines of the mouldings.

ANNIE MINET STALL 62BIS. ✆ 01 40 11 33 56
African and Oriental furniture and artefacts.

STALL 65 ✆ 01 40 11 29 69
The engravings on sale here are mainly of fruit and flowers, plus some fashion plates.

ELISABETH STALL 66. ✆ 01 40 11 12 00
Gallé-style vases. If it's pâte de verre that you're interested in, then this market is a good place to come.

BENOÎT STALL 70. ✆ 01 40 11 58 45
Another early 20th-century glass and pâte de verre specialist.

STALL 72 ✆ 01 40 12 14 18
Small items of Art Nouveau furniture and Gallé-style lighting – two specialities that go well together.

STANY HOFFMANN STALL 75. ✆ 01 40 12 87 29
Gilt-wood or painted furniture on a grand scale: tall pier glasses, console tables and pillars. Tapestries and chandeliers are also on display.

PAUL MILGEN STALL 75BIS. ✆ 01 40 12 89 56
Curious marquetry pictures in a variety of different woods.

GILBERT FISCHER STALL 75TER. ✆ 01 40 12 40 46
A good source for pictures.

STALL 81 ✆ 01 40 10 00 85
Twenties- and Thirties-style furniture, mirrors and seating.

STALL 83
Engravings, including old maps of the French provinces and regions. You can see how regions like Puisaye and Soissonais have changed over the centuries.

BRUDASZ STALL 86BIS. ✆ 01 40 12 87 04

This stall sells an array of haute-couture costume jewelry from the Thirties to the present day, plus haute-couture bags – many by Hermès, others by Chanel and Dior.

ALAIN CICAL STALL 93

Vases, statues and large dishes in fine porcelain. To fill you in on a bit of historical background: the Chinese discovered porcelain in the 7th or 8th century AD, but it was not until 1709, a thousand years later, that Johann Friedrich Böttger first made it in Europe.

STALL 94 ✆ 01 40 12 20 17

Specializes in Lalique vases and other work by René, Marc and Marie-Claude Lalique, a dynasty of gifted craftsmen.

ALEXIA SAY STALL 100. ✆ 01 40 12 11 07

Art Nouveau-style furniture and objects. Alexia Say also specializes in Daum, Gallé and Lalique glass.

LARGEAULT STALL 107. ✆ 01 40 12 83 54

A very colourful stall stocking stained glass at the back, but also objects in glass and pâte de verre, which are evidently a speciality at the Marché Biron.

HÉLÈNE JORDAN STALL 117 ✆ 01 40 12 53 73

Dealing mainly in jewelry, Hélène Jordan also has various styles of pictures and furniture.

CLAUDE BOYER STALL 119
(ALSO AT MARCHÉ DES ROSIERS, STALL 3.)

Large flowered barbotine ware from the early 20th century. Pâte de verre vases and lighting.

STALL 123 ✆ 01 40 10 29 80

This tiny cluttered stall is the only one in the market to sell hangings, fabrics and trimmings. It's fascinating rummaging through them.

STALL 125 ✆ 01 40 12 82 38

A real portrait gallery, with 19th-century pictures of soberly dressed members of the bourgeoisie on the walls. Furniture is also on sale.

LE CURIEUX STALL 126. ✆ 01 40 10 83 97

Dozens of fans and all the kinds of appealing trinkets that today's society no longer uses: parasols, seals, lorgnettes, cosmetic and shaving kits and hand mirrors.

BROPHY STALL 135BIS (ON RUE DES ROSIERS)

Brophy stocks an impressive assortment of scientific instruments, astronomical, nautical and optical: bright copper and shiny metal compasses, astrolabes, logs, globes, barometers, telescopes and sextants. For the non-scientist, many of the objects are a complete mystery; you wonder what on earth they could be used for.

BLANDINE LEFÈVRE

AISLE 2

STALL 136 ✆ 01 40 11 35 29

The ceiling of this stall is high enough to accommodate large pieces of furniture, such as tall corner cupboards and deep armoires, and a variety of styles are stocked. It is interesting to learn that wardrobes with mirrors did not appear until around 1830.

STALL 140 ✆ 01 40 11 93 85

A selection of pristine posters, extolling the virtues of everything from Kub stock cubes and Suze pastis to the film *Visiteurs du Soir* and cruises on board the *Normandie*. They are mounted on canvas to protect them.

STALL 142 ✆ 01 40 10 00 57

This furniture stall is covered in a predominantly yellow Jacquard weave, which complements the decor of its small mezzanine.

BLANDINE LEFÈVRE STALL 148BIS

✆ 01 40 12 53 82

The limited size of the stall means that the 18th- and 19th-century furniture that Blandine sells is small-scale. Chairs, particularly wing chairs, are a speciality and Philippe, her husband, explains that their wonderful mirrors and pier glasses are never on the walls for long. Equally charming is her shop in central Paris, near the Hôtel Drouot auction house (8 rue Grange Batelière ✆ 01 48 00 02 11).

STALL 150

This stall offers a variety of fine gilt-wood or painted objects: pillars, mirrors and statues.

STALL 155 ✆ 01 40 11 32 17
High-quality painted or inlaid furniture. If you are shown a piece with a marble top, you can tell whether the marble is genuinely old by feeling the back. If it is hatched, it is old; if it is smooth, it means it has been machine-cut, so be careful.

PHILIPPE LACHAUX STALL 156. ✆ 01 40 12 09 40
This stunningly decorated stall is actually made of three stands which have been knocked together. Lachaux changes the decor frequently and, even though it is fascinating to learn that he specializes in good spiral staircases which he repairs himself and then has installed by professionals, you can't help but be distracted by the panelling, mirrors, lanterns, handmade furniture and latticework that he has arranged with consummate skill to look like a stage set. Highly original; don't miss it.

STALL 160 ✆ 01 40 12 43 75
A good selection of traditional-style furniture: chestnut from central France, lime from Provence, oak from the north, cherry from the west and walnut from the south. A tour of France's forests.

AU FIL DES TEMPS STALL 161. ✆ 01 40 11 78 77
Engravings and small pieces of furniture.

STALLS 164–65 ✆ 01 40 10 23 56
Painted furniture, a lot of it from northern and eastern Europe, and a few seats.

STALLS 167–68 ✆ 01 40 10 25 94
A few interesting tapestry cartoons, but mainly furniture: breadboxes, china cabinets, cupboards and chests. The selection varies depending on what the owner finds.

STALL 171
Old-fashioned office furniture and fittings; an antique shop's cashier's desk in carved wood; roll-top desks for the study; and huge sturdy drapers' tables that make marvellous dining-room tables for weekend retreats.

STALL 173 ✆ 01 40 12 48 85
All sorts of naval artefacts: terrestrial globes, boats, telescopes, small cases. This stall, with its ocean-blue walls, has a very nautical air about it.

STALL 179
This stall evokes the mysterious Orient, with statues of Buddha, red-and-black lacquered furniture and oval baskets in which to carry your teapot on journeys or picnics.

STALL 180 ✆ 01 40 11 24 42
Desks, secretaires and *bonheurs du jour* for old-timers or 'scribblers' who still like to use pen and paper and keep well away from the ubiquitous computer mouse.

STALL 190 ✆ 01 40 11 15 73
Rustic-style sideboards and a few lamps.

STALL 194TER ✆ 01 40 11 26 09
Massive high-quality bookcases and desks and the occasional splendid trunk.

MICHEL MUSSON STALLS 196–97
Fine desks in all sizes – a *bonheur du jour*, a lady's bureau, a roll-top and a pedestal. All have plenty of drawers, some of which may be secret.

EDWIGE LELOUCH STALL 198
Edwige Lelouch sells good carved-wood rustic-style furniture: sideboards, china cabinets and attractive little chairs. Some folk art too.

STALL 200
This stall stocks large, highly carved armoires and superb chests of drawers. Its owner, Thierry de Rydder, regularly sells provincial furniture from Lorraine, Brittany, Provence, etc. and the scale of his pieces makes them ideal for rooms with high ceilings.

STALL 202 ✆ 01 40 11 63 67
A motley collection: armoires and sideboards, jewelry and walking sticks.

DOMINIQUE STALL 203. ✆ 01 40 11 99 49
This meagre space is crammed with pieces of small furniture (highly rated at the moment), pictures, objects and trinkets, all of which are lit by chandeliers. A real mélange.

MARCHÉ JULES VALLÈS

In 1938 a Venetian by the name of Amadeo Cesana bought a plot of land at 7 rue Jules Vallès and started renting out spaces to secondhand dealers. The traders soon began setting up wooden booths along the two beaten-earth aisles and before long had them roofed over for the convenience of their customers – an idea that was later copied in other markets. The small Marché Jules Vallès is still the cheapest of the markets and the one where stallholders from the other markets like to buy. Unfortunately, it is difficult to predict when stalls will be open but Friday morning (when other dealers go) is probably the best time to try.

LA GROSSE HORLOGE STALL 13. ℰ 01 40 12 57 67
Clocks to mark our happiest hours, from grandfather to the Swiss cuckoo variety, and others in more conventional styles.

STALL 21
Children's toys: dominoes, Pope Joan cards and little clockwork metal cars.

STALL 25
Wonderful implements for country houses or showpiece gardens and everyday objects for traditional-style kitchens. A useful source for presents to give people when you go and stay for the weekend.

STALL 31
A real bric-a-brac stall that you can browse through while the stallholder tells you all about his stock. He has been dealing here for over forty years and is remarkably knowledgeable.

STALL 34
Damask and fine linen embroidered in (mostly red) cross stitch. The stock is generally in good condition, but it's always as well to unfold things to make sure.

STALL 40
'*Aux armes citoyens!*' Another specialist in uniforms, kepis and medals. Curiously enough, late 19th-century Prussian helmets are still much sought after. The defeats seem to have been completely forgotten!

STALL 48
Panels of colourful stained glass which, whatever the size, can be incorporated as ornamental features into doors or walls. Also fireplaces.

STALL 52
Some weapons, but also American college rings (for those who feel like showing off a bit).

STALL 54
If you want to lay claim to some ancestors, you can always buy some well-painted family portraits. And how about a chandelier to light your picture gallery?

CHOISI POUR VOUS STALLS 55–57

A marvellous Aladdin's cave right at the end of the market, which has sabres and swords hanging from the ceiling, stacks of cane chairs, rows of carved wooden frames and, when I visited, a teddy bear peeping out of a trunk. A book on how to get your own back on annoying people has been mischievously stuck in a vice by the stallholder. A huge selection.

STALL 78 ☏ 01 40 11 54 41

Trinkets and magnificent candelabra, some of which have undoubtedly been used in religious services. Whether they're made of silver plate, brass or copper, you'll need plenty of elbow grease if you want to polish these objects up to their former lustre.

STALL 80

This stallholder hangs his military frock coats, greatcoats and mess jackets in every available space and they billow in the frequent draughts. But were they really worn by bona fide soldiers? Or were they perhaps costumes for extras in *The Longest Day* or, more recently, Spielberg's *Saving Private Ryan*? Judging by their good condition, the latter seems more likely.

MICHEL STALL 96. ☏ 06 81 32 31 87

37

An attractive stall with early works of art, folk art, tools and a few toys. People collect the decorations for roof ridges, usually made of zinc, which are sold here.

FRÉDÉRIQUE COUQUE STALL 100. (ALSO AT MARCHÉ MALASSIS, RONDEUR DES JOURS, STALL 60, GROUND FLOOR.)

Couque opened this stall, selling ceramics, lots of folk art and curios, at the beginning of 1998.

CHOISI POUR VOUS   LA GROSSE HORLOGE

MARCHÉ PAUL BERT

This enormous open-air market opened in 1949, shortly after World War II. Rag-and-bone merchants had set up business in a field that was once a vineyard. This proved impracticable when it rained, so the stallholders got together and had the aisles between their stalls tarred over. The market is in an inverted L-shape, with seven aisles and entrances at 104 rue des Rosiers and at 18 rue Paul Bert.

VINGTIÈME SIÈCLE

ERIC LENTZ

AISLE 1

CARPENTIER STALL 11. ℰ 01 40 11 33 30

Superb chandeliers and mirrors that would add elegance to any home. They go so well together that maybe if you have one, you should have both. Ask for someone to come and hang them for you, because with pieces of this quality, it's not advisable to do so yourself.

BACHELIER ANTIQUITÉS STALL 17. ℰ 01 40 11 89 98

One of the best places to buy French folk artefacts, china cabinets and sideboards, crammed with rustic pottery, copper, chopping blocks and baskets. Americans go mad about the stock, especially for the wine-related objects which are kept on the first floor. In fact, its owner François Bachelier opened a shop in Connecticut in April 1997.

MICHEL MORIN STALL 20. ℰ 01 40 11 19 10

Another specialist in French folk art, who has a varied selection of painted armoires, gardening tools, baskets, glazed-clay dishes and ornaments for roof ridges.

40

MICHEL PERACHES ET ERIC MIEL

STALL 21. ℰ 01 40 12 30 05

Only dealing since spring 1998, their customers already include buyers from Ralph Lauren – a truly impressive recommendation. On their stand – complete with creaky floorboards – they display objects that are invariably original and usually large-scale: a Portuguese statue of the Virgin to be carried in processions, a propellor aeroplane, tables for large gatherings, big cupboards, old shop fittings and office furniture and a small selection of folk

BACHELIER ANTIQUITÉS   MICHEL PERACHES ET ERIC MIEL

art. Michel and Eric also buy and sell paintings, sculptures and engravings of hunting scenes, plus stuffed animals and stags' antlers, which are either made into chandeliers or incorporated into walking sticks. Tally-ho!

PAUL KHORMAÏAN STALL 27. ✆ 01 40 12 77 22
This folk art stall is particularly popular with American visitors. It also sells a few pieces of furniture, tools and even some toys.

STALL 41
20th-century lighting and furniture in a variety of styles.

STALL 59
Firedogs and tongs – essential accessories for the country house – are displayed alongside lighting and attractive candlesticks.

CHANTAL DAGOMMER STALL 71. ✆ 01 40 11 09 29
This stall resembles an elegant boudoir, with haute-couture dresses hanging next to embroidered 19th-century waistcoats and laced corsets, and goffered lace next to hats, buttons and dolls.

STALL 122
This stall stocks a selection of large pots for the garden.

AISLE 2

PERLE JALLOT STALL 32. ✆ 01 49 45 14 87
A friendly and knowledgeable stallholder who specializes in fabrics: from early silks, tapestries and hangings to 19th-century trimmings and 1920s curtains. The stall which she shares with Jane Bernard, who deals in interesting small furniture and objects, is a riot of colours and luxurious materials.

H.P. STALL 131. ✆ 01 40 11 94 09
Gilt-wood and Baroque objects. But, be warned; this stall only opens occasionally.

STALL 135 ✆ 01 40 11 72 03
An extensive selection of stemmed glasses, available in sets of four or six. Choose tall slender ones, or something more chunky, but be sure that they complement the proportions of your table – the combination can prove most attractive.

JEAN BEAUMARIÉ (CORNER OF AISLES 2 AND 6). ✆ 01 47 09 68 02
Among Beaumarié's selection of architectural salvage in wrought iron and stone are gates, latticework, balustrades, statues, large pots, windows and fireplaces. He also has huge premises at Ville d'Avray.

AISLE 3

STALL 58
Trinkets, trinkets and more trinkets. Also faïence and porcelain crockery.

LA MARTINIÈRE STALL 58TER
If you find Michel Busson's 18th-century-style painted furniture, bookcases and

wrought-iron chandeliers appealing and you'd like to see more, you will find an even larger selection in Auvers-Saint-Georges in the department of Essonne.

STALL 59
White patinated furniture in the attractive Gustavian style.

POTRON MINET STALL 159. ✆ 01 40 11 77 12
Stéphane and Carole Borraz have only recently opened their stall in Paul Bert. Fresh from studying history of art, they admit that they 'have been fascinated by antiques from an early age'. On their attractive tiled stand, their objects 'to die for' hark back to the 18th and 19th centuries: there's a delightful array of patinated furniture, china, folk art and master pieces to be unearthed. The music they play in the background is as well chosen as their stock.

CHRISTOPHE GAIGNON STALL 169. ✆ 01 49 45 03 74
A very motley collection: old-fashioned office furniture, fine latticework and wrought ironwork.

AISLE 4

PAPILLON STALL 172. ✆ 01 40 11 17 22
The business card for this stall is a playing card – logically enough, because Papillon is devoted to games, toys, dolls and dolls' furniture. Plenty of miniature objects and the kind of beans you find in the Twelfth Night cake – ideal for people who are fed up with eating cake all the year round, just so that they can add to their collection of beans!

STALL 180
Sixties objects and furniture, plenty of plastic and bright colours. Baby boomers will love it.

FLORIS HOUWINCK STALL 213. ✆ 01 40 11 79 79
Behind the ivy-covered frontage of his stand, this friendly young Dutchman, who grew up in Burgundy, sells things that he likes and that are a bit out of the ordinary. He likes to mix styles and points out that the good thing about unusual objects is that the prices are flexible. 'I often have massive pieces', he explains, 'like this enormous rectangular wooden-framed mirror with bone studs.'

STALL 215 ✆ 01 40 10 11 21
A large selection of pictures.

CYRIL ET MARIE GRIZOT STALL 218. ✆ 01 40 10 82 13
They find interesting things from their period – the Twenties to the Fifties – and always have furniture and items by designers such as André Leleu, Jean Royère and Florence Knoll in stock.

CATHERINE MILLANT STALLS 219–21. ✆ 01 40 11 87 83
Catherine and her partner, Danièle Eisenstein, sell anything that appeals to them, from the 18th century through to the 1940s. They have a very small display but change it frequently. An unusual and interesting range of high-quality things.

CATHERINE MILLANT

AISLE 5

OLIVIER DEBOSCKER STALL 204BIS. ℂ 01 40 11 86 94

Deboscker frames his late 19th- and early 20th-century herbarium plates beautifully. In a completely different category, he also has superb wooden shutters
which would make perfect cupboard doors.

BRIGITTE PERRUCHOT STALL 206. ℂ 01 40 10 09 34

Her dainty dressing tables go perfectly with the curtains and hangings that she
displays around them.

MARC BOUCHETARD STALL 222. ℂ 01 40 11 35 55

Marc Bouchetard specializes in ironwork: firedogs, tongs, fireguards and firebacks. He also stocks superb metal 19th-century furniture.

ERIC LENTZ STALL 237. ℂ 06 07 35 99 14

A lover of all things monumental, Lentz began dealing in the summer of 1998
and sells 20th-century objects, from the Twenties to the Seventies. He
sometimes has animal hides lying on the floor and be prepared to meet a
peculiar concrete monkey climbing up a tree trunk – a concrete one, of
course.

STALL 239 ℂ 01 40 10 95 20

An enormous range of chandeliers, lamps and mirrors are on offer here.

LAURENCE LENGLARE STALL 241. ℂ 01 40 11 91 47

Silvered-glass objects, mirrors and curios. The selection is highly original.

MARTINE REYNAUD STALL 247. ℂ 01 40 12 28 40

Attractive painted and handcrafted furniture, with plenty of drawers and leaves.

LITS ET LAMPES

44

CERVANTÈS STALL 251. ℂ 01 40 11 32 11

This stallholder, dealing from a delightful yellow-decorated stand, is a well-known specialist in Forties furniture, including mirrors.

M.L.V. STALL 257. ℂ 01 45 56 90 06

Engravings of birds, butterflies, soldiers, women and horse riders for collectors of these and similar subjects.

PATRICE MAYER STALL 261. ℂ 01 45 43 92 57

Deals mainly in handcrafted painted or natural wood furniture, such as old shop counters. He also has a few fine pier glasses and mirrors.

AISLE 6

PATRICK FOURTIN STALL 81

A Forties specialist who displays his finest pieces in the distinctly minimalist setting of his Paris gallery at 9 rue des Bons Enfants.

CHRISTIAN SAPET STALL 81BIS. ℂ 01 40 12 29 12

This stall resembles a house in a stage set and is an essential port of call for leading interior designers and antique dealers, from both Paris and abroad. You enter via an ivy-covered glass frontage and find yourself in a cavern on two levels. Sapet's collection of Arts and Crafts-style furniture and furnishings, which are always immensely popular with the English and Americans, reflects his exquisite taste.

MARC MAISON STALL 83. ℂ 06 60 62 61 90

Marc Maison stocks typical examples of what's come to be known as the 'grand style': pillars, ornaments for roof ridges and large stone pots to put on a balustrade.

DÉCO BISTRO STALL 87. ✆ 01 49 45 01 02

Jean-Luc Perrier sells bar fittings and accessories, from pedestal tables and counters to glasses and ashtrays; everything is in pristine condition. 'Think of this as the shop window for the 50,000 square feet of bars that one finds at Tournus [in the great wine-growing district of Burgundy]', explains Jean-Luc.

VINGTIÈME SIÈCLE STALL 93. ✆ 01 49 45 11 09

Bruno Ract-Madoux deals in the best furniture and objects from the Fifties, Sixties and Seventies. His stock includes work by Pierre Paulin (who designed rooms in the Elysée Palace for President Pompidou), Olivier and Pascal Mourgue, Knoll Associates, Charles Eames, Harry Bertoia and all the major modern designers. His list of clients is equally impressive and features, among others, Tom Ford, Gucci's design director, and Chloé's Stella McCartney. If he recognizes you as an enthusiast, Bruno will take you to a tiny house at the entrance to the Marché Paul Bert where he stores the rest of his stock.

LITS ET LAMPES STALL 232. ✆ 01 40 12 76 69

For Odile Fouchard, sleeping is a serious business. A flea market dealer for years, she has now set up a stall in Paul Bert selling ornate metal beds. Mainly 19th-century, the majority are from provincial France or England. Many of the pieces are not standard size, but Odile can tell you where to buy the appropriate bed linen. Her small folding beds make attractive little sofas and, besides beds, she also sells small pedestal tables that can be used as bedside tables, chandeliers, lamps and textiles. And don't miss her delightful children's beds, perfect to decorate with a white piqué coverlet and an organdie canopy.

AISLE 7

RENAUD TESSIER STALL 286. ✆ 01 40 12 31 83

A military theme pervades the postcards, decorations and weapons in stock.

SYLVIE CORBELIN STALL 291. ✆ 01 40 12 03 28

A gemmologist who says she 'likes things from every period', but has a particular fondness for pearls and turquoises.

STALL 402 ✆ 01 40 11 33 01

Furniture and lighting from 1900 to 1930 – well worth a browse.

STALLS 403–5 ✆ 01 40 10 95 65

High-quality inlaid and painted furniture.

MARC DELIGNY STALL 406. ✆ 06 08 98 10 72

How about a row of pillars or a fountain? The only problem is that you need the grounds to display them in. Also statues, monumental vases, fireplaces and decorative stonework of all kinds.

CHRISTOPHE REYNAL STALL 421. ✆ 01 34 79 15 55

Frames in every style and size, and also mirrors which Reynal skilfully restores.

NE PAS TOUCHER
MERCI

MARCHÉ CAMBO

The Marché Cambo at 75 rue des Rosiers takes its name from the French pronunciation of Israël Elkembaum, an antique dealer who set up sixty stalls in his huge store in the early 1970s. The market burned down in 1992, reopening four years later. The courtyard is awaiting restoration and will eventually house about fifteen more stalls.

GROUND FLOOR

THÉORÈME STALLS 3-4. ℭ 01 40 12 32 97
Rustic-style ceramics, some of them from Moustiers, Nevers, Rouen and Strasbourg, the largest French factories to produce faïence.

DANIEL ET CLAUDINE BOUR STALL 6. ℭ 01 49 48 04 97
High-quality (and white, naturally) embroidered and monogrammed linen, displayed in magnificent countryish armoires that are often beautifully carved.

HERVÉ CHONIGBAUM STALL 9. ℭ 01 40 11 44 41
Chonigbaum willingly admits that he doesn't specialize. His stock, however, is delightful: large painted wooden benches, chandeliers and attractive silverware.

PATRICK GARANJOUD ℭ 01 40 11 26 69
Interesting curios and furniture: small bronzes, carvings and porcelain.

FIRST FLOOR

ANTIQUITÉS CAMILLE STALL 12. ℭ 01 49 45 91 71
Furniture in every style. It's useful to know that if the joints of a piece appear to have been cut too precisely, the work must date to after 1840, the year in which the mechanical saw was invented.

LE CAMPHRIER STALL 18. ℭ 01 40 11 23 75
19th-century veneer furniture and Art Deco pâte de verre.

WALFREDO BARTH STALL 20. ℭ 01 49 45 06 56
Art Nouveau and Art Deco ceramics and 19th- and 20th-century drawings.

LA MAISON DU ROY STALL 21. ℭ 01 42 97 47 14
Fine 18th-century furniture. In terms of the decorative arts in France, the 1700s are heralded as *the* great century, since they produced both the elegant Régence style and wonderfully exuberant Louis XV marquetry.

CORINNE TONELLI STALL 22. ℭ 01 40 12 36 53
Before putting her furniture – chests of drawers, tables, consoles – on sale, Tonelli carefully strips each piece. 'That way they look good in a contemporary setting', she says.

MARCHÉ DES ROSIERS

The Marché des Rosiers is a grandiose title for the group of twelve tiny stalls set up on the ground floor of a small modern building at 3 rue Paul Bert in 1976. All or most of the stallholders specialize in pâte de verre and Art Nouveau furniture (six of the seven listed below sell furniture, objects and lighting in that vein) and some have stalls in the larger Saint-Ouen markets as well. In France, Art Nouveau is also known as *'style 1900'*. Its creator, Emile Gallé, was a ceramicist, a glassmaker and a cabinet maker whose sinuous designs were inspired by plants.

CLAUDE BOYER STALL 3. ℂ 01 40 12 98 55
(ALSO AT MARCHÉ BIRON, STALL 119, AISLE 1.)
Lighting is Claude Boyer's specialist field.

BERNARD LIAGRE STALL 6. ℂ 06 09 93 47 92
Lighting, vases and small items of furniture inlaid with blond wood.

MICHEL GIRAUD STALL 7
Art Nouveau vases and lighting.

CHRISTIAN SERRES STALL 8. ℂ 01 40 12 97 65
Small inlaid tables and glassware.

J.-P. RICHARD STALL 9. ℂ 01 40 12 86 79
Visit for lighting and crockery.

A. GAUTHIER STALL 10
Once again, lighting is the speciality, with a large selection of wall lamps.

TRANSPARENCES STALL 14. ℂ 01 40 12 59 44
Aurélia and Laurence Thévenin's stall is the odd one out here; they sell paintings from the Provençal school, plus a few pieces of silverware and glass.

MARCHÉ SERPETTE

Another fairly new market that was set up by Alain Serpette, an antique weapons specialist, in a huge coachbuilder's workshop at 110 rue des Rosiers in 1977. It is covered and comprises six aisles.

AISLE 1

DANIEL DELÉTRAIN STALL 2. ✆ 01 40 11 25 09
A delightful stand with small bronzes, pictures, silver and a few chandeliers.

STALL 4 ✆ 01 40 10 03 40
Mainly pistols – apparently firearms are the most popular weapons with collectors. A few pictures, engravings and drawings of military subjects are also stocked.

CABOTSE STALL 6. ✆ 01 40 11 29 16
Mostly Thirties crockery, which may seem rather plain when compared with wares from the preceding Art Nouveau period.

LA GARDE STALL 8. ✆ 01 40 10 17 88
Napoleon will always have his admirers. His bust adorns this stall, alongside medals, sabres, swords and uniforms.

THOMAS BONZOM ET PIERRE NICOLAS STALL 10. ✆ 06 09 92 66 97
In their blue-draped stand, stag's antlers crown an enormous semicircular stained-glass window and on top of some lacquered panelling, little birds seem to be twittering away with a stuffed monkey. A highly eclectic choice. 'We try to add a bit of wit to what we do', they explain.

LE SAVOIR FER STALL 16. ✆ 01 40 12 13 58
Firebacks and firedogs. Once purely functional, firedogs have become increasingly ornamental over the centuries. Also highly decorative old locks.

STALL 26 ✆ 01 40 10 13 50
At this stall everything is giant-sized: pier glasses, gilded mirrors and a superb carved wooden stag's head, a huntsman's dream.

STALL 27 ✆ 01 40 11 63 60
Beautiful mirrors and pier glasses, fine chandeliers and tapestries to decorate vast expanses of wall.

ARTÉMISE ET CUNÉGONDE STALL 28. ✆ 01 40 10 02 21
No sign of the comic-strip heroines of *La Famille Fenouillard* here. No books at

all, in fact, but it does sell attractive household linen with white or coloured embroidery. The dresses, on the other hand, are in fairly poor condition, so you need to be handy with a needle.

PATRICIA TIMSIT STALL 30BIS. ✆ 01 40 10 18 94
Exquisite signed 19th- and 20th-century jewelry. It is worth remembering that Patricia Timsit has a good repairer working for her and she also designs her own range of jewelry.

MAHÉ STALL 31. ✆ 01 40 12 81 22
High-quality furniture, mirrors and pictures.

STALL 35 ✆ 01 40 12 45 05
All kinds of tables. You're bound to find both one small enough to squeeze into a tiny space and one big enough to accommodate a large gathering.

CARMINA ANTIQUITÉS STALL 38. ✆ 01 49 45 11 24
Carole Minassian loves collecting anything on a monumental scale: pillars, chandeliers and tables for luxury flats or large country houses.

SAINT-OUEN ANTIQUITÉS STALL 39. ✆ 01 40 12 83 39
As well as his romantic jewelry, Claude Moraglia sells all kinds of bibelots and small pieces of furniture.

STALL 40 ✆ 01 40 11 26 92
Lots of silverware, much of it highly ornamental, from attractive formal pieces to useful serving sets. If you become a regular visitor to flea markets, it is worth learning about hallmarks.

THOMAS BONZOM ET PIERRE NICOLAS   MICHÈLE PERCEVAL

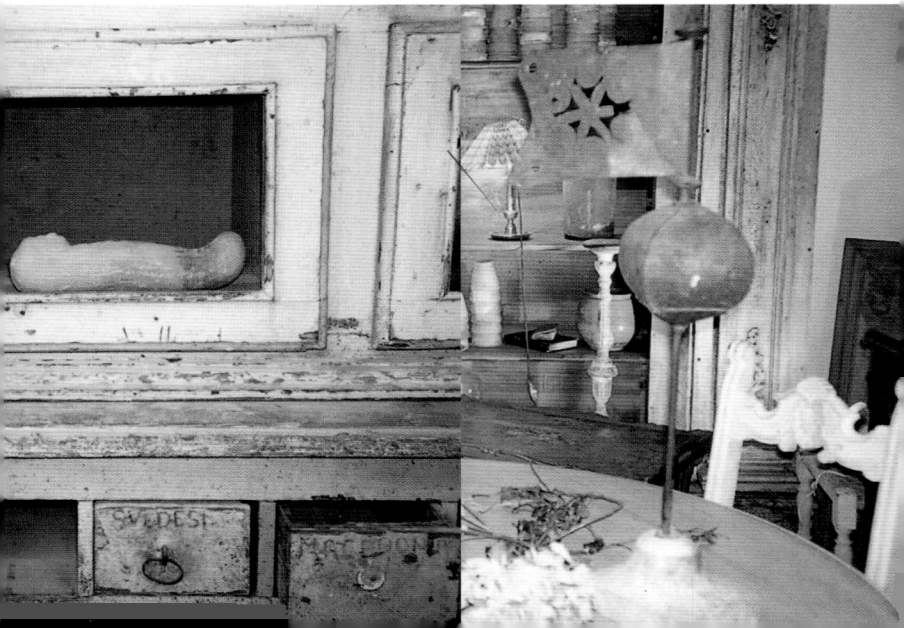

STALL 41 ✆ 01 40 10 02 43
A good source for furniture: armoires, bookcases, console tables, chandeliers and pier glasses. There's something to suit every taste.

AISLE 2

JEAN-YVES BARCZYK, STALL 3
Fine chandeliers and wrought iron.

STALL 5 ✆ 01 40 12 05 63
Plunge in and hunt through cheap junk, secondhand clothes and thousands of little bits and pieces, all jumbled together.

RENAUD VUAILLAT ET XAVIER CHOLLET
STALL 9 (ALSO AT STALL 11, AISLE 6). ✆ 01 40 12 22 14
These two dealers love 'anything unusual and unexpected': masses of large metal lamps, a fine wrought-iron sofa frame, a pair of beautiful Italian 18th-century high-backed wooden benches and a pair of enormous chandeliers with coloured glass beads that used to hang in a casino. A real find.

FRANÇOISE RENOULT STALL 17. ✆ 01 40 11 30 65
Charming objects, with pictures of flowers hanging above place settings in silver plate, pretty bottles in a leather vanity case and *verre églomisé* (gilded glass) balls.

AISLE 3

JEAN-PAUL COSTEY STALLS 2-4. ✆ 40 12 26 38
Wonderful home bars straight from the Thirties, in a variety of burr woods, that are inlaid with ivory or chrome. They come in all sizes, from counters to buffets and cocktail bars, and are in impeccable condition. Plus, of course, cocktail shakers, glasses and ice buckets from the same glamorous period.

OLWEN FOREST STALLS 5 AND 7. ✆ 01 40 11 96 38
Olwen Forest is English but used to be a dancer and actress in Hollywood. She has always collected the amazing jewelry designed – for American movie stars and for the roles they played – by Joseff of Hollywood, Miriam Haskell, Elsa Schiaparelli and Hattie Carnegie. Olwen's favourite period is the Thirties and Forties, but her selection ranges right through from 1920 to 1970.

VOYAGES STALL 10. ✆ 01 49 45 09 56
The insides of these Vuitton and Hermès trunks, suitcases and hatboxes, some of which are over a hundred years old, are masterpieces of ingenuity.

LE MONDE DU VOYAGE STALL 15. ✆ 01 40 12 64 03
The Bristol in Oslo, Reed's in Madeira, the Astoria in Vienna: these are just some of the evocative labels to be found on the old wooden-framed trunks here, many of which are by Vuitton. It also sells Hermès bags and even Hermès belts and ties.

ANNE-MARIE DESPAS STALL 16
A specialist in Italian 18th-century Arte Povera ('poor man's art' using lacquered cut-outs to imitate decorative paintwork). Occasionally she has a few well-preserved waistcoats from the same period.

PIERRETTE ET PIERRE QUITARD STALL 18
✆ 01 40 10 00 24

Like a stage set in the making, this stand displays a few wood panels, two fire-places back to back, a painted pillar and attractive 18th-century regional furniture, all of it restored by the stallholder. You are also told (just to whet your appetite) that you can see more in the impasse du Boeuf Couronné, in Bazainville, Yvelines.

ART ET DESIGN STALL 19. ✆ 01 40 10 12 83
Ralph Kochemann is an interior designer and his enthusiasm for Art Deco is the inspiration for this stall.

DOMINIQUE HEIDENGER STALL 24. ✆ 01 46 23 11 70
Although Heidenger is only a small lady, the things she salvages – windows, mirrors and pillars – are massive.

AISLE 4

DU BILLARD AU COMPTOIR STALL 9. ✆ 01 40 12 85 68

Fine antique billiard tables, restored for the modern rules of the game, are sold here with all the accessories, plus chandeliers.

MARIE-EVE ROSENTHAL STALL 11. ✆ 01 40 12 04 85
This lady is mad about mirrors. There are stacks of them wherever you look, transforming her huge stall into a gilded labyrinth in which your image is reflected endlessly. I was suddenly dazzled by an enormous Régence mirror that conjured up images of the palace where it had hung and the beauties that had been reflected in it. 'It's a Biennale mirror', said Marie-Eve softly. 'I'd love it to stay in France.'

STALL 12
A very cluttered stall but absolutely delightful and beautifully arranged, with a huge Danish desk, an Oriental vase and marvellous pictures.

L'INSOLITE, L'AUTRE PAS STALL 17. ✆ 01 49 45 16 18
Old-fashioned toys. But would modern children know how to play with them?

AISLE 5

ARTE STALL 2. ✆ 01 40 12 04 88
Catherine Choucroun likes anything decorative and she often has beautifully patinated antique furniture alongside Forties pieces, plus a selection of carved-wood and wrought-iron objects and 18th-century wood panelling. The combination is most beguiling.

LUCIEN PINEAU STALL 4. ✆ 01 40 11 45 75
Oriental pictures, with beautiful odalisques reclining on silken cushions and dreaming of dark-eyed warriors slaying infidels.

STALL 11 ✆ 01 40 11 39 42
Statues and busts in a variety of media: clay, bronze, marble and wood.

STALL 17

This stall stocks beautiful and unusual bedheads along with a large selection of impressively sized chandeliers.

STALL 18 ✆ 01 49 48 00 47

Another stall which is full of delights, with its large wooden shutters hung with wall lamps, lanterns and wooden objects. When you look inside and see the stacks of crockery under large chandeliers, it makes you feel like inviting a crowd of friends round.

CARIATIDES STALL 20. ✆ 01 40 10 15 40

Catherine Chagnon-Lartige specializes in stained-glass windows of all sizes.

MICHÈLE PERCEVAL STALL 26

Perceval loves patinated wood and collects examples of it from every period: panelling, pier glasses, etc.

AISLE 6

J.-P. JANKOVSKY STALL 6. ✆ 01 40 11 99 16

This is the stall to go to if you want a retro-style bathroom. Monsieur Jankovsky has all the accessories you need: soapdishes and hooks, mirrors and wall lights. He also stocks washbasins.

NICOLAS GIOVANNONI ET FRANCIS TOUSSAINT STALLS 8 AND 10 (ALSO AT MARCHÉ VERNAISON, STALL 146, AISLE 7.) ✆ 01 40 12 79 45

These two stallholders say that they deal in anything that goes on the table, from any period: canteens of cutlery in silver and silver plate, porcelain dinner services and complete sets of crystalware. They sometimes have a few fine chandeliers.

MARCHÉ ANTICA

Located at 99 rue des Rosiers, the Marché Antica is one of the smallest markets and also one of the newest. It was set up in 1985.

GISÈLE VAURY-SOURMAIS ✆ 01 40 10 09 93
Magnificent walking sticks from the 1700s to 1930. In the display cases, Vaury-Sourmais has high-quality trinkets, seals, opaline glass, etc.

DANIÈLE BOUILLOT
A boudoir oozing with femininity, selling 19th-century or early 20th-century perfume bottles, boxes for face powder, bags and little hats with veils.

HIER... ENCORE ✆ 01 49 45 03 24
A large selection of chairs, pictures and china, spread over three stalls.

TRACE DE CHINE ✆ 01 53 82 17 25 AND 06 07 64 78 48
Liu Jia Yin imports elm, cypress or camphor furniture from her homeland and most of her stock dates from the 18th and 19th centuries. Much older are her beautiful and unadorned ceramics, among them some Sung bowls. She also sells a few rugs.

MARCHÉ MALASSIS

The market's name comes from the Malassis plain, where rag-and-bone merchants set up in 1860 after they had been driven out of Paris. The site, accessed via 142 rue des Rosiers, is one of the newest and trading started here in 1989. On two levels and covered by a huge glass roof, the market has its own restaurant, Le Saint Framboise, and the news-stand stocking local papers at the entrance also sells books. Not whodunnits or literary prizewinners though; this is a flea market, after all, and the only books available are about collectors' items, fine furniture and pictures. You can even order Emmanuel Bénézit's multi-volume dictionary, the definitive guide to painting, sculpture, drawing and engraving. Let's hope *this* book will be prominently displayed there too!

GROUND FLOOR

LA COLLECTIONNITE STALL 5. ✆ 01 40 11 87 69
An assortment of games and toys, dolls and model soldiers. Your whole childhood at a glance.

JEAN-PIERRE CAIETTA STALLS 9 AND 10
Trinkets, small pieces of inlaid furniture, a few pieces of silverware and folk-style crockery.

MOURAD AMEZAL STALL 13. ✆ 01 49 45 13 46
This stall, decorated with a marvellous photo of Gary Cooper dressed as a cowboy and posing as a member of the paparazzi, sells photographic equipment. Everything, except for the very oldest items, is in working order. It also has projectors and films.

ALICE STALLS 16–17. ✆ 01 40 11 43 33
A wonderful mixture of small furniture, folding fireguards, frames and trinkets.

N.V.M. NADINE COTTINET STALL 18. ✆ 01 40 11 54 74
Nadine Cottinet and her husband Pierre have paved their stall with salvaged terracotta, azulejos, stone and enamel tiles from the 17th and 18th centuries. If you still want to see more, they will tell you to go to Sols Majeurs, which is run by their son (12 rue Jacques Cœur, 75004 Paris ✆ 01 42 71 74 28).

STALLS 19–20 ✆ 01 49 48 06 69
Furniture and objects from the Thirties and Forties, including toilet articles; worth a browse.

CARTE BLANCHE   STÉPHANE BARDOT ET PATRICIA ATTWOOD

LE CLUB CENTRAL PATIO. ℂ 01 40 10 13 90

Olivier Rosenthal and Bernard Legris only sell leather club armchairs and they have masses of them. As you will see, they are fairly well-padded – the chairs, that is – and some of their seat cushions have brown velvet covers. Rosenthal and Legris recommend applying slightly coloured beeswax to the leather upholstery every six months and rubbing it in well. You might see them doing it.

STALL 30 ℂ 01 40 12 10 48

Wonderful mirrors and frames.

VEYRET STALL 33. ℂ 01 40 10 07 96

A typical mixture of fascinating bric-a-brac: a white faïence stove, some banisters, an astronomical telescope, window wainscotting, etc.

CARTE BLANCHE STALLS 34–36. ℂ 01 41 11 63 81

A hotchpotch of styles and provenances, in which carved chairs, large pictures and objects that have been dug up from under the ground are all displayed together.

TRÉSORS DE PERSE STALL 41. ℂ 01 40 11 10 30

Monsieur Givili goes to Syria to find his beautiful furniture inlaid with mother-of-pearl: stools, chairs, small tables, chests and mirrors. To complement them, he stocks magnificent carpets and textiles, also from the Middle East.

STÉPHANE BARDOT ET PATRICIA ATTWOOD
STALLS 42–43. ℂ 01 40 11 61 78

These two Oriental enthusiasts share their finds. Patricia seeks out porcelain in China and Japan, while Stéphane travels the length and breadth of India in search of decorative pieces: panelling from Gujarat, furniture from Goa, huge basins and fountains from Rajastan and also furniture from the colonial era and primitive Indonesian works of art.

L'ESCALIER DE CRISTAL STALL 45. ℂ 01 40 11 37 34

Evelyne Bastok sells tableware and painted furniture. And yes, she says, she will also look out for missing pieces of a service if you ask her to.

RONDEUR DES JOURS STALL 60. ℂ 01 40 11 48 98
(ALSO AT MARCHÉ JULES VALLÈS, STALL 100)

Frédérique Couque sells Palissy wares, magnificent 16th- and 17th-century ceramics decorated with highly naturalistic *trompe l'œil* devices that were inspired by the great Renaissance visionary Bernard Palissy. He was imitated in the 19th century by artists such as Charles-Jean Avisseau and J. Landais. Couque also stocks attractive ceramics from the South of France and her partner, Jean Dreyfus, specializes in antique watches.

SYLVIANE CRISTOBAL STALL 61. ℂ 01 43 62 00 10
(ALSO AT STALL 138, FIRST FLOOR.)

Cristobal's tapestry cartoons were used as guides by weavers at Aubusson in the 18th and 19th centuries. Painted in gouache on paper or oil on canvas, they are both works of art and practical tools and show whole full-size designs. She has them in all shapes and sizes and mounts some in frames.

SYCOMORE STALL 62. ✆ 01 40 11 48 29
This stall sells Art Deco objects and also items that were salvaged when the Parisian nightclub Le Lido was refurbished.

CATHERINE DIAN-DUMOND STALL 66. ✆ 01 40 10 13 60
A large selection of barbotine ware (vases, flowerpot holders and umbrella stands, most of them large) and a few pieces of cane furniture.

D.W. ANTIQUITÉS STALLS 68–69. ✆ 06 60 68 63 25
Art Deco furniture and lighting.

K.F.J. STALL 72
Perfume flacons – some with scent still in them – and enchanting powder boxes.

COLLECTION'S STALL 79. ✆ 01 40 11 47 67
The name says it all. This stall has everything: spectacles and corkscrews, small 19th-century bronzes, rattles, and so on. They will tell you that there are exactly 146 categories of collectors' items, although I haven't counted them.

G.L.B. STALL 80. ✆ 01 40 11 00 22
Fine silverware, some by Jean-Baptiste-Claude Odiot and by Charles Christofle (including canteens of cutlery and formal pieces). Also glassware, with many of the pieces by Lalique and Daum.

AUX LIBELLULES STALL 81. ✆ 01 40 11 44 36
Interesting bric-a-brac. The stock includes intricate belt buckles, little mesh purses in silvered metal and a few small lamps and vases.

ZERLINE STALL 84. ✆ 01 40 10 92 51
Doors that can be re-used in rooms or for cupboards, attractive painted furniture and pier glasses.

EMAIL ET PUCES STALL 87. ✆ 01 40 10 14 29
Dominique Chrétien's stall, selling advertising paraphernalia, has enamelled placards on the walls and piles of silk-screen printed metal boxes, framed advertisements and posters extolling the virtues of products such as Kub stock cubes, Menier chocolate and Postillon wines.

AS TIME GOES BY… AND SPIRIT STALLS 89–90
✆ 01 40 12 40 18
Franck Menier and Harry Aaron have salvaged the glossiest Americana from the Thirties to the Fifties: chewing-gum dispensers, jukeboxes, enormous refrigerators with rounded corners, furniture and all kinds of accessories emblazoned with the Coca-Cola logo. Everything is in working order and comes with a guarantee. It's a kind of American dream.

AIRE DU TEMPS STALL 92. ✆ 01 40 12 49 24
Postcard collectors will find an assortment of subjects here.

LE BRICK À BARC STALL 95. ✆ 01 40 11 32 31
The name is a play on words for a stall that sells nautical and scientific equipment.

MARIE-THÉRÈSE NAYS-FAVRE STALL 102

☎ 01 40 10 29 02

A fine collection of silverware and jewelry, bottles with silver casing, mirrors and pictures.

GILDA SAIMAN STALLS 113–14

☎ 01 40 11 47 50

If you are nostalgic for the Thirties and Forties, this is the place to find furniture, carpets, lighting and pictures. Everything goes together.

REBIÈRE ANTIQUITÉS STALLS 115–17

☎ 01 40 12 68 43

To furnish retro-style bathrooms, there are attractive washstands with swivelling basins. Also sofas and small Napoleon III tables.

NICOLE AKER STALL 119. ☎ 01 40 11 79 83

This stall feels like an old-fashioned kitchen, as it is filled with enamelled-metal objects, red check linen and every size of spice jar. Aker attracts a large Japanese clientele who have christened her look the 'poor country style'. They are mad about the things she sells, as are fashionable young Parisians.

FIRST FLOOR

FRANCK BERGÉ STALLS 123–25

☎ 06 80 40 18 22

The crockery and glass sold by this young stallholder are of extremely good quality, so it's not surprising that he numbers New York's Metropolitan Museum of Art among his customers. Everything is in impeccable condition, the services are always complete and he regularly has about forty on display.

MALASSIS, SAINT-OUEN PARIS

PRESTIGE-ART DU TEXTILE STALL 126. ☎ 01 40 10 16 25
(ALSO AT MARCHÉ DAUPHINE, STALL 56, GROUND FLOOR.)
Tapestries, hangings, carpets and curtains, some of which are Oriental.

PARISSA STALLS 130–31
A good choice of carpets and hangings. Similar to Stall 126.

CHRISTIAN LECLERC STALL 161. ☎ 06 60 43 78 49
Attractive painted furniture that has been well restored and distressed where
necessary.

CIRCÉ STALL 164. ☎ 01 40 12 14 93
A tribute to femmes fatales and to the woman who tried to snatch Ulysses from
the arms of Penelope. Did she use alluring perfumes from precious flacons and
keep her cosmetics in seductively pretty boxes?

LA LIBRAIRIE DU LOUVRE STALLS 166–67. ☎ 01 34 16 41 59
Jean-Pierre Bauer is an expert who sells engravings and prints, with an emphasis
on the regional.

JADIS À MALASSIS STALLS 183–85. ☎ 01 42 28 00 34
An enormous and fascinating stall where you will find an extraordinary stock of
fleurs du Berry, the flowers used to make bouquets and the type of bridal headdresses that newly married couples often preserved under glass and kept on
their mantelpiece as a souvenir of their wedding day. Plus chandeliers, patinated bedsteads, pretty painted furniture (also from Berry), chandeliers and
mirrors.

GHISLAIN ANTIQUES   L'HOMME DE PLUME

GHISLAIN ANTIQUES STALL 190. ℰ 06 09 04 41 13

Large 18th- and 19th-century tapestries and seat coverings in good condition.
The owner can also recommend a good upholsterer if you need one.

ATTITUDES STALL 201

A fascinating stall, with carved candelabra hanging above couches and chandeliers that are reflected in the surrounding mirrors.

L'HOMME DE PLUME STALL 211. ℰ 01 40 11 49 33

At her enormous stall, Françoise Leray has everything you need to furnish your
study or library: a wide selection of large flat tête-à-tête desks, paperknives, magnifying glasses, penholders, writing cases, inkwells, small revolving bookshelves
or larger bookcases and library steps. She also restores screens. Everything is top
quality.

HUMEURS STALL 214

This stall stocks a selection of unusual and fascinating objects, including, when I
visited, a small painted chest, a wooden stork, an old mannequin and a number
of firebacks.

STALLS 229–30

With its half-open writing desks and bead hanging lamps, architects' drawings
and portraits (that you might want to pass off as being of your ancestors), there's
a wealth of fascinating things to be discovered at this stall.

LIBRAIRIE BOULOUIZ-FEREZ STALL 235
ℰ 01 40 11 49 21

A bookseller who compiles catalogues and organizes sales focusing on Greece,
Egypt and the Middle East. His particular fields of interest are art and travel.

ACHAT
PHOTOGRAPHIES
ANCIENNES
'Au Bonheur du Jour'
Stand 11   40 11 64 30

TOUTES NOS PHOTOGRAPHIES
SONT DES TIRAGES D'ÉPOQUE
THÈMES DIVERS :
. NUS FÉMININS MASCULINS
. VOYAGES XIX ème XX ème
    → TURQUIE ÉGYPTE ALGÉRIE
    TUNISIE PALESTINE GRÈCE AFRIQUE
    ASIE INDOCHINE CHINE INDONÉSIE...
. SECOND EMPIRE
. CINÉMA · THÉATRE · OPÉRA
. ÉCRIVAINS · PEINTRES
. SPORTS
. PERSONNALITÉS
    FAMILLE D'ORLÉANS DE RUSSIE
. SURRÉALISME · INSOLITE

MARCHÉ DAUPHINE

This, the newest of the big Saint-Ouen flea markets, opened at 140 rue des Rosiers in 1991. It is on two levels and has a glass roof. The shops upstairs open on to narrow gangways in which the dealers sometimes keep the overflow from their stalls. Expert valuation certificates have been available since September 1997.

GROUND FLOOR

AU BONHEUR DU JOUR STALLS 10–11. ℰ 01 40 11 64 30
First and foremost, this stall sells good-quality old black-and-white photos, many of them nudes – from the theatre, from music halls and from the silver screen. What exotic foreign beauties! I also discovered some really curious items: tokens for brothels in Cambodia and Arizona, on which was written 'Good for all night'.

SHANAZ STALLS 12–13. ℰ 01 40 11 39 70
In terms of carving on furniture, every French province has its own particular motif: foliage in Île de France, hearts in Alsace, daisies in Champagne, wild roses in Picardy, etc. On this stand you will find – and be able to identify – some wonderful armoires and commodes. It also has a few chandeliers.

PRÉSENTS PASSÉS STALL 23. ℰ 01 40 12 87 36
From her fascinating stall Isabelle Maleval sells old tools in good condition. The stand's name is well chosen, since these tools from the past are still very much in use today. A new generation of craftsmen relishes the opportunity to work with such beautiful objects, polished by years of service in traditional crafts. A real expert like Guillaume Pellerin – *the* authority on old tools and author of a book about them – comes here regularly, looking for items for his personal collection.

SCHWARTZ STALL 25. ℰ 01 49 45 14 36
Antique clothes, household linen, embroidery and lace.

MAYA ANTIQUITÉS STALL 32. ℰ 01 40 12 62 14
Small items, to give to friends or to add to a collection: a little cup with a delicate pattern, a graceful statuette, a bud vase or perhaps an ivory or bone paperknife.

COUESPEL & GALLOT STALL 36. ℰ 01 40 11 52 21
A huge selection of small pieces of furniture and objects. The patinated and gilded leather that is sold to cover tables and writing desks is extremely useful. If you need to replace any, remember to take measurements with you.

AU RÉVERBÈRE STALL 43. ℰ 01 40 10 00 46
Bernard Lazarovici is an engraving and lithography expert. Much of his stock is

68

decorative, or has a Parisian or gastronomic theme. He also specializes in original lithographs by the caricaturist Sem.

CÉLESTIN-HENRI DEVOT STALL 55. ✆ 01 40 11 46 22
Commodes, lit by chandeliers, with pictures which might be described as being in a fairly conventional style.

PRESTIGE STALL 56. ✆ 01 40 11 14 64
(**ALSO AT MARCHÉ MALASSIS, STALL 126, FIRST FLOOR**)
Monsieur Ahi displays an excellent choice of carpets, similar to those at Malassis.

THIERRY AMBLARD STALL 74. ✆ 01 40 11 18 19
In the old-fashioned style of Pullman travellers and of passengers on luxury liners, be sure to take a mountain of elegant leather and wooden luggage wherever you go. Here you will find trunks and suitcases by Louis Vuitton and Hermès, as well as smaller bags by them and by Chanel.

RÉTRO PUB STALL 76
The smile of the little Alsatian girl, with her big bow and rosette, eclipses all the other posters, advertising paraphernalia and enamel placards promoting Dijon mustard, Jacquet cognac, Barros port and Père Noël wools.

NORMAND STALL 77. ✆ 01 40 11 52 92
If real Parisian postcards are what you're interested in, this is where to find them, arranged by area. Also a superb collection of beer mats from bars.

DANIEL LONGUEVILLE STALL 79. ✆ 06 80 87 26 02
With his wife Marie-Odile, Daniel has recently set up this small stall selling 18th- and 19th-century furniture, silver and pretty trinkets. There's always a good selection of paintings and chandeliers too. If you want to see more, visit

their shop near the Château de Maisons-Lafitte (21 place de la Vieille Eglise, 78600 Maisons Laffitte ✆ 01 39 62 09 96).

ISABELLE FEUGÈRE STALL 91. ✆ 01 40 12 10 18
Feugère happily admits that she is a 'general practitioner, like a doctor'. But no doctor has ever discovered such delightful objects: a fireguard, a little painted chest, flower paintings and a carved armoire.

DIAMANTINA STALL 98. ✆ 01 40 12 71 79
The big names of the place Vendôme and the rue de la Paix, such as Cartier, Van Cleef & Arpels and Poiray, have pride of place among the beautiful pieces of jewelry and watches here. Don't be put off, as they are not necessarily unaffordable.

BOUTIQUE LYDIA STALL 101. ✆ 01 40 11 49 51
This stall stocks dresses and hats by fashion legends such as Givenchy and Chanel, but also earlier (pre-1920) designers. Everything is in excellent condition and Lydia Chapelier, herself a former couturière, lists museums among her customers. Also haute-couture jewelry, gloves, shoes and Hermès scarves.

ABJ STALL 105. ✆ 01 40 11 44 78
The fireplaces, mirrors and chandeliers on display here will whet your appetite for a visit to the shop a little further along in Saint-Ouen (4 rue Lécuyer).

AMBIANCE STALL 108. ✆ 01 40 10 98 55
The stall is called Ambiance and it has a delightful one, with its ornate mirrors, marble busts and a few fine pieces of 18th-century furniture.

STALL 121 ✆ 06 07 76 40 27
There is an air of traditional comfort to the club armchairs and billiard table lights that are stocked here. There is some china too, and, with any luck, you might turn over a plate and discover the mark of a little horn – which proves its provenance from Chantilly – or the initials 'D.V.' if it was made in Mennecy.

STALLS 128–29 ✆ 01 40 10 83 46
One of the best places to find chromolithographs, postcards, buttons and ribbons.

LUC BOUVERET STALLS 149–50. ✆ 01 40 12 89 80
A decorated piano stands on a large 18th-century carpet, surrounded by tapestries and prints. Original engravings are signed and numbered.

MICHEL KLEIN STALL 151. ✆ 01 40 11 58 51
15th- to 17th-century sideboards, chairs and high-backed benches in dark carved wood, plus early pictures, pewter dishes and tapestries in the Haute Epoque style.

CHRISTIAN ARNOUX STALL 156. ✆ 01 40 11 04 21
Pâte de verre bottles, vases, lighting and mirrors.

FIRST FLOOR

STALL 179 ✆ 01 34 71 19 62
Traditional enamel kitchen utensils and crockery. The Japanese are mad about

them; they buy up everything on the flea market stalls and then use the stock to open their own shops.

STALL 180 ℂ 01 34 71 19 62
Rows of old-fashioned wooden roll-top office furniture, ideal for the study.

P.B. STALLS 181–82. ℂ 01 40 11 93 80
Art Deco coloured-glass lighting and engraved mirrors. Those little glass balls that are so easily broken can be bought separately and replaced here.

GIRAUD STALLS 183–84. ℂ 01 49 45 94 61
Forties and Fifties furniture and glassware. The objects are fetching much higher prices now and have become popular with the younger generation, ever since the revival of Forties and Fifties fashion a few years ago.

L'ARMADA STALL 185
The name speaks for itself on this stall for naval buffs. Michel Martin salvages portholes, lanterns, barometers and navigational equipment straight from ships. He also stocks scientific instruments: globes, graphometers, telescopes, etc.

GÉRARD LEPRÊTRE STALL 187. ℂ 06 85 96 98 59
Charming carved-wood or horn objects from Germany's Black Forest: small mirrors, shelves, frames, pipe racks and coat hooks. Leprêtre also likes the soft curves of Michael Thonet's bent-wood furniture.

HABIB ARFAOUI STALL 189. ℂ 01 46 34 66 56
Sells books and engravings that will delight both real and armchair travellers.

FRANÇOISE RÉMY STALL 190. ℂ 01 40 12 81 98
She says she finds it hard to pin herself down to any particular kind of book, but it's obvious which subjects she prefers: literature, history and travel.

AU PASSÉ SIMPLE STALLS 191–92. ℂ 06 86 05 61 43
Records, posters and some wonderful glass slides for magic lanterns, from the days before cinema.

AU PIED DE LA LETTRE STALL 194. ℂ 01 49 48 02 18
Jean-Claude Fayon aims to 'find interesting books in good condition, leather-bound of course, on literature and history. In short, good contents in a good container.' He has complete sets.

PAPIERS ANCIENS STALLS 196–97. ℂ 01 40 11 27 00
In addition to books, Alain Rodelet sells engravings, medals and paintings. Also autographs, which have interested collectors since the 19th century.

ANTHARE DE SCHUYTER STALL 218. ℂ 01 40 11 17 25
Books, including ones for children, engravings and a large range of Images d'Epinal (precursors of modern strip cartoons).

EXOTIC KALAGAS STALLS 224–25. ℂ 01 40 12 86 28
It was purely by chance that her son Vincent's trip to Asia sparked off Edith

Bodart's career. He still goes off in search of furniture from India and from the Himalayan border of Pakistan: Afghan beds made from woven leather, wonderful little multicoloured cupboards from the Swat valley, nomads' chests from Nuristan, Pakistani spice boxes on feet, a handsome laundry stone from Jaisalmer and even furniture from the era when India was an English colony. Edith, meanwhile, imports rugs from Egypt and above all from Morocco, produced by tribes from the South, plus earth-coloured pottery made by Kabyle women.

STALL 236 ✆ 01 40 10 26 39
Charming traditional French objects, like baskets, embroidered household linen, simple and attractive pottery and enamel kitchen utensils – ideal for anyone with an aversion to all things high-tech.

MONIQUE GERMANO STALL 241.
✆ 01 40 12 95 29
Monique Germano has an eclectic approach, attracting at least three sorts of collector to her stall which sells inkwells, penholders and even desks, plates, barbotine flowerpot holders and enamel kitchen utensils.

MAMMOTH ANTIEK STALLS 250–57 AND 284–85
Joke and Jos Walters own Holland's largest antique shop and their premises in Dauphine are enormous. Their speciality is 19th-century pine German, Austrian, Dutch and Scandinavian furniture. They offer benches, chests, sideboards, desks, windows and display cabinets, all restored and often stripped, although they leave the painted floral motifs on some pieces. Well worth a browse.

JANE DE LIVRON STALL 270. ✆ 01 40 11 26 88
This English stallholder has a vast selection of liqueur cabinets, as well as silver-ware and attractive engraved crystal glasses.

MARCHÉ LÉCUYER-VALLÈS

At 20 rue Jules Vallès, a painted sign depicting Simone Signoret and Charlie Chaplin alongside reels of film hangs above the entrance to a tiny alleyway leading to the rue Lécuyer. It is a friendly 'lucky dip' of a market, with its small stalls and simple tarpaulin-covered portable tables. Have a brief look around before embarking on the larger Saint-Ouen markets. There's not an enormous array of stock, but you never know your luck….

STALL 3
Books and crockery.

JELLAL KESRAOUI STALL 5
A mix of bibelots and miniatures, crockery and silverware.

STALL 6
If you're interested in Thirties furniture, then this stall is worth a browse.

ALBERT STALL 9
Albert is also known as the Prince, he tells you. His stall has a mixture of bags, suitcases, medals, bottles and a few fur coats.

STALL 10
There's an extremely feminine slant to the dresses, ribbons, lace, junk beads, hats and hatpins on sale here.

STALL 12
Come and have a look at the old newsreel films, radios, cameras and photographic and projection equipment on sale at this stall.

STALL 15
Books, with the emphasis on regional literature.

STALL 16
A stand selling an array of pendulum clocks and vases for the mantelpiece, but also wall clocks and chandeliers.

SHOPS IN SAINT-OUEN

In the streets around the markets traders still spread out their wares on temporary stalls or directly on the ground, just as the rag-and-bone merchants did in the early 1900s. Others have shops.

RUE DES ROSIERS

L'ENTREPÔT 80 RUE DES ROSIERS

L'Entrepôt used to belong to a secondhand dealer and scrap-metal merchant, but in 1990 three antique sellers got together and took over the site, which was partly occupied by sheds. It now sells fireplaces, staircases, wood panelling, handcrafted furniture, chandeliers, clocks, tables and pier glasses, all of very high quality. The site is huge and the atmosphere tranquil. It's a far cry from the crowds and frenetic activity in the more popular markets.

LA GALERIE DES GLACES 87 RUE DES ROSIERS
✆ 01 40 11 17 52

This shop specializes in Rococo mirrors but has examples in every imaginable style, in gilt wood or plaster. There are also a few gilt-wood armchairs to choose from.

MIROIRS 109 RUE DES ROSIERS
✆ 01 40 10 25 29

As the name indicates, it sells mirrors, with gilt-wood frames.

MAISON BEYS 118 RUE DES ROSIERS
✆ 01 40 12 69 99 OR 01 40 12 42 71

A long warehouse that offers a little bit of everything: an engraved Venetian mirror, a portrait of a distinguished person wearing a tricolour belt, a Louis XVI secretaire, gilt-wood candelabra, a stone *pietà*, an Empire pedestal table, a pair of shepherdesses, a silver-gilt monstrance, a praying figure of a saint and a carved wooden cradle. Pure theatre.

LA BOUTIQUE 75 122 RUE DES ROSIERS. ✆ 01 40 12 56 70

Sophie Trébuchet salvages pillars, pots, wrought iron, wooden latticework and balustrades. She also has a few large pictures of flowers and fruit. There are pairs of stone dogs and lions at the entrance, guarding the stock.

DISCOPHILIE 125 RUE DES ROSIERS
Vinyl records, both singles and albums, arranged by category (and it stocks every type of music you can think of).

MURIEL 133–35 RUE DES ROSIERS. ✆ 01 40 12 75 17
A motley collection, with Chinese watercolours next to little Wedgwood vases, jade fibulas, silver crucifixes, jewelry, place settings and small trinkets.

ALPHA COLLECTIONS 139 RUE DES ROSIERS
✆ 01 42 85 07 08
A jumble of vinyl records, postcards and small perfume bottles.

MEUBLES ANCIENS DE NOS GRAND-MÈRES
140 RUE DES ROSIERS. ✆ 01 40 11 62 26
The kind of attractive traditional fruitwood furniture that, as the name suggests, your grandmother might have owned.

L'AIDJOLATE ANTIQUITÉS 140 RUE DES ROSIERS
✆ 01 40 10 10 86
Trinkets and barbotine ware in all sizes.

141 RUE DES ROSIERS
An array of secondhand clothes and fashion accessories.

LES VIEILLES PIERRES DU MELLOIS 152 RUE DES ROSIERS
✆ 01 40 12 54 79
Wonderful fireplaces and stone garden benches.

156 RUE DES ROSIERS
A large selection of secondhand clothes and fashion accessories, but a wider choice than at no. 141, with dresses hung across the wall. Lots of hats, both feathered and velvet, bags, lace, buttons and a few ivory brushes.

RUE PAUL BERT

LA PETITE MAISON AUX PUCES 10 RUE PAUL BERT
✆ 01 40 10 56 69
Antique dealer Annick Clavier moved to Saint-Ouen from the fashionable rue de Verneuil in central Paris in 1997. Since then, she has been living in this charming little house with a small garden from which she sells any of the expertly chosen objects, paintings or pieces of furniture on display, replacing them whenever she needs to. 'Turnover is very quick', she says. Ring at the garden gate and you can be sure of a warm welcome. Both the mistress of the house and her ephemeral decor are enchanting.

SEMA 13 RUE PAUL BERT. ✆ 01 40 11 25 69
Stone and marble mantelpieces, wrought-iron trelliswork, Medici vases and some splendid pier glasses.

ANTILOPE 17 RUE PAUL BERT. ✆ 01 40 11 39 41
Art Deco period furniture, objects and lighting.

ERIC HEITZMANN 21 RUE PAUL BERT. ℂ 01 43 25 71 33
Fine 18th- and 19th-century furniture and mirrors.

GALERIE CAILLEUX 24TER RUE PAUL BERT
A large selection of 19th-century paintings, secretaires, inlaid tables and trinketry.

VIOLETTE ET SARAH 42 RUE PAUL BERT. ℂ 01 40 12 33 78
This family has been selling secondhand clothes here since 1946, when Violette's
mother Minouche ran the shop. 'We used to sell American clothes then', says
Sarah, Violette's daughter. Now they specialize in old European clothes, lace and
stylish fashion accessories and also stock plenty of ribbons and trimmings.

RUE JULES VALLÈS

AU ROI DES ANTIQUAIRES 20 RUE JULES VALLÈS
ℂ 01 40 11 57 05
A huge secondhand shop with a large selection of lighting and copper pans.

MAZEAUX, AUX VIEUX MÉTAUX 28 RUE JULES VALLÈS
ℂ 01 40 11 63 92
Latticework and baths, balconies and banisters, washbasins and firebacks, all piled
up higgledy-piggledy. Also remnants of metal, hence the name.

31 RUE JULES VALLÈS
A real odds-and-ends shop, with pleated nightdresses and beautifully goffered lace
blouses next to china dolls, silverware and trinkets.

LA PETITE MAISON AUX PUCES   LA PETITE MAISON AUX PUCES

78

DOCKS DE LA RADIO 34 RUE JULES VALLÈS. ✆ 01 40 11 09 90
The radios, cameras, hi-fi systems and turntables on sale are all in working order, but they also stock spare parts for people who want to do their own repairs. There are records too for those who still have their old players.

SURPLUS MILITAIRE GARBA 42 RUE JULES VALLÈS
✆ 01 40 11 76 53
Combat fatigues, parkas, caps and heavy boots, both new and secondhand.

LE MARCHÉ DES ANTIQUAIRES 46 RUE JULES VALLÈS
A varied range of secondhand stock, but it is particularly good for small items of hardware, either new or old.

SURPLUS SIMON 48 RUE JULES VALLÈS
More modern army uniforms.

COPA MUSIC 52 RUE JULES VALLÈS
Records – all types of music – for those who still listen to vinyl.

DOMINIQUE BORY STALL 5
Good-quality secondhand clothes, mostly from the Forties and Fifties. Twenty-somethings love them, especially the elegant dresses which include quite a selection of little black numbers.

NEARBUYS

Avenue Michelet, pretentiously named the Marché Michelet, is another cheap market, with stalls on one side and, on the other, shops that only sell leather and denim. Not worth even a ten-minute stroll.

Don't forget that lunch begins early at the markets and first sittings start at 11.30am. Although the stalls don't open as early as they used to – I remember getting up at dawn when I was about fifteen or sixteen to get to the Marché Malik by 6am to look for shetland sweaters – the stallholders still arrive very early, as do some of their major customers, the antiques dealers and interior designers.

LE BIRON
85 RUE DES ROSIERS
✆ 01 40 12 65 65
The 'chic' place to eat, recommended and patronized by the more expensive dealers, important customers and foreign visitors.

LA BRASSERIE BIRON
120 AVENUE MICHELET
✆ 01 40 11 18 72
This opened in 1931 and is now an institution. It is located at one of the exits from the Marché Biron.

CHEZ LOUISETTE
136 AVENUE MICHELET (OR ENTER VIA MARCHÉ VERNAISON, AISLE 10)
✆ 01 40 12 10 14
An open-air café for tourists. The story is that Edith Piaf started out here. Lunch is served from 11.30am to 5.30pm.

LA CHOPE DES PUCES
122 RUE DES ROSIERS
✆ 01 40 11 02 49
Tourists eat to the strains of the Les Manouches orchestra, who play from 2 to 7pm.

P'TIT LANDAIS
96 RUE DES ROSIERS
✆ 01 49 45 11 55
This café at the corner of the Marché Paul Bert is popular with stallholders. The atmosphere is always friendly and informal.

LE SAINT FRAMBOISE
FIRST FLOOR MARCHÉ MALASSIS 142 RUE DES ROSIERS
✆ 01 40 11 27 38
Facing on to the Marché Malassis, this restaurant has a small terrace where you can sit outside on fine days. Provençal-print tablecloths, a friendly atmosphere and good home cooking.

PUCES DE MONTREUIL

There are only a handful of real secondhand dealers left in what has now become a regular market (although it doesn't sell food). They are the last descendants of the Maubert rag-and-bone merchants who had to move out of Paris in the 19th century to the little villages east of the city. When you come out of the metro station, cross over the top of the ring road; the market runs along the pavement of the avenue du Professeur André Lemierre, parallel to the ring road in the 20e arrondissement. Much of what's on sale on the sunshade-covered temporary stalls – jeans and trainers, saucepans and cassettes, watches and plates, caftans and spices – need not detain you for long.

HOW & WHEN TO GO TO THE
PUCES DE MONTREUIL

PUCES DE MONTREUIL
AVENUE DU PROFESSEUR
ANDRÉ LEMIERRE, 20ᵉ

OPEN
Saturday to Monday,
9am–7pm

BY METRO
Porte de Montreuil (line 9
Sèvres–Montreuil)

BY BUS
On the PC, no. 351
(Nation–Roissy pôle RER) or
no. 26 (Gare Saint Lazare–
Cours de Vincennes)

PARKING
This may cause problems.
Take the Porte de Montreuil
exit from the ring road and try
your luck.

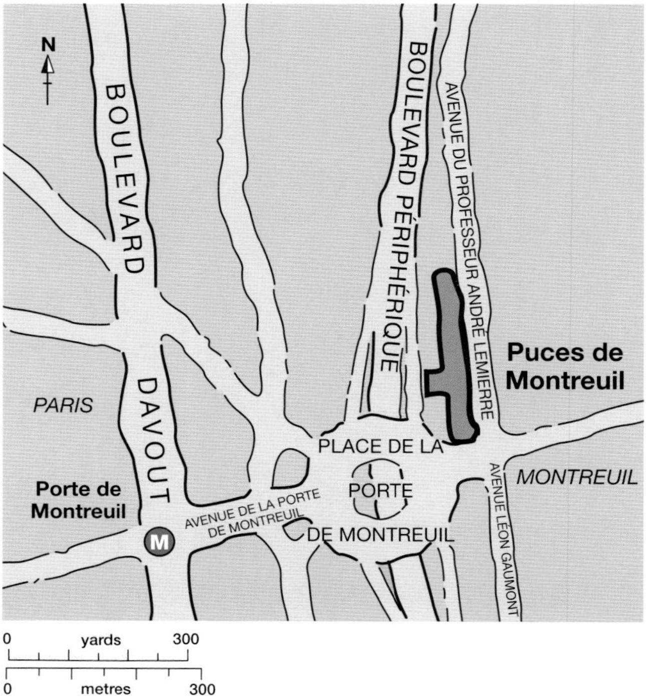

IRMA ET ANDRÉ STALL 794

Embroidered household linen, nightshirts and blouses, all in good condition.

NADINE BUY STALL 832

Well-preserved clothes from the Thirties to the present. Buy also has some children's clothes from the turn of the 20th century and household linen, but is particularly good for elegant black dresses and underwear – very popular with the youngsters.

NORDINE STALL 833

He has been selling clothes (from the early 1900s to the 1970s) for fourteen years. All are in good condition, but will need ironing. He also has theatrical costumes and some household linen.

KIMONO-DÔ ☎ 01 46 81 20 56

Everything Mel Boyer stocks is in silk or cotton, in good condition and superbly designed. He always wears one of his kimonos or a *haori*, a traditional Japanese jacket: the *bakama*, combined skirt and trousers for men, he also sells are more unusual. Many of his customers work in show business.

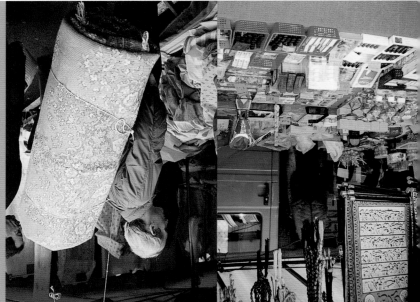

PUCES DE VANVES

At one time, from 1920 onwards, the rag-and-bone merchants traded in Vanves itself, but they have moved closer to Paris over the years because of all the building work (demolition of the fortifications and later the construction of cheap housing). It was the ring road that brought them to their present site on the Paris side of the Porte de Vanves in 1965. The little temporary stalls – folding tables with sunshades and sometimes just tarpaulins on the ground – extend along the whole length of the avenue Marc Sangnier and the avenue Georges Lafenestre. Although some of the stalls don't have names, the owners generally use the same site each week and some even display their identity permits. The Vanves flea markets are open all day every Saturday and Sunday, but morning is the best time to go. Although the dealers bring as much as they can fit into their cars or vans, the choice at Vanves is obviously more limited than at Saint-Ouen and it doesn't take nearly as long to walk round.

HOW & WHEN TO GO TO THE PUCES DE VANVES

PUCES DE VANVES
AVENUE MARC SANGNIER AND AVENUE GEORGES LAFENESTRE, 14^E

OPEN
Saturday and Sunday, 9am–7pm, but it's best to go in the morning.

BY METRO
Porte de Vanves (line 13 Châtillon Montrouge–Saint Denis Basilique). Take the avenue Marc Sangnier exit.

BY BUS
On the PC, no. 48 (Porte de Vanves–Gare du Nord) or no. 58 (Vanves Lycée Michelet–Châtelet). No. 95 (Porte de Vanves–Porte de Montmartre) on Sundays.

PARKING
Leave the ring road at the Porte de Vanves exit and then the problems begin; finding a parking space is difficult.

AVENUE MARC SANGNIER

JEAN-LOUIS HEITZMANN
A dealer selling nice engravings and carved wooden frames.

JEAN-PIERRE BEAUJEAN
Jean-Pierre Beaujean specializes in small sets of tableware. Mixing different sets of crockery over the course of a meal is highly recommended by the trendy style magazines.

SIMONE FABRE
Come for silverware and small objects in carved wood.

BOULIN
A good selection of crockery.

YVES BARUCHEL
Baruchel sells attractive jewelry, but don't expect to find pieces designed by the big names from the place Vendôme.

F. MAGISTRY
A rather mixed selection, with small pieces of furniture and some everyday ceramics.

FLAO
Bar accessories and beer mats, some of them designed and autographed by famous people.

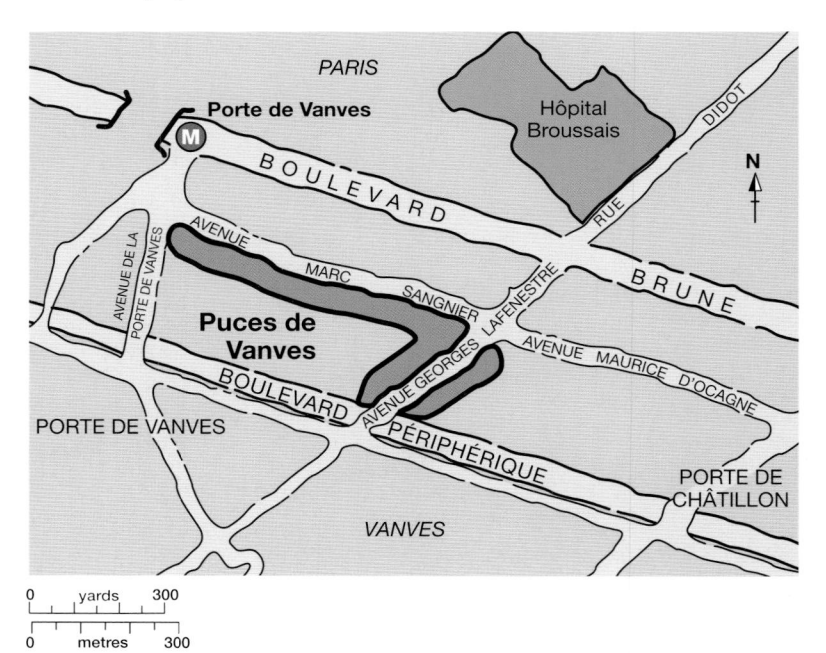

DANIÈLE ENGLIZ-BEY
A dealer in flower pictures and bouquets in glass domes. Posies presented to actresses were sometimes preserved in this way, as were bridal bouquets.

FANTAZIO
This stall specializes in designs from the Sixties and Seventies, particularly Scandinavian furniture, plus lighting and crockery.

GABRIELLE
Gabrielle is interested in Art Deco ceramics and glass made in Longwy in northeast France. The quality of her stock is high.

ZERROUKI
A large selection of cutlery, but you have to be prepared to polish pieces up or even have them resilvered. Remember that English and French hallmarks are different.

MONNIER
An eclectic and extraordinary mix of stock that brings a collection of coffee mills together with small pictures of boats. There's also a massive selection of hatpins, if you are looking for a lapel brooch.

LES TEMPLIERS
An apt name for a stall selling old candles, baroque pendant lighting and assorted trinkets.

CLAIRE LAVOINE
This is one of the best stalls at Vanves. Lavoine has been here since the mid-1980s and travels as far afield as Spain in search of glasses, bottles, decanters and boxes. She can have damaged glassware repaired and will even find replacement

MICHELINE ROLLAND

decanter stoppers if you ask her. She also has attractive jewelry, napkin rings and silver or silver-plate egg cups. I even found the tiny bone dice that I needed for my mah-jong set here.

JOSETTE ET GILBERT ANTOINE

This pair combine folk art and rustic tableware. Their stand is a real treasure trove for anyone with a house in the country and an ideal source for gifts – particularly if you have been invited to go and stay with friends and can't think what to take them.

LOUISE ROYER

A wide range of kitchen utensils in enamelled metal and copper. Old-fashioned scales are fairly useless without a full set of weights, so replace any you might have lost here.

ROBERT JONARD ET BRIGITTE OLIVIER

They sell attractive silver- or ivory-mounted costume jewelry from the turn of the 20th century, plus a few trinkets.

BARBEAU

Curios and trinkets.

MARIE MOULIS

The superb selection of household linen that is on display provides the perfect complement to the china and chromolithographs that Marie Moulis also stocks.

RENÉ MARIE

He specializes in ceramics, odds and ends of metal and pictures, sharing a stall with Marie Moulis.

ABEC
Superb walking sticks with carved handles, cigarette holders, little boxes, belt buckles and a few pieces of jewelry.

DANIEL SANZ
Daniel Sanz always stocks ceramics, attractive pictures frames, engravings and photos. He may also have scraps of antique textiles or lace.

LES CHEVAUX DU VENT
Horses of the Wind is a marvellous name for a stall specializing in jewelry and objects from the Orient, souvenirs of all those places you've dreamed of visiting.

PHILIPPE LAMBERT
Pictures in various genres; well worth a look.

PATRICE BODZEN
Come and browse through this extensive range of real and costume jewelry.

GRIBOUILLE
Silver, crockery and decorative faïence pottery wares.

CATHERINE MANOCI
Catherine Manoci seeks out both little pieces of jewelry and other small-scale precious objects.

A. & G. ROY
A selection of good crockery.

AVENUE GEORGES LAFENESTRE

PARISOT
A good display of carved wood and crockery.

SCARLETT
This stand, presumably named after the heroine of *Gone with the Wind*, is worth a visit by anyone looking for clothes and accessories by top designers. It also has a large selection of bags.

MICHELINE ROLLAND
A good display of linen, curtains and lace.

FRANÇOISE CHATELAIN
Chatelain changed careers to become an antique dealer and has developed a talent for unearthing 19th-century crockery, glass and silver.

CHRISTIAN JACQUOT
A large range of very good linen. Look for your monogram on a pillowcase, napkin or tablecloth. He also stocks some clothes and fabrics.

ESPINOSA
The Puces de Vanves have very few furniture stalls (there obviously isn't enough

room to display large-scale pieces), but here you will find small pieces, such as occasional tables, shelves and corner cupboards.

POISSON ✆ 06 07 02 38 64 OR 02 54 82 43 09

Each week Jean-François, the father, Jean-Christophe, the son, and Sophie, the daughter-in-law, bring along a superb collection of paintings and sculpture – 14th- to 18th-century – and extremely well-restored furniture, which they display in the back of their two vans, sheltered from the bad weather. When I visited, there was a magnificent sundial with cabbalistic figures, dating from 1560.

JACQUELINE SCACCIA

Embroidered linen with lace or openwork borders. A pair of beautiful antique pillowcases will look pretty on the bed in the daytime, but don't actually sleep on them if you want to keep them in good condition.

GRÉMION

Folk-style household linen, much of it in red and white. Perfect for the kitchen and bathroom.

M.-T. COLINET

M.-T. Colinet sells timbale moulds, which you can collect in the normal way or use for little bunches of flowers, as water glasses or to keep pencils in.

SYLVIE CABLAT

A large selection of picture postcards. These have been popular since the late 19th century and some major painters have tried their hands at designing them.

NEARBUYS

On two Sundays a month, from May to October, painters without a gallery can display and sell their work for a very modest charge in the little square on the avenue Georges Lafenestre; it is known as the artists' square.

AUX DÉLICES DU PALAIS
60 BOULEVARD BRUNE (CORNER OF AVENUE GEORGES LAFENESTRE)
☏ **01 45 39 48 68**

The tearoom in the corner of this bakery is popular with the dealers. When you learn that the bread here was awarded first prize in the Best Baguette of Paris competition in 1998, pure greed will make you stop off here and you'll have no regrets about obeying their no smoking policy.

MARCHÉ D'ALIGRE
VIADUC DES ARTS

The secondhand dealers in the place d'Aligre (close to Paris's place de la Bastille) have the nuns of the abbey of Saint Antoine to thank for their market. The last abbess donated the site just before the French Revolution. There are about thirty dealers in total – although not always the same ones – who mainly sell small-scale bric-a-brac, plus some household linen and books. They are only open in the mornings and tend to pack up their *barnums*, or stands, quickly if the weather is bad. Dealers from Saint-Ouen are attracted here by the possibility of the occasional interesting find.

Nearby, under arches which at one time supported the tracks of a little suburban railway, forty or so craftsmen and restorers have opened workshops and boutiques. The area is known as the Viaduc des Arts and runs the length of the avenue Daumesnil. It's a useful place to know about in case any of your flea market buys needs a spot of repair work.

HOW & WHEN TO GO TO THE

MARCHÉ D'ALIGRE
VIADUC DES ARTS

MARCHÉ D'ALIGRE

PLACE D'ALIGRE, 12ᴱ

OPEN
Tuesday to Sunday,
8.30am–1pm

VIADUC DES ARTS

AVENUE DAUMESNIL, 12ᴱ

OPEN
Tuesday to Saturday,
10.30am–7pm. Some
boutiques are also open on
Sundays and Mondays.

BY METRO
Bastille (line 1 La Défense–
Château de Vincennes,
line 5 Bobigny Pablo
Picasso–Place d'Italie
and line 8 Créteil Préfecture–
Balard) or Ledru Rollin
(line 8 Créteil Préfecture–
Balard). On the RER, Gare
de Lyon (lines A and D).

BY BUS
No. 20 (Gare Saint Lazare–
Bastille), no. 29 (Gare Saint
Lazare–Porte Montempoivre),
no. 65 (Gare d'Austerlitz–
Aubervilliers), no. 69 (Place

Gambetta–Champs de
Mars), no. 76 (Louvre–
Bagnolet) and no. 86 (Saint
Germain des Prés–Saint
Mandé). No. 91 (Gare
Montparnasse–Bastille)
runs on Sundays.

PARKING
The nearest car park is
on the corner of avenue
Daumesnil and boulevard
Diderot.

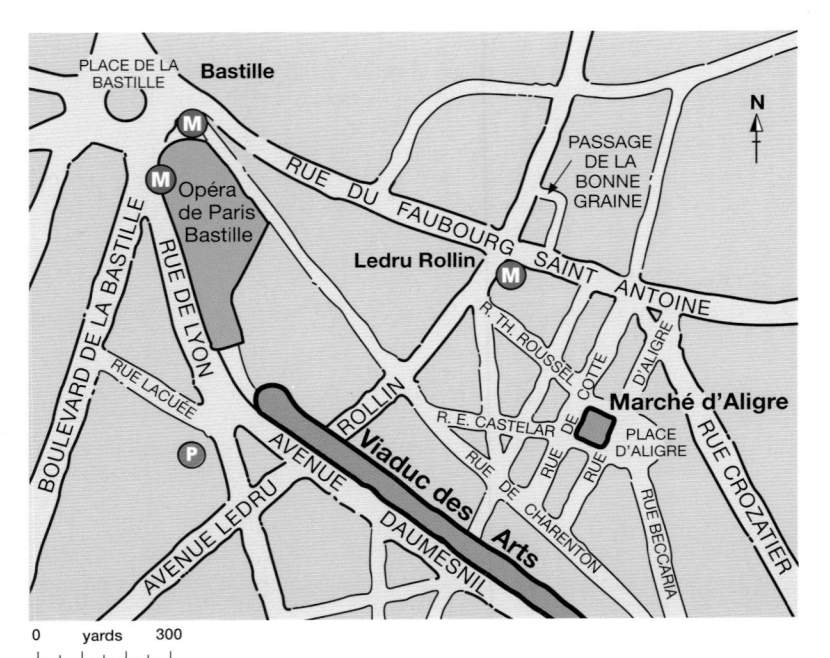

PLACE DE LA BASTILLE · Bastille · Opéra de Paris Bastille · RUE DU FAUBOURG SAINT ANTOINE · PASSAGE DE LA BONNE GRAINE · Ledru Rollin · R. TH. ROUSSEL · R. E. CASTELAR · RUE DE LA BASTILLE · RUE DE LYON · RUE LACUÉE · BOULEVARD DE LA BASTILLE · ROLLIN · Viaduc des Arts · AVENUE LEDRU · AVENUE DAUMESNIL · RUE DE CHARENTON · RUE DE COTTE · RUE D'ALIGRE · Marché d'Aligre · PLACE D'ALIGRE · RUE CROZATIER · RUE BECCARIA · N

0 yards 300
0 metres 300

VIADUC DES ARTS

LORENOVE NO. 11. ✆ 01 40 01 90 01
Restores period windows. An invaluable place to know about for those with old houses.

RIPAMONTI NO. 13. ✆ 01 43 40 80 80
A stone cutter and sculptor who will, for example, copy a damaged statue.

L'ATELIER MICHEL FEY NO. 15. ✆ 01 43 41 22 22
A specialist in covering furniture and in gilding leather.

LE BONHEUR DES DAMES NO. 17. ✆ 01 43 42 06 27
This boutique sells wonderful samplers.

MÉTIER COSTUMIER NO. 19. ✆ 01 43 40 38 38
Designs and makes costumes for both the theatre and the cinema; the displays in its shop windows are always magnificently arranged.

L'ATELIER N'O NO. 21. ✆ 01 43 46 26 26
In this workshop, Marc and Evelyne Viladrich create delightful objects from the pebbles, shells and driftwood that they have collected on their travels.

HOULÈS NO. 27. ✆ 01 43 46 25 50
An excellent specialist in furniture trimmings.

LE VIA NOS. 29–37. ✆ 01 46 28 11 11
Le Via was set up to help young designers realize their ideas. The work they produce is then exhibited in the extremely attractive vaulted rooms.

CÉCILE ET JEANNE NO. 49. ✆ 01 43 41 24 24
These two jewelry designers, whose creations are as appealing as they are original, sell to major museums. Both the Musée du Louvre in Paris and the National Gallery in London are among their customers.

YAMAKADO NO. 65. ✆ 01 43 40 79 79
Yamakado is a talented Japanese furniture designer who produces highly imaginative pieces.

L'ATELIER ROBIN TOURENNE NO. 71.
✆ 01 43 07 59 25
If you've picked up some posters or old paper at a flea market and they are in need of some attention, bring them along to Tourenne and he'll restore them to their former glory.

BAGUÈS NO. 73. ✆ 01 43 41 53 53
This established specialist in beautiful period lighting also produces contemporary pieces, in bronze and wrought iron.

LE CADRE D'OR NO. 79. ✆ 01 43 45 71 71
This workshop will frame and mount anything that you bring along.

L'ATELIER N'O   L'ATELIER N'O

L'ATELIER GUIGUE LOCCA NO. 81. ℰ 01 43 44 99 55

A selection of painted furniture and objects in Northern- and Eastern-European styles. Another speciality is units for hi-fis and speakers that are custom-built to blend into the decor of your room.

MARIE LAVANDE NO. 83. ℰ 01 44 67 78 78

Embroidered and lace-edged linen can be washed, ironed and repaired here. Joëlle Serres's great passion in life is textiles and her customers, who entrust magnificent examples to her, are often famous. Peer in through the window and watch them hard at work, ironing away.

PASCAL MAINGOURD NO. 85. ℰ 01 43 41 46 46

Pascal Maingourd is a decorator. He gives advice on how to display your *chines*, or finds, to their best advantage.

L'ATELIER LE TALLEC NOS. 93–95. ℰ 01 43 40 61 55

Hand-painted porcelain.

AUTOMATES ET POUPÉES NO. 97. ℰ 01 43 42 22 33

Restorers of automata and old dolls, who also produce their own new models.

ALLAIN CADINOT NO. 99. ℰ 01 43 41 43 43

Allain Cadinot makes and repairs flutes.

ROGER LANNE NO. 103.
ℰ 01 43 40 67 67

If, on the other hand, it's a violin or cello that you want to buy or have repaired, this is the place to come. You occasionally find secondhand violins in the flea markets that need a bit of attention.

ASTIER DE VILLATTE NO. 107. ℰ 01 43 45 72 72

Produces imaginative furniture and smaller objects – frames, mirrors, boxes and even crockery – sometimes reusing old materials.

L'ATELIER DU CUIVRE ET DE L'ARGENT NO. 113
ℰ 01 43 40 20 20

An attractive selection of stock, in either copper or silver, as the name suggests.

L'ATELIER LEBEAU NO. 117. ℰ 01 43 45 96 05

As well as making them from scratch, this workshop also repairs carved- and gilt-wood frames.

MATIÈRES PREMIÈRES NO. 123. ℰ 01 44 74 01 05

Masters of imitation – *trompe l'œil*, fake marble, fake lapis lazuli, fake burr, etc.

ARTEFACT NO. 125. ℰ 01 44 74 76 77

Architectural models are designed, produced and restored here.

DIX HEURES DIX NO. 127. ℰ 01 43 40 74 60

It was Fabrice Berreux, a young designer making furniture, accessories and lighting, who named this shop Ten Past Ten.

JEAN-CHARLES BROSSEAU NO. 129. ℰ 01 53 33 82 00

Jean-Charles Brosseau is an extremely well-known milliner who works in felt and straw. He also produces perfume and tableware.

NEARBUYS

It's lovely to walk along the former railway line, beneath the brick, stone and glass arches of the Viaduc des Arts. The old tracks have now been converted into a garden that, high above the road, winds the length of the avenue Daumesnil.

AU PÈRE TRANQUILLE
75–77 AVENUE DAUMESNIL
℡ 01 43 43 64 58
This restaurant has been serving delicious meals for many years and was established long before the craftsmen set up their workshops along the Viaduc des Arts. Whenever it is warm enough, they set up tables and chairs on the pavement, creating a friendly atmosphere.

LE PASSAGE
18 PASSAGE DE LA BONNE GRAINE (AT THE LEVEL OF 117 RUE DU FAUBOURG SAINT ANTOINE)
℡ 01 47 00 73 30
A delightful restaurant recommended for its wines, cheeses and *andouillettes* (small sausages made from chitterlings). Traditional bistro decor displaying rows of prestigiously labelled magnums, hidden behind a wooden facade with red curtains.

LE VIADUC CAFÉ
41–43 AVENUE DAUMESNIL
℡ 01 44 74 70 70
Feeling weary and your legs are tired? Stop off at the Viaduc Café for a much-needed break.

VIADUC DES ARTS

A

FRANÇOIS BARBAUD

1862 - 1938

L'INDUSTRIE CHEVALINE

Le Marché
du
Livre ancien
et
d'occasion
de Paris

Tous les Samedis
et Dimanches

MARCHÉ DU
LIVRE ANCIEN

The Marché du Livre Ancien has been held here every weekend since 1987. It takes place in two covered markets that were once part of the Vaugirard abattoirs and adjoins the delightful Parc Georges Brassens.

Around sixty booksellers set up their trestle tables side by side, offering an extremely wide choice of rare editions and leather-bound books, along with paperbacks and strip cartoons. The books are arranged alphabetically, by author or by subject, or stacked in untidy piles. One specializes in Pléïade books, another two in military subjects and politics, others in the arts. Only two sell children's books. You can also find newspapers, engravings, maps and even a bookbinder, Stéphanie Thomas (© 01 45 26 07 03), who displays a few examples of her work. Fragile or valuable books are covered with glassine and when it's windy everyone secures their books with elastic bands to stop the pages blowing about. There is even a letterbox in which anyone looking for a particular book or rare edition or wanting to sell books can leave their address.

Que des *Spécialité*
VIANDE EXTRA

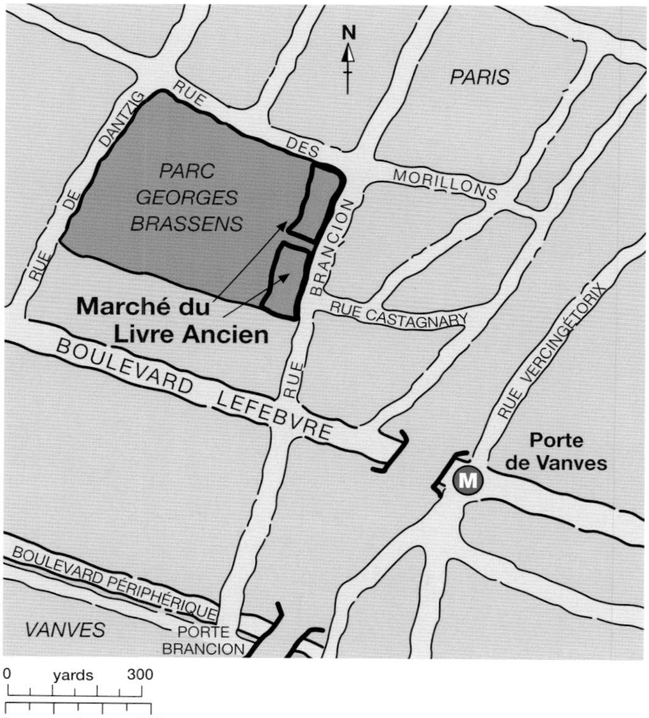

N

PARIS

RUE DANTZIG

RUE DES

MORILLONS

RUE DE

PARC
GEORGES
BRASSENS

BRANCION

**Marché du
Livre Ancien**

RUE CASTAGNARY

RUE VERCINGÉTORIX

BOULEVARD LEFEBVRE

RUE

**Porte
de Vanves**

BOULEVARD PÉRIPHÉRIQUE

VANVES

PORTE
BRANCION

| 0 | yards | 300 |
| 0 | metres | 300 |

HOW & WHEN TO GO TO THE

MARCHÉ DU LIVRE ANCIEN

MARCHÉ DU LIVRE ANCIEN
89–101 RUE BRANCION, 15ᴱ

OPEN
Saturday and Sunday, 8.30am–6.30pm

BY METRO
Porte de Vanves
(line 13 Châtillon Montrouge–Saint Denis Basilique)

BY BUS
No. 48 (Porte de Vanves–Gare du Nord), no. 89 (Vanves Lycée Michelet–Bibliothèque de France) and no. 62 (Cours de Vincennes–Porte de Saint Cloud). No. 95 (Porte de Vanves–Porte de Montmartre) runs on Sundays.

PARKING
Parking spaces are available in the side streets off the rue Brancion.

NEARBUYS

MAX POILÂNE
87 RUE BRANCION
☎ 01 48 28 45 90
If you're feeling a little peckish, try the delicious *matefaims* (a type of pancake) from the baker Max Poilâne. Baking seems to run in the family, as it's his brother who makes the famous *pain Poilâne* (Poilâne bread), which is now marketed as far afield as New York.

CHEZ VICTORIA
101 RUE BRANCION
☎ 01 44 19 05 25
Victoria sells savoury or sweet tarts and pies that you can either eat in or take away.

MAX POILÂNE

WHERE TO BUY INDEX **PARIS**

*Numerals refer to pages in
the Paris end of the book.*

Abec, *Vanves* 89
ABJ, *Dauphine, St-O* 69
L'Aidjolate Antiquités,
  rue des Rosiers, St-O 76
Aire du Temps,
  Malassis, St-O 62
Nicole Aker, *Malassis, St-O* 63
Albert,
  Lécuyer-Vallès, St-O 73
Alice, *Malassis, St-O* 60
Alpha Collections,
  rue des Rosiers, St-O 76
Ambiance,
  Dauphine, St-O 69
Thierry Amblard,
  Dauphine, St-O 68
Mourad Amezal,
  Malassis, St-O 60
Anthare de Schuyter,
  Dauphine, St-O 70
Antik Art, *Vernaison, St-O* 15
Antilope,
  rue Paul Bert, St-O 76
Antiquités Camille,
  Cambo, St-O 47
Josette et Gilbert Antoine,
  Vanves 88
Habib Arfaoui,
  Dauphine, St-O 70
L'Armada, *Dauphine, St-O* 70
Christian Arnoux,
  Dauphine, St-O 69
Arte, *Serpette, St-O* 54
Artefact, *Viaduc des Arts* 98
Artémise et Cunégonde,
  Serpette, St-O 51
Art et Cristal,
  Vernaison, St-O 13
Art et Design,
  Serpette, St-O 54
Astier de Villatte,
  Viaduc des Arts 98
As Time Goes By... and Spirit,
  Malassis, St-O 62
L'Atelier du Cuivre
  et de l'Argent,
  Viaduc des Arts 98
L'Atelier Guigue Locca,
  Viaduc des Arts 97
L'Atelier Lebeau,
  Viaduc des Arts 98
L'Atelier le Tallec,
  Viaduc des Arts 97
L'Atelier Michel Fey,
  Viaduc des Arts 96
L'Atelier N'O,
  Viaduc des Arts 96
L'Atelier Robin Tourenne,
  Viaduc des Arts 96

Attitudes, *Malassis, St-O* 65
Patricia Attwood *see*
  Stéphane Bardot
Au Bonheur du Jour,
  Dauphine, St-O 67
Au Fil des Temps,
  Biron, St-O 32
Au Grenier de Lucie,
  Vernaison, St-O 16, 18
Au Passé Simple,
  Dauphine, St-O 70
Au Pied de la Lettre,
  Dauphine, St-O 70
Au Réverbère,
  Dauphine, St-O 67
Au Roi des Antiquaires,
  rue Jules Vallès, St-O 77
Automates et Poupées,
  Viaduc des Arts 97
Aux Libellules,
  Malassis, St-O 62
Bachelier Antiquités,
  Paul Bert, St-O 40
Baguès, *Viaduc des Arts* 96
Denise Balbon,
  Vernaison, St-O 21
Jean-Luc Balleur,
  Vernaison, St-O 21
Barbeau, *Vanves* 88
Jean-Yves Barczyk,
  Serpette, St-O 53
Stéphane Bardot
  et Patricia Attwood,
  Malassis, St-O 61
Walfredo Barth,
  Cambo, St-O 47
Yves Baruchel, *Vanves* 86
Jean-Pierre Beaujean,
  Vanves 86
Jean Beaumarié,
  Paul Bert, St-O 41
Benoît, *Biron, St-O* 29
Franck Bergé,
  Malassis, St-O 63
Biron 28, *Biron, St-O* 28
Jacques Bitoun,
  Biron, St-O 27
Patrice Bodzen,
  Vanves 89
Le Bonheur des Dames,
  Viaduc des Arts 96
Thomas Bonzom et Pierre
  Nicolas, *Serpette, St-O* 51
Dominique Bory,
  rue Jules Vallès, St-O 78
Marc Bouchetard,
  Paul Bert, St-O 43
Danièle Bouillot,
  Antica, St-O 57
Boulin, *Vanves* 86
Daniel et Claudine Bour,
  Cambo, St-O 47

Boutique Lydia,
  Dauphine, St-O 69
La Boutique 75,
  rue des Rosiers, St-O 75
Luc Bouveret,
  Dauphine, St-O 69
Claude Boyer, *Biron* and
  Rosiers, St-O 30, 49
Le Brick à Barc,
  Malassis, St-O 62
Brophy, *Biron, St-O* 30
Jean-Charles Brosseau,
  Viaduc des Arts 98
Brudasz, *Biron, St-O* 30
F. Bruyneel, *Biron, St-O* 28
Nadine Buy, *Montreuil* 83
Sylvie Cablat, *Vanves* 90
Cabotse, *Serpette, St-O* 51
Allain Cadinot,
  Viaduc des Arts 97
Le Cadre d'Or,
  Viaduc des Arts 96
Jean-Pierre Caietta,
  Malassis, St-O 60
Le Camphrier,
  Cambo, St-O 47
Cariatides, *Serpette, St-O* 55
Carmina Antiquités,
  Serpette, St-O 52
Carpentier, *Paul Bert, St-O* 40
Carte Blanche,
  Malassis, St-O 61
Catan, *Vernaison, St-O* 22
Cécile et Jeanne,
  Viaduc des Arts 96
Cervantès,
  Paul Bert, St-O 44
Françoise Chappuy,
  Vernaison, St-O 17
Françoise Chatelain,
  Vanves 89
Chauvet, *Vernaison, St-O* 14
Cheval Collection,
  Vernaison, St-O 20
Les Chevaux du Vent,
  Vanves 89
Choisi pour Vous,
  Jules Vallès, St-O 37
Xavier Chollet *see*
  Renaud Vuaillat
Hervé Chonigbaum,
  Cambo, St-O 47
Alain Cical, *Biron, St-O* 30
Circé, *Malassis, St-O* 64
Le Club, *Malassis, St-O* 61
M.-T. Colinet, *Vanves* 90
La Collectionnite,
  Malassis, St-O 60
Collection's,
  Malassis, St-O 62
Copa Music,
  rue Jules Vallès, St-O 78

Sylvie Corbelin,
Paul Bert, St-O 45
Jean-Paul Costey,
Serpette, St-O 53
Couespel & Gallot,
Dauphine, St-O 67
Frédérique Couque,
Jules Vallès, St-O 37
Sylviane Cristobal,
Malassis, St-O 61
Le Curieux, *Biron, St-O* 30
Béatrice Cuvelier,
Vernaison, St-O 22
Chantal Dagommer,
Paul Bert, St-O 41
D'Autreppe,
Vernaison, St-O 22
Olivier Deboscker,
Paul Bert, St-O 43
Déco Bistro,
Paul Bert, St-O 45
Daniel Delétrain,
Serpette, St-O 51
Marc Deligny,
Paul Bert, St-O 45
Jane de Livron,
Dauphine, St-O 71
Anne-Marie Despas,
Serpette, St-O 53
Célestin-Henri Devot,
Dauphine, St-O 68
Diamantina,
Dauphine, St-O 69
Catherine Dian-Dumond,
Malassis, St-O 62
Ursula M. Dieterich,
Vernaison, St-O 17
Discophilie,
rue des Rosiers, St-O 76
Dix Heures Dix,
Viaduc des Arts 98
Docks de la Radio,
rue Jules Vallès, St-O 78
Dominique, *Biron, St-O* 33
Jean Doutrepont,
Biron, St-O 28
Du Billard au Comptoir,
Serpette, St-O 54
D.W. Antiquités,
Malassis, St-O 62
Jacqueline Edouard,
Biron, St-O 28
Clara Eliane,
Vernaison, St-O 16
Elisabeth, *Biron, St-O* 29
Email et Puces,
Malassis, St-O 62
Henri Emberger,
Biron, St-O 28
Danièle Engliz-Bey, *Vanves* 87
L'Entrepôt,
rue des Rosiers, St-O 75
L'Escalier de Cristal,
Malassis, St-O 61
Espinosa, *Vanves* 89
Exotic Kalagas,
Dauphine, St-O 70
Simone Fabre, *Vanves* 86
Fantazio, *Vanves* 87
Mireille Favre,
Vernaison, St-O 20
Isabelle Feugère,
Dauphine, St-O 69
Gilbert Fischer, *Biron, St-O* 29

Flao, *Vanves* 86
Olwen Forest,
Serpette, St-O 53
Patrick Fourtin,
Paul Bert, St-O 44
Francine, *Vernaison, St-O* 18
Françoise (I),
Vernaison, St-O 13
Françoise (II),
Vernaison, St-O 14
Gabrielle, *Vanves* 87
Christophe Gaignon,
Paul Bert, St-O 42
Galerie ABC,
Vernaison, St-O 15
Galerie Cailleux,
rue Paul Bert, St-O 77
La Galerie des Glaces,
rue des Rosiers, St-O 75
Galerie V.,
Vernaison, St-O 20
Patrick Garanjoud,
Cambo, St-O 47
La Garde, *Serpette, St-O* 51
Garry, *Biron, St-O* 28
A. Gauthier, *Rosiers, St-O* 49
Monique Germano,
Dauphine, St-O 71
Ghislain Antiques,
Malassis, St-O 65
Janine Giovannoni,
Vernaison, St-O 18
Nicolas Giovannoni,
Vernaison, St-O 19
Nicolas Giovannoni
et Francis Toussaint,
Serpette, St-O 55
Giraud, *Dauphine, St-O* 70
Michel Giraud,
Rosiers, St-O 49
Gisèle, *Biron, St-O* 29
G.L.B., *Malassis, St-O* 62
Grémion, *Vanves* 90
Gribouille, *Vanves* 89
Cyril et Marie Grizot,
Paul Bert, St-O 42
La Grosse Horloge,
Jules Vallès, St-O 35
La Guimandie,
Vernaison, St-O 15
Monsieur Harry,
Malik, St-O 25
Dominique Heidenger,
Serpette, St-O 54
Eric Heitzmann,
rue Paul Bert, St-O 77
Jean-Louis Heitzmann,
Vanves 86
Hier… Encore, *Antica, St-O* 57
Stany Hoffmann,
Biron, St-O 29
L'Homme de Plume,
Malassis, St-O 65
Olga Horde,
Vernaison, St-O 17
Houlès, *Viaduc des Arts* 96
Floris Houwinck,
Paul Bert, St-O 42
H.P., *Paul Bert, St-O* 41
Humeurs, *Malassis, St-O* 65
L'Insolite, L'Autre Pas,
Serpette, St-O 54
Irma, *Vernaison, St-O* 22
Irma et André, *Montreuil* 83

Christian Jacquot, *Vanves* 89
Jadis à Malassis,
Malassis, St-O 64
Perle Jallot, *Paul Bert, St-O* 41
J.-P. Jankovsky,
Serpette, St-O 55
Robert Jonard et Brigitte
Olivier, *Vanves* 88
Pierre Jonchères,
Vernaison, St-O 18
Hélène Jordan, *Biron, St-O* 30
Jellal Kesraoui,
Lécuyer-Vallès, St-O 73
K.F.J., *Malassis, St-O* 62
Paul Khormaïan,
Paul Bert, St-O 41
Kimono-Dô, *Montreuil* 83
Michel Klein,
Dauphine, St-O 69
Philippe Lachaux,
Biron, St-O 32
Philippe Lambert, *Vanves* 89
Roger Lanne,
Viaduc des Arts 97
Largeault, *Biron, St-O* 30
Claire Lavoine, *Vanves* 87
Christian Leclerc,
Malassis, St-O 64
Blandine Lefèvre,
Biron, St-O 31
Edwige Lelouch,
Biron, St-O 33
Laurence Lenglare,
Paul Bert, St-O 43
Eric Lentz, *Paul Bert, St-O* 43
Gérard Leprêtre,
Dauphine, St-O 70
Lhomond, *Vernaison, St-O* 13
Bernard Liagre,
Rosiers, St-O 49
Librairie Boulouiz-Ferez,
Malassis, St-O 65
La Librairie du Louvre,
Malassis, St-O 64
Lits et Lampes,
Paul Bert, St-O 45
Daniel Longueville,
Dauphine, St-O 68
Lorenove, *Viaduc des Arts* 96
Luggage, *Vernaison, St-O* 18
F. Magistry, *Vanves* 86
Mahé, *Serpette, St-O* 52
Pascal Maingourd,
Viaduc des Arts 97
Maison Beys,
rue des Rosiers, St-O 75
La Maison du Roy,
Cambo, St-O 47
Maison Jacques,
Vernaison, St-O 13
Marc Maison,
Paul Bert, St-O 44
Maïté Poupées,
Vernaison, St-O 23
Mammoth Antiek,
Dauphine, St-O 71
Catherine Manoci,
Vanves 89
Le Marché des Antiquaires,
rue Jules Vallès, St-O 78
Marie, *Vernaison, St-O* 21
Marie Lavande,
Viaduc des Arts 97
René Marie, *Vanves* 88

La Martinière,
Paul Bert, St-O 41
Matières Premières,
Viaduc des Arts 98
Maya Antiquités,
Dauphine, St-O 67
Patrice Mayer,
Paul Bert, St-O 44
Mazeaux, aux Vieux Métaux,
rue Jules Vallès, St-O 77
Métier Costumier,
Viaduc des Arts 96
Meubles Anciens de
nos Grand-mères,
rue des Rosiers, St-O 76
Michel, *Jules Vallès, St-O* 37
Eric Miel *see* Michel Peraches
Mikael, *Malik, St-O* 25
Paul Milgen, *Biron, St-O* 29
Catherine Millant,
Paul Bert, St-O 42
Annie Minet, *Biron, St-O* 29
M.L.V., *Paul Bert, St-O* 44
Miroirs,
rue des Rosiers, St-O 75
Le Monde du Vogage,
Serpette, St-O 53
Monnier, *Vanves* 87
Violette Morel,
Vernaison, St-O 21
Morel-Zysset,
Vernaison, St-O 14
Michel Morin,
Paul Bert, St-O 40
Jane Moufflet,
Biron, St-O 27
Marie Moulis, *Vanves* 88
Muriel,
rue des Rosiers, St-O 76
Michel Musson,
Biron, St-O 33
Natlyne, *Biron, St-O* 29
Marie-Thérèse Nays-Favre,
Malassis, St-O 63
Pierre Nicolas *see*
Thomas Bonzom
Nordine, *Montreuil* 83
Normand, *Dauphine, St-O* 68
Novella, *Vernaison, St-O* 13
N.V.M. Nadine Cottinet,
Malassis, St-O 60
Brigitte Olivier *see*
Robert Jonard
Papiers Anciens,
Dauphine, St-O 70
Papillon, *Paul Bert, St-O* 42
Un Parfum d'Aventure,
Vernaison, St-O 15
Parisot, *Vanves* 89
Parissa, *Malassis, St-O* 64
P.B., *Dauphine, St-O* 70
Michel Peraches et Eric Miel,
Paul Bert, St-O 40
Michèle Perceval,
Serpette, St-O 55
Brigitte Perruchot,
Paul Bert, St-O 43
La Petite Maison aux Puces,
rue Paul Bert, St-O 76
Philippe,
Vernaison, St-O 20
Lucien Pineau,
Serpette, St-O 54
Poisson, *Vanves* 90

Potron Minet,
Paul Bert, St-O 42
Présents Passés,
Dauphine, St-O 67
Prestige, *Dauphine, St-O* 68
Prestige-Art du Textile,
Malassis, St-O 64
Pierrette et Pierre Quitard,
Serpette, St-O 54
Rebière Antiquités,
Malassis, St-O 63
Nicolas Rémon,
Vernaison, St-O 19
Françoise Rémy,
Dauphine, St-O 70
Françoise Renoult,
Serpette, St-O 53
Rétro Pub,
Dauphine, St-O 68
Christophe Reynal,
Paul Bert, St-O 45
Martine Reynaud,
Paul Bert, St-O 43
F.-G. Richard,
Vernaison, St-O 17
J.-P. Richard,
Rosiers, St-O 49
Ripamonti,
Viaduc des Arts 96
Yvette Robert,
Biron, St-O 28
Robert et Fils,
Vernaison, St-O 14
Micheline Rolland, *Vanves* 89
Rondeur des Jours,
Malassis, St-O 61
Marie-Eve Rosenthal,
Serpette, St-O 54
A. & G. Roy, *Vanves* 89
Louise Royer, *Vanves* 88
Gilda Saiman,
Malassis, St-O 63
Saint-Ouen Antiquités,
Serpette, St-O 52
Patrice Salet,
Vernaison, St-O 17
Daniel Sanz, *Vanves* 89
Christian Sapet,
Paul Bert, St-O 44
Le Savoir Fer,
Serpette, St-O 51
Alexia Say, *Biron, St-O* 30
Jacqueline Scaccia,
Vanves 90
Scarlett, *Vanves* 89
Schwartz,
Dauphine, St-O 67
SEMA, *rue Paul Bert, St-O* 76
Christian Serres,
Rosiers, St-O 49
Guy-Laurent Setruk,
Vernaison, St-O 20
Shanaz, *Dauphine, St-O* 67
Surplus Militaire Garba,
rue Jules Vallès, St-O 78
Surplus Simon,
rue Jules Vallès, St-O 78
Sycomore, *Malassis, St-O* 62
Sylvie et Pierre-Gilles,
Vernaison, St-O 15
Les Templiers, *Vanves* 87
Renaud Tessier,
Paul Bert, St-O 45
Théorème, *Cambo, St-O* 47

Stéphanie Thomas,
Marché du Livre Ancien 101
Patricia Timsit,
Serpette, St-O 52
Corinne Tonelli,
Cambo, St-O 47
R. Toupenet, *Biron, St-O* 27
Francis Toussaint *see*
Nicolas Giovannoni
Trace de Chine,
Antica, St-O 57
Tradition, *Biron, St-O* 29
La Tranchée Militaire,
Malik, St-O 25
Transparences,
Rosiers, St-O 49
Trésors de Perse,
Malassis, St-O 61
Gisèle Vaury-Sourmais,
Antica, St-O 57
Les Verres de nos Grand-
mères, *Biron, St-O* 27
Veyret, *Malassis, St-O* 61
Le Via, *Viaduc des Arts* 96
Les Vieilles Pierres du Mellois,
rue des Rosiers, St-O 76
Vingtième Siècle,
Paul Bert, St-O 45
Violette et Sarah,
rue Paul Bert, St-O 77
Voyages, *Serpette, St-O* 53
Renaud Vuaillat et Xavier
Chollet, *Serpette, St-O* 53
Yamakado,
Viaduc des Arts 96
Zerline, *Malassis, St-O* 62
Zerrouki, *Vanves* 87
Zoé, *Vernaison, St-O* 18

RESTORERS

Novella, *Vernaison, St-O* 13
Ursula M. Dieterich,
Vernaison, St-O 17
Maïté Poupées,
Vernaison, St-O 23
Christophe Reynal,
Paul Bert, St-O 45
Claire Lavoine, *Vanves* 87
Lorenove, *Viaduc des Arts* 96
Ripamonti, *Viaduc des Arts* 96
L'Atelier Michel Fey,
Viaduc des Arts 96
L'Atelier Robin Tourenne,
Viaduc des Arts 96
Le Cadre d'Or,
Viaduc des Arts 96
Marie Lavande,
Viaduc des Arts 97
Automates et Poupées,
Viaduc des Arts 97
Allain Cadinot,
Viaduc des Arts 97
Roger Lanne,
Viaduc des Arts 97
L'Atelier Lebeau,
Viaduc des Arts 98
Artefact, *Viaduc des Arts* 98
Stéphanie Thomas,
Marché du Livre Ancien 101

WHAT TO BUY INDEX

When a category lists dealers in both cities, Paris stalls precede the London ones, separated by a rule. Numerals refer to page numbers in their respective ends of the book. Since some categories are more typically French, while others are more English, not every category lists stalls in both cities.

ADVERTISING ART
Françoise Chappuy,
   Vernaison, St-O 17
Philippe, *Vernaison, St-O* 20
Galerie V., *Vernaison, St-O* 20
Email et Puces,
   Malassis, St-O 62
Rétro Pub, *Dauphine, St-O* 68

David Huxtable, *Alfies* 19
Paul Arnold, *Camden Lock* 36
Nic Costa, *Camden Passage* 42
Posters for Collectors,
   Grays 60
Andy's Tin City, *Portobello* 80
Liz Farrow, *Portobello* 83

AFRICA *see* **TRIBAL ART**

AMERICANA
La Tranchée Militaire,
   Malik, St-O 25
Stall 52, *Jules Vallès, St-O* 36
As Time Goes By... and Spirit,
   Malassis, St-O 62

Sparkle Moore, *Alfies* 22

ANTIQUITIES
Poisson, *Vanves* 90

Hilary Kashden,
   Covent Garden 51
Nigel Mills, *Covent Garden* 51
Jane Stewart, *Grays* 60
Helios Gallery, *Portobello* 85
Tetragon Antiquities,
   Portobello 90

ARCHITECTURAL SALVAGE
see **FIREPLACES**

ART DECO *see also*
CERAMICS
Alexia Say, *Biron, St-O* 30
Stall 402, *Paul Bert, St-O* 45
Walfredo Barth,
   Cambo, St-O 47
Art et Design,
   Serpette, St-O 54
Sycomore, *Malassis, St-O* 62
D.W. Antiquités,
   Malassis, St-O 62
P.B., *Dauphine, St-O* 70
Antilope,
   rue Paul Bert, St-O 76

Geoffrey Robinson, *Alfies* 22
Rojeh Antiques, *Alfies* 22

ARTISTS' MATERIALS
Michael Oliphant,
   Bermondsey 29
Green & Stone, *Antiquarius* 71
Atlantis Art Supplies,
   Brick Lane 101

ART NOUVEAU
R. Toupenet, *Biron, St-O* 27
Jean Doutrepont,
   Biron, St-O 28
Stall 72, *Biron, St-O* 29
Alexia Say, *Biron, St-O* 30
Stall 402, *Paul Bert, St-O* 45
Walfredo Barth,
   Cambo, St-O 47
Claude Boyer,
   Rosiers, St-O 49
Bernard Liagre,
   Rosiers, St-O 49
Michel Giraud,
   Rosiers, St-O 49
Christian Serres,
   Rosiers, St-O 49
J.-P. Richard, *Rosiers, St-O* 49
A. Gauthier, *Rosiers, St-O* 49

Raul Arantes,
   Camden Passage 42

ARTS AND CRAFTS
Christian Sapet,
   Paul Bert, St-O 44

Furniture + Designs
   1870–1970, *Alfies* 19
Keith Roughton,
   Camden Lock 36

BARBOTINE WARE
see **CERAMICS**

BAR ACCESSORIES
Galerie V., *Vernaison, St-O* 20
Déco Bistro,
   Paul Bert, St-O 45
Jean-Paul Costey,
   Serpette, St-O 53
Du Billard au Comptoir,
   Serpette, St-O 54
Normand,
   Dauphine, St-O 68
Jane de Livron,
   Dauphine, St-O 71
Flao, *Vanves* 86

BASKETS
Bachelier Antiquités,
   Paul Bert, St-O 40
Michel Morin,
   Paul Bert, St-O 40
Stall 236, *Dauphine, St-O* 71

H&C, *Covent Garden* 50
Putnams, *Columbia Road* 103

BATHROOM ACCESSORIES
Brigitte Perruchot,
   Paul Bert, St-O 43
J-P. Jankovsky,
   Serpette, St-O 55
Stalls 19–20,
   Malassis, St-O 60

Rebière Antiquités,
   Malassis, St-O 63
Mazeaux, Aux Vieux Métaux,
   rue Jules Vallès, St-O 77

Dudley and Genie, *Alfies* 19

BEADS AND BEADWORK
Maison Jacques,
   Vernaison, St-O 13

Kit Smith, *Covent Garden* 52
Sultani Antiques, *Grays* 60
Nicholas Donn, *Portobello* 82
David Lewin, *Portobello* 86
Michael Telfer-Smollett,
   Portobello 90

BICYCLES
G Whizz, *Old Crowther* 68

BILLIARDS *see* **SPORT**

BOOKS
Nicolas Rémon,
   Vernaison, St-O 19
Stall 181, *Vernaison, St-O* 21
Violette Morel,
   Vernaison, St-O 21
Monsieur Harry,
   Malik, St-O 25
Librairie Boulouiz-Ferez,
   Malassis, St-O 65
Habib Arfaoui,
   Dauphine, St-O 70
Françoise Rémy,
   Dauphine, St-O 70
Au Pied de la Lettre,
   Dauphine, St-O 70
Papiers Anciens,
   Dauphine, St-O 70
Anthare de Schuyter,
   Dauphine, St-O 70
Stall 3,
   Lécuyer-Vallès, St-O 73
Stall 15,
   Lécuyer-Vallès, St-O 73
temporary stalls,
   Marché d'Aligre 93
temporary stalls,
   Marché du Livre Ancien 101

Bibliopola, *Alfies* 18
Gardiner & Gardiner, *Alfies* 19
Archive Bookstore, *Alfies* 23
Stephen Foster's Bookshop,
   Alfies 23
Kay Books, *Bermondsey* 29
Sandy Field,
   Covent Garden 50
The Dover Bookshop,
   Covent Garden 53
Zwemmers,
   Covent Garden 53
Harrison's Books, *Grays* 60
Don Kelly, *Antiquarius* 70

108

Susan Biltcliffe, *Portobello* 81
Historical Impressions,
 Portobello 85
Books for Cooks,
 Portobello 90
Magpie Bookshop,
 Spitalfields 100
One Eye Books,
 Spitalfields 100
 TRADE CATALOGUES
 Don Kelly, *Antiquarius* 70
 Susan Biltcliffe,
  Portobello 81

BOTTLES
Clara Eliane,
 Vernaison, St-O 16
Denise Balbon,
 Vernaison, St-O 21
Françoise Renoult,
 Serpette, St-O 53
Danièle Bouillot,
 Antica, St-O 57
K.F.J., *Malassis, St-O* 62
Marie-Thérèse Nays-Favre,
 Malassis, St-O 63
Circé, *Malassis, St-O* 64
Christian Arnoux,
 Dauphine, St-O 69

BOUTIQUES DE CHARME
Sylvie et Pierre-Gilles,
 Vernaison, St-O 15
Stall 105bis,
 Vernaison, St-O 17
Irma, *Vernaison, St-O* 22
Maïté Poupées,
 Vernaison, St-O 23
Le Curieux, *Biron, St-O* 30
Blandine Lefèvre,
 Biron, St-O 31
Philippe Lachaux,
 Biron, St-O 32
Dominique, *Biron, St-O* 33
Michel Peraches et Eric Miel,
 Paul Bert, St-O 40
Potron Minet,
 Paul Bert, St-O 42
Floris Houwinck,
 Paul Bert, St-O 42
Catherine Millant,
 Paul Bert, St-O 42
Martine Reynaud,
 Paul Bert, St-O 43
Christian Sapet,
 Paul Bert, St-O 44
Hervé Choningbaum,
 Cambo, St-O 47
Daniel Delétrain,
 Serpette, St-O 51
Françoise Renoult,
 Serpette, St-O 53
Anne-Marie Despas,
 Serpette, St-O 53
Stall 12, *Serpette, St-O* 54
Arte, *Serpette, St-O* 54
Stall 18, *Serpette, St-O* 55
Alice, *Malassis, St-O* 60
Sylviane Cristobal,
 Malassis, St-O 61
Aux Libellules,
 Malassis, St-O 62
Zerline, *Malassis, St-O* 62
Jadis à Malassis,
 Malassis, St-O 64

Attitudes, *Malassis, St-O* 65
Humeurs, *Malassis, St-O* 65
Stalls 229–30,
 Malassis, St-O 65
Couespel & Gallot,
 Dauphine, St-O 67
Isabelle Feugère,
 Dauphine, St-O 69
Ambiance, *Dauphine, St-O* 69
Gérard Leprêtre,
 Dauphine, St-O 70
La Petite Maison aux Puces,
 rue Paul Bert, St-O 76
L'Atelier N'O,
 Viaduc des Arts 96
Pascal Maingourd,
 Viaduc des Arts 97
Astier de Villatte,
 Viaduc des Arts 98
Matières Premières,
 Viaduc des Arts 98
Artefact, *Viaduc des Arts* 98

BRASS *see* **METALWARE**

BRIC-A-BRAC
La Guimandie,
 Vernaison, St-O 15
Stall 69, *Vernaison, St-O* 15
Guy-Laurent Setruk,
 Vernaison, St-O 20
Stall 220, *Vernaison, St-O* 22
Stall 7, *Biron, St-O* 27
Dominique, *Biron, St-O* 33
Stall 31, *Jules Vallès, St-O* 36
Choisi pour Vous,
 Jules Vallès, St-O 37
Thomas Bonzom et Pierre
 Nicolas, *Serpette, St-O* 51
Stall 5, *Serpette, St-O* 53
Veyret, *Malassis, St-O* 61
Maya Antiquités,
 Dauphine, St-O 67
Célestin-Henri Devot,
 Dauphine, St-O 68
Stalls 128–29,
 Dauphine, St-O 69
temporary stalls,
 Lécuyer-Vallès, St-O 73
Albert, *Lécuyer-Vallès, St-O* 73
Muriel,
 rue des Rosiers, St-O 76
31 *rue Jules Vallès, St-O* 77
Le Marché des Antiquaires,
 rue Jules Vallès, St-O 78
F. Magistry, *Vanves* 86
temporary stalls,
 Marché d'Aligre 93

Chris Bennett,
 Bermondsey 28
Richard Perry,
 Bermondsey 29
print dealer,
 Bermondsey 30
Chad Sansean,
 Bermondsey 30
M. Von Taubenheim,
 Bermondsey 30

BRIDAL HEADDRESSES
Stall 105bis,
 Vernaison, St-O 17
Jadis à Malassis,
 Malassis, St-O 64
Danièle Engliz-Bey, *Vanves* 87

BUTTONS
Galerie ABC,
 Vernaison, St-O 15
Irma, *Vernaison, St-O* 22
Stall 250, *Vernaison, St-O* 22
Chantal Dagommer,
 Paul Bert, St-O 41

Moya Smith, *Bermondsey* 30
H&C, *Covent Garden* 50
Judith Pollitt, *Portobello* 89
Rita Stephenson, *Portobello* 90

**CARPETS, RUGS
AND TAPESTRIES**
Stall 29, *Vernaison, St-O* 14
Stany Hoffmann,
 Biron, St-O 29
Stall 27, *Serpette, St-O* 51
Trésors de Perse,
 Malassis, St-O 61
Prestige-Art du Textile,
 Malassis, St-O 64
Parissa, *Malassis, St-O* 64
Ghislain Antiques,
 Malassis, St-O 65
Prestige, *Dauphine, St-O* 68
Luc Bouveret,
 Dauphine, St-O 69
Exotic Kalagas,
 Dauphine, St-O 70

N. Davalou Carpets,
 Bermondsey 28
Christopher Farr,
 Portobello 92
Roughneck & Thug,
 Spitalfields 101

CERAMICS
Stall 27, *Vernaison, St-O* 14
Morel-Zysset,
 Vernaison, St-O 14
Stall 110, *Vernaison, St-O* 17
Nicolas Giovannoni, *Vernaison*
 and *Serpette, St-O* 19, 55
Alain Cical, *Biron, St-O* 30
Frédérique Couque,
 Jules Vallès, St-O 37
Stall 58, *Paul Bert, St-O* 41
J-P. Richard, *Rosiers, St-O* 49
Stall 18, *Serpette, St-O* 55
Hier… Encore, *Antica, St-O* 57
Trace de Chine,
 Antica, St-O 57
Jean-Pierre Caietta,
 Malassis, St-O 60
Stéphane Bardot et Patricia
 Attwood, *Malassis, St-O* 61
L'Escalier de Cristal,
 Malassis, St-O 61
Rondeur des Jours,
 Malassis, St-O 61
Franck Bergé,
 Malassis, St-O 63
Stall 121, *Dauphine, St-O* 69
Exotic Kalagas,
 Dauphine, St-O 70
Stall 236, *Dauphine, St-O* 71
Stall 3,
 Lécuyer-Vallès, St-O 73
Jellal Kesraoui,
 Lécuyer-Vallès, St-O 73
Jean-Pierre Beaujean,
 Vanves 86
Boulin, *Vanves* 86

Gabrielle, *Vanves* 87
Marie Moulis, *Vanves* 88
René Marie, *Vanves* 88
Daniel Sanz, *Vanves* 89
Gribouille, *Vanves* 89
A & G. Roy, *Vanves* 89
Parisot, *Vanves* 89
Françoise Chatelain, *Vanves* 89
L'Atelier Le Tallec,
  Viaduc des Arts 97
Astier de Villatte,
  Viaduc des Arts 98

print dealer, *Bermondsey* 30
M. Von Taubenheim,
  Bermondsey 30
The Home Service,
  Camden Lock 36
Vinci Antiques, *Grays* 61
Green & Stone, *Antiquarius* 71
R.A. Barnes, *Portobello* 80
ART DECO
Susie Cooper Ceramics,
  Alfies 22
Radford-Muir, *Grays* 60
BARBOTINE WARE
Claude Boyer,
  Biron, St-O 30
Catherine Dian-Dumond,
  Malassis, St-O 62
Monique Germano,
  Dauphine, St-O 71
L'Aidjolate Antiquités,
  rue des Rosiers, St-O 76
BLUE AND WHITE
Sue Norman,
  Antiquarius 70
**EARLY (DELFT, CREAMWARE,
JACKFIELD, ETC.)**
Gardiner & Gardiner,
  Alfies 19
Gordon Gridley,
  Camden Passage 43
Patrick Boyd-Carpenter,
  Grays 58
Guest and Gray, *Grays* 59
Appleby Antiques,
  Portobello 80
Aurea Carter, *Portobello* 81
Jo De Sousa Macedo,
  Portobello 82
Agnes Fox, *Portobello* 83
Garland Antiques,
  Portobello 84
Mike Handford,
  Portobello 85
Erna Hiscock and John
  Shepherd, *Portobello* 85
Alan Milford,
  Portobello 86
Susana Montiel,
  Portobello 87
MAJOLICA
Britannia, *Grays* 58
ORIENTAL *see* **ORIENTAL ART**
STAFFORDSHIRE
Jacqueline Oosthuizen,
  Portobello 88

CHAIRS *see* **FURNITURE**

CHANDELIERS *see*
LIGHTING

CHINA *see* **CERAMICS
AND TABLEWARE**

CHROME *see* **METALWARE**

CHROMOLITHOGRAPHS
see **PRINTS**

**CIRCUS AND FAIRGROUND
DECORATION**
Henri Emberger, *Biron, St-O* 28

CLOCKS
Stall 238, *Vernaison, St-O* 22
Jacqueline Edouard,
  Biron, St-O 28
La Grosse Horloge,
  Jules Vallès, St-O 35
Stall 16,
  Lécuyer-Vallès, St-O 73

The Old Father Time Clock
  Centre, *Portobello* 88

CLOTHES *see also*
**FASHION ACCESSORIES,
HATS AND HANDBAGS**
Françoise, *Vernaison, St-O* 14
Francine, *Vernaison, St-O* 18
Béatrice Cuvelier,
  Vernaison, St-O 22
Chantal Dagommer,
  Paul Bert, St-O 41
Artémise et Cunégonde,
  Serpette, St-O 51
Schwartz, *Dauphine, St-O* 67
Boutique Lydia,
  Dauphine, St-O 69
Stall 10,
  Lécuyer-Vallès, St-O 73
Dominique Bory,
  rue Jules Vallès, St-O 78
141 *rue des Rosiers, St-O* 76
156 *rue des Rosiers, St-O* 76
Violette et Sarah,
  rue Paul Bert, St-O 77
Irma et André, *Montreuil* 83
Nadine Buy, *Montreuil* 83
Nordine, *Montreuil* 83
Kimono-Dô, *Montreuil* 83
Scarlett, *Vanves* 89

Victory Motorcycles,
  Camden Lock 37
Annie's Vintage Costume
  and Textiles,
  Camden Passage 42
Browns, *Grays* 61
TNT, *Old Crowther* 68
Graham and Dani,
  Portobello 76
A.P.C., *Portobello* 92
Graham & Green,
  Portobello 93
Paul Smith, *Portobello* 93
Vent, *Portobello* 93
Roughneck & Thug,
  Spitalfields 101
COSTUME
Anne-Marie Despas,
  Serpette, St-O 53
Nordine, *Montreuil* 83
Métier Costumier,
  Viaduc des Arts 96

Gallery of Antique Costume
  & Textiles, *Alfies* 23
Linda Wigglesworth,
  Grays 61
David Ireland, *Portobello* 85

Sheila Cook Textiles,
  Portobello 92
**COUTURE AND
DESIGNER LABELS**
Chantal Dagommer,
  Paul Bert, St-O 41
Boutique Lydia,
  Dauphine, St-O 69
Scarlett, *Vanves* 89

Linda Bee, *Grays* 58
Paul Smith Sale Shop,
  Grays 61
Steinberg & Tolkein,
  Antiquarius 71
Identity, *Portobello* 76
Paul Smith, *Portobello* 93
MENSWEAR ONLY
The Duffer of St George,
  Covent Garden 53
Paul Smith Sale Shop,
  Grays 61
C.D. Arnold, *Brick Lane* 101
WOMENSWEAR ONLY
Bebe, *Alfies* 18
Persiflage, *Alfies* 21
Sparkle Moore, *Alfies* 22
Linda Bee, *Grays* 58
Steinberg & Tolkein,
  Antiquarius 71
Affinity, *Portobello* 76
Viva Barnett, *Portobello* 76
Sheila Cook Textiles,
  Portobello 92
Bernstock Speirs,
  Columbia Road 102
VIVIENNE WESTWOOD
Identity, *Portobello* 76

COINS
Nigel Mills, *Covent Garden* 51
Sultani Antiques, *Grays* 60
Helios Gallery, *Portobello* 85

COMMEMORATIVE WARES
Britannia, *Grays* 58
Titanic, *Old Crowther* 68

COPPER *see* **METALWARE**

CORKSCREWS
Turning Worms, *Portobello* 91

COSTUME *see* **CLOTHES**

COUNTRY ANTIQUES
see also **FOLK ART**
Anne Gormley, *Alfies* 19
Laraine Plummer, *Alfies* 21
Katherine Pole, *Alfies* 21
Garland Antiques,
  Portobello 84
David Lewin, *Portobello* 86

COUTURE *see* **CLOTHES**

CRYSTALS *see* **SHELLS**

CURIOS *see* **WORKS OF ART**

CUTLERY *see* **TABLEWARE**

DECORATIVE ACCESSORIES
Gillian Danz, *Alfies* 18
Francesca Martire, *Alfies* 20
Jessica Ward, *Alfies* 22

M. Von Taubenheim,
Bermondsey 30
Graham & Green,
Camden Lock 37
The Corner Room,
Camden Passage 42
John Goodison and
Chris Paraskeva,
Camden Passage 43
Shane Meredith,
Camden Passage 44
World, *Covent Garden* 53
Helray Ltd, *Lillie Road* 69
Colin Smith and Gerald
Robinson, *Portobello* 89
Bazar Antiques & Decorative
Items, *Portobello* 92
Emma Bernhardt,
Portobello 92
Graham & Green, *Camden
Lock* and *Portobello* 37, 93
Roughneck & Thug,
Spitalfields 101
Putnams, *Columbia Road* 103

DECORATIVE ANTIQUES
Gardiner & Gardiner, *Alfies* 19
Anne Gormley, *Alfies* 19
Laraine Plummer, *Alfies* 21
Katherine Pole, *Alfies* 21
Catherine Wallis, *Alfies* 22
Madeline Crispin Antiques,
Alfies 23
The Corner Room,
Camden Passage 42
Tony D'Almeida,
Camden Passage 42
John Goodison and
Chris Paraskeva,
Camden Passage 43
Gordon Gridley,
Camden Passage 43
Shane Meredith,
Camden Passage 44
Baroque 'n' Roll, *Lillie Road* 68
Andrew Bewick and Jonathan
Lee, *Lillie Road* 69
Zal Davar, *Lillie Road* 69
Decorative Antiques,
Lillie Road 69
Helray Ltd, *Lillie Road* 69
Catherine Nimmo,
Lillie Road 69
Bourbon-Hanby Antiques
Centre, *Antiquarius* 71
Green & Stone, *Antiquarius* 71
Garland Antiques, *Portobello* 84
Bazar Antiques & Decorative
Items, *Portobello* 92

DESKS AND PENS
Marie, *Vernaison, St-O* 21
Stall 171, *Biron, St-O* 32
Stall 180, *Biron, St-O* 32
Stall 194ter, *Biron, St-O* 33
Michel Musson,
Biron, St-O 33
Christophe Gaignon,
Paul Bert, St-O 42
L'Homme de Plume,
Malassis, St-O 65
Couespel & Gallot,
Dauphine, St-O 67
Stall 180,
Dauphine, St-O 70

Monique Germano,
Dauphine, St-O 71
L'Atelier Michel Fey,
Viaduc des Arts 96
Phyllis Gorlick-King,
Portobello 84

DOLLS see TOYS

DRAWINGS
Patrice Salet,
Vernaison, St-O 17
Pierre Jonchères,
Vernaison, St-O 18
Charlie, *Bermondsey* 28
Phyllis Gorlick-King,
Portobello 84

EIGHTIES
CO_2, *Camden Lock* 36

ENAMEL
Olga Horde,
Vernaison, St-O 17
Nicole Aker, *Malassis, St-O* 63
Stall 179, *Dauphine, St-O* 69
Stall 236, *Dauphine, St-O* 71
Monique Germano,
Dauphine, St-O 71
Louise Royer, *Vanves* 88
Kitchen Bygones, *Alfies* 20
Jonathan's Belowstairs,
Camden Passage 44
Kim Sinclair,
Portobello 89

ENGRAVINGS see PRINTS

EROTICA
Béatrice Cuvelier,
Vernaison, St-O 22
Au Bonheur du Jour,
Dauphine, St-O 67

FABRICS see TEXTILES

FANS
Françoise, *Vernaison, St-O* 14
Le Curieux, *Biron, St-O* 30
Barbara Springall,
Bermondsey 30

FASHION see CLOTHES

FASHION ACCESSORIES
see also **HATS, HANDBAGS**
Francine, *Vernaison, St-O* 18
Janine Giovannoni,
Vernaison, St-O 18
Béatrice Cuvelier,
Vernaison, St-O 22
Brudasz, *Biron, St-O* 30
Chantal Dagommer,
Paul Bert, St-O 41
Danièle Bouillot,
Antica, St-O 57
Boutique Lydia,
Dauphine, St-O 69
Stall 10, *Lécuyer-Vallès, St-O* 73
141 *rue des Rosiers, St-O* 76
156 *rue des Rosiers, St-O* 76
Violette et Sarah,
rue Paul Bert, St-O 77

Scarlett, *Vanves* 89

Bebe, *Alfies* 18
Cristobal, *Alfies* 18
Francesca Martire, *Alfies* 20
Persiflage, *Alfies* 21
Sparkle Moore, *Alfies* 22
Annie's Vintage
Costume and Textiles,
Camden Passage 42
Kit Smith, *Covent Garden* 52
World, *Covent Garden* 53
Linda Bee, *Grays* 58
Affinity, *Portobello* 76
Viva Barnett, *Portobello* 76
Graham and Dani,
Portobello 76
Margaret and Kim,
Portobello 77
Sarah and Jo,
Portobello 77
Emma Bernhardt,
Portobello 92
Sheila Cook Textiles,
Portobello 92
Paul Smith, *Portobello* 93
Vent, *Portobello* 93
P.R.K. Blackmans Shoes,
Brick Lane 101
Bernstock Speirs,
Columbia Road 102

FIFTIES
Cyril et Marie Grizot,
Paul Bert, St-O 42
Eric Lentz, *Paul Bert, St-O* 43
Vingtième Siècle,
Paul Bert, St-O 45
As Time Goes By… and Spirit,
Malassis, St-O 62
Giraud, *Dauphine, St-O* 70
Bruna Naufal, *Alfies* 21
Paola and Iaia, *Alfies* 21
Geoffrey Robinson,
Alfies 22
Sparkle Moore, *Alfies* 22
Susie Cooper Ceramics,
Alfies 22
The Home Service,
Camden Lock 36
Planet Bazaar,
Camden Lock 36
Stable Five, *Camden Lock* 36
Annie's Vintage Costume
and Textiles,
Camden Passage 42
Linda Bee, *Grays* 58
TNT, *Old Crowther* 68
Betty and Len Wiltshire,
Portobello 91
Vent, *Portobello* 93

**FIREGUARDS see
METALWARE**

**FIREPLACES, PILLARS,
ARCHITECTURAL SALVAGE**
Stall 163, *Vernaison, St-O* 21
Stall 176, *Vernaison, St-O* 21
Stall 253, *Vernaison, St-O* 23
Stall 263, *Vernaison, St-O* 23
Stall 48, *Jules Vallès, St-O* 36
Stall 59, *Paul Bert, St-O* 41
Jean Beaumarié,
Paul Bert, St-O 41

Marc Maison,
    Paul Bert, St-O 44
Marc Deligny,
    Paul Bert, St-O 45
Le Savoir Fer,
    Serpette, St-O 51
Carmina Antiquités,
    Serpette, St-O 52
Pierrette et Pierre Quitard,
    Serpette, St-O 54
Dominique Heidenger,
    Serpette, St-O 54
ABJ, *Dauphine, St-O* 69
L'Entrepôt,
    rue des Rosiers, St-O 75
La Boutique 75,
    rue des Rosiers, St-O 75
Les Vieilles Pierres du Mellois,
    rue des Rosiers, St-O 76
SEMA, *rue Paul Bert, St-O* 76
Lorenove, *Viaduc des Arts* 96
Ripamonti, *Viaduc des Arts* 96
Matières Premières,
    Viaduc des Arts 98

Les Coussis du Chien,
    Portobello 76

FISHING see **SPORT**

FLATWARE see
TABLEWARE

FLOORING see **TILES**

FOLK ART see also
COUNTRY ANTIQUES
Edwige Lelouch, *Biron, St-O* 33
Michel, *Jules Vallès, St-O* 37
Frédérique Couque,
    Jules Vallès, St-O 37
Bachelier Antiquités,
    Paul Bert, St-O 40
Michel Morin,
    Paul Bert, St-O 40
Paul Khormaïan,
    Paul Bert, St-O 41
Potron Minet,
    Paul Bert, St-O 42
Théorême, *Cambo, St-O* 47
Jean-Pierre Caietta,
    Malassis, St-O 60
Stall 236, *Dauphine, St-O* 71
Josette et Gilbert Antoine,
    Vanves 88
L'Atelier Guigue Locca,
    Viaduc des Arts 97

FORTIES
Cyril et Marie Grizot,
    Paul Bert, St-O 42
Eric Lentz, *Paul Bert, St-O* 43
Cervantès, *Paul Bert, St-O* 44
Patrick Fourtin,
    Paul Bert, St-O 44
Arte, *Serpette, St-O* 54
Gilda Saiman,
    Malassis, St-O 63
Giraud, *Dauphine, St-O* 70

Bebe, *Alfies* 18
Bruna Naufal, *Alfies* 21
Paola and Iaia, *Alfies* 21
Susie Cooper Ceramics,
    Alfies 22
The Home Service,
    Camden Lock 36

Stable Five,
    Camden Lock 36
Annie's Vintage Costume
    and Textiles,
    Camden Passage 42
Linda Bee, *Grays* 58
Affinity, *Portobello* 76
Betty and Len Wiltshire,
    Portobello 91
Vent, *Portobello* 93

FOSSILS
Mireille Favre,
    Vernaison, St-O 20

Dale Rogers, *Portobello* 89

FRAMES
Stall 29, *Vernaison, St-O* 14
Stall 95, *Vernaison, St-O* 17
Stall 99bis, *Vernaison, St-O* 17
Stall 163, *Vernaison, St-O* 21
Violette Morel,
    Vernaison, St-O 21
Stall 195, *Vernaison, St-O* 22
Christophe Reynal,
    Paul Bert, St-O 45
Stall 30, *Malassis, St-O* 61
Jean-Louis Heitzmann,
    Vanves 86
Daniel Sanz, *Vanves* 89
Le Cadre d'Or,
    Viaduc des Arts 96
L'Atelier Lebeau,
    Viaduc des Arts 98

Jones and Campbell, *Alfies* 19
Hayman & Hayman,
    Antiquarius 69
Emerich Vidich, *Antiquarius* 70
Green & Stone, *Antiquarius* 71
Charles Daggett Gallery,
    Portobello 82
David Levi Antiques,
    Portobello 86
Paul Treadaway, *Portobello* 90
Lacy Gallery, *Portobello* 93

FURNITURE see also
SHOP FITTINGS
Stall 27, *Vernaison, St-O* 14
Stall 29, *Vernaison, St-O* 14
Sylvie et Pierre-Gilles,
    Vernaison, St-O 15
Stall 95, *Vernaison, St-O* 17
Catan, *Vernaison, St-O* 22
Stall 253, *Vernaison, St-O* 23
Stall 255, *Vernaison, St-O* 23
Stall 263, *Vernaison, St-O* 23
Natlyne, *Biron, St-O* 29
Gisèle, *Biron, St-O* 29
Tradition, *Biron, St-O* 29
Stall 60, *Biron, St-O* 29
Stany Hoffmann,
    Biron, St-O 29
Hélène Jordan, *Biron, St-O* 30
Stall 125, *Biron, St-O* 30
Stall 136, *Biron, St-O* 31
Stall 142, *Biron, St-O* 31
Stall 155, *Biron, St-O* 32
Philippe Lachaux,
    Biron, St-O 32
Stall 160, *Biron, St-O* 32
Au Fil du Temps,
    Biron, St-O 32
Stalls 164–65, *Biron, St-O* 32
Stalls 167–68, *Biron, St-O* 32

Stall 171, *Biron, St-O* 32
Stall 190, *Biron, St-O* 32
Stall 194ter, *Biron, St-O* 33
Edwige Lelouch,
    Biron, St-O 33
Stall 200, *Biron, St-O* 33
Stall 202, *Biron, St-O* 33
Choisi pour Vous,
    Jules Vallès, St-O 37
Bachelier Antiquités,
    Paul Bert, St-O 40
Michel Morin,
    Paul Bert, St-O 40
Michel Peraches et Eric Miel,
    Paul Bert, St-O 40
Paul Khormaïan,
    Paul Bert, St-O 41
Stall 41, *Paul Bert, St-O* 41
La Martinière,
    Paul Bert, St-O 41
Stall 59, *Paul Bert, St-O* 42
Potron Minet,
    Paul Bert, St-O 42
Christophe Gaignon,
    Paul Bert, St-O 42
Cyril et Marie Grizot,
    Paul Bert, St-O 42
Catherine Millant,
    Paul Bert, St-O 42
Marc Bouchetard,
    Paul Bert, St-O 43
Martine Reynaud,
    Paul Bert, St-O 43
Patrice Mayer,
    Paul Bert, St-O 44
Patrick Fourtin,
    Paul Bert, St-O 44
Christian Sapet,
    Paul Bert, St-O 44
Vingtième Siècle,
    Paul Bert, St-O 45
Lits et Lampes,
    Paul Bert, St-O 45
Stalls 403–5,
    Paul Bert, St-O 45
Daniel et Claudine Bour,
    Cambo, St-O 47
Patrick Garanjoud,
    Cambo, St-O 47
Antiquités Camille,
    Cambo, St-O 47
Le Camphrier,
    Cambo, St-O 47
La Maison du Roy,
    Cambo, St-O 47
Corinne Tonelli,
    Cambo, St-O 47
Bernard Liagre,
    Rosiers, St-O 49
Christian Serres,
    Rosiers, St-O 49
Mahé, *Serpette, St-O* 52
Stall 41, *Serpette, St-O* 53
Renaud Vuaillat et Xavier
    Chollet, *Serpette, St-O* 53
Pierrette et Pierre Quitard,
    Serpette, St-O 54
Arte, *Serpette, St-O* 54
Stall 17, *Serpette, St-O* 55
Trace de Chine, *Antica, St-O* 57
Stalls 19-20, *Malassis, St-O* 60
Carte Blanche,
    Malassis, St-O 61
Stéphane Bardot et Patricia
    Attwood, *Malassis, St-O* 61
Zerline, *Malassis, St-O* 62

112

Christian Leclerc,
  Malassis, St-O 64
L'Homme de Plume,
  Malassis, St-O 65
Shanaz, *Dauphine, St-O* 67
Daniel Longueville,
  Dauphine, St-O 68
Michel Klein,
  Dauphine, St-O 69
Gérard Leprêtre,
  Dauphine, St-O 70
Exotic Kalagas,
  Dauphine, St-O 70
Mammoth Antiek,
  Dauphine, St-O 71
L'Entrepôt,
  rue des Rosiers, St-O 75
Maison Beys,
  rue des Rosiers, St-O 75
Meubles Anciens de
  nos Grand-mères,
  rue des Rosiers, St-O 76
La Petite Maison aux Puces,
  rue Paul Bert, St-O 76
Eric Heitzmann,
  rue Paul Bert, St-O 77
Galerie Cailleux,
  rue Paul Bert, St-O 77
Espinosa, *Vanves* 89
Poisson, *Vanves* 90
Le Via, *Viaduc des Arts* 96
Yamakado, *Viaduc des Arts* 96
Astier de Villatte,
  Viaduc des Arts 98
Dix Heures Dix,
  Viaduc des Arts 98

Furniture + Designs
  1870–1970, *Alfies* 19
Gardiner & Gardiner, *Alfies* 19
Anne Gormley, *Alfies* 19
Connie Margrie, *Alfies* 20
Laraine Plummer, *Alfies* 21
Katherine Pole, *Alfies* 21
Rojeh Antiques, *Alfies* 22
Catherine Wallis, *Alfies* 22
Madeline Crispin Antiques,
  Alfies 23
Keith Roughton,
  Camden Lock 36
Graham & Green, *Camden
  Lock* and *Portobello* 37, 93
The Corner Room,
  Camden Passage 42
Tony D'Almeida,
  Camden Passage 42
Carlton Davidson Antiques,
  Camden Passage 42
John Goodison and
  Chris Paraskeva,
  Camden Passage 43
Gordon Gridley,
  Camden Passage 43
After Noah,
  Camden Passage 45
Baroque 'n' Roll,
  Lillie Road 68
Andrew Bewick and Jonathan
  Lee, *Lillie Road* 69
Zal Davar, *Lillie Road* 69
Decorative Antiques,
  Lillie Road 69
Catherine Nimmo,
  Lillie Road 69
Bourbon-Hanby Antiques
  Centre, *Antiquarius* 71

Bazar Antiques & Decorative
  Items, *Portobello* 92
CHAIRS
Blandine Lefèvre,
  Biron, St-O 31
Stalls 164–65,
  Biron, St-O 32
Edwige Lelouch,
  Biron, St-O 33
Renaud Vuaillat et
  Xavier Chollet,
  Serpette, St-O 53
Hier… Encore,
  Antica, St-O 57
Rebière Antiquités,
  Malassis, St-O 63
Le Club, *Malassis, St-O* 61
Ghislain Antiques,
  Malassis, St-O 65
Stall 121, *Dauphine, St-O* 69
Michel Klein,
  Dauphine, St-O 69
Le Via, *Viaduc des Arts* 96
Yamakado,
  Viaduc des Arts 96

Connie Margrie, *Alfies* 20
Keith Roughton,
  Camden Lock 36
John Goodison and
  Chris Paraskeva,
  Camden Passage 43
twentytwentyone,
  Camden Passage 45
GARDEN
S. Brunswick, *Alfies* 18
Chelsea Gardener,
  Antiquarius 71
MODERN
Bruna Naufal, *Alfies* 21
CO₂, *Camden Lock* 36
The Home Service,
  Camden Lock 36
Planet Bazaar,
  Camden Lock 36
Unit 78, *Camden Lock* 36
After Noah,
  Camden Passage 45
twentytwentyone,
  Camden Passage 45
Aram Designs,
  Covent Garden 53
Helray Ltd, *Lillie Road* 69
Les Coussis du Chien,
  Portobello 76
Christopher Farr,
  Portobello 92
Graham & Green,
  Portobello 93
Andreas Schmid,
  Spitalfields 101
PAINTED
Patrice Mayer,
  Paul Bert, St-O 44
L'Escalier de Cristal,
  Malassis, St-O 61
Exotic Kalagas,
  Dauphine, St-O 70
Mammoth Antiek,
  Dauphine, St-O 71
L'Atelier Guigue Locca,
  Viaduc des Arts 97

Anne Gormley, *Alfies* 19
Laraine Plummer, *Alfies* 21
Katherine Pole, *Alfies* 21

Gordon Gridley,
  Camden Passage 43
Baroque 'n' Roll,
  Lillie Road 68
Andrew Bewick and
  Jonathan Lee,
  Lillie Road 69
Decorative Antiques,
  Lillie Road 69
Catherine Nimmo,
  Lillie Road 69
David Lewin, *Portobello* 86
Bazar Antiques &
  Decorative Items,
  Portobello 92
TABLES
Stall 27, *Vernaison, St-O* 14
Olga Horde,
  Vernaison, St-O 17
Catan, *Vernaison, St-O* 22
Stall 255,
  Vernaison, St-O 23
Gisèle, *Biron, St-O* 29
Stall 171, *Biron, St-O* 32
Michel Peraches et Eric
  Miel, *Paul Bert, St-O* 40
Stall 35, *Serpette, St-O* 52
Carmina Antiquités,
  Serpette, St-O 52
Mammoth Antiek,
  Dauphine, St-O 71
L'Entrepôt,
  rue des Rosiers, St-O 75
Le Via, *Viaduc des Arts* 96
Yamakado,
  Viaduc des Arts 96

Furniture + Designs
  1870–1970, *Alfies* 19
Keith Roughton,
  Camden Lock 36
twentytwentyone,
  Camden Passage 45
UPHOLSTERED
Textilean, *Alfies* 22
Connie Margrie, *Alfies* 20

GAMES *see* **TOYS**

GARDEN WARES
S. Brunswick, *Alfies* 18
Chelsea Gardener,
  Antiquarius 71
Cranborne Antiques,
  Portobello 82
Mike Handford, *Portobello* 85
S & B Evans & Sons,
  Columbia Road 102
Organics, *Columbia Road* 103
Putnams, *Columbia Road* 103
GARDEN FURNITURE
see **FURNITURE**
GARDEN ORNAMENTS
Stall 163,
  Vernaison, St-O 21
Stall 176,
  Vernaison, St-O 21
Stall 122,
  Paul Bert, St-O 41
Jean Beaumarié,
  Paul Bert, St-O 41
Marc Maison,
  Paul Bert, St-O 44
Marc Deligny,
  Paul Bert, St-O 45
Stall 11, *Serpette, St-O* 54

Stéphane Bardot
et Patricia Attwood,
Malassis, St-O 61
Ripamonti,
Viaduc des Arts 96

John Goodison and
Chris Paraskeva,
Camden Passage 43
Baroque 'n' Roll,
Lillie Road 68
Helray Ltd, *Lillie Road* 69

GEM STONES see **SHELLS**

GILT WOOD see **WOOD**

GLASS AND CRYSTALWARE
Robert et Fils,
Vernaison, St-O 14
Sylvie et Pierre-Gilles,
Vernaison, St-O 15
Stall 110, *Vernaison, St-O* 17
Nicolas Giovannoni, *Vernaison*
and *Serpette, St-O* 19, 55
Denise Balbon,
Vernaison, St-O 21
Violette Morel,
Vernaison, St-O 21
Irma, *Vernaison, St-O* 22
Les Verres de nos Grand-
mères, *Biron, St-O* 27
Stall 135, *Paul Bert, St-O* 41
L'Escalier de Cristal,
Malassis, St-O 61
G.L.B., *Malassis, St-O* 62
Franck Bergé,
Malassis, St-O 63
Jane de Livron,
Dauphine, St-O 71
Gabrielle, *Vanves* 87
Claire Lavoine, *Vanves* 87
Françoise Chatelain,
Vanves 89

Geoffrey Robinson, *Alfies* 22
print dealer, *Bermondsey* 30
Planet Bazaar, *Camden Lock* 36
Christopher Pearce,
Camden Passage 44
Templar Antiques,
Camden Passage 44
Green & Stone, *Antiquarius* 71
Mike Handford, *Portobello* 85
Alan Milford, *Portobello* 86
 DOMES
 The Old Father Time Clock
 Centre, *Portobello* 88
 LALIQUE
 Stall 94, *Biron, St-O* 30
 Alexia Say, *Biron, St-O* 30
 G.L.B., *Malassis, St-O* 62

Susie Cooper Ceramics,
Alfies 22
Raul Arantes,
Camden Passage 42
 PÂTE DE VERRE
 Stalls 241–43,
 Vernaison, St-O 22
 Jean Doutrepont,
 Biron, St-O 28
 Elisabeth, *Biron, St-O* 29
 Benoît, *Biron, St-O* 29
 Stall 94, *Biron, St-O* 30
 Alexia Say, *Biron, St-O* 30
 Largeault, *Biron, St-O* 30

Claude Boyer, *Biron* and
Rosiers, St-O 30, 49
Le Camphrier,
Cambo, St-O 47
Bernard Liagre,
Rosiers, St-O 49
Michel Giraud,
Rosiers, St-O 49
Christian Serres,
Rosiers, St-O 49
J-P. Richard,
Rosiers, St-O 49
A. Gauthier,
Rosiers, St-O 49
Christian Arnoux,
Dauphine, St-O 69
 STAINED GLASS
 Largeault, *Biron, St-O* 30
 Stall 48,
 Jules Vallès, St-O 36
 Dominique Heidenger,
 Serpette, St-O 54
 Cariatides,
 Serpette, St-O 55

Neil Phillips, *Portobello* 89

HANDBAGS
Brudasz, *Biron, St-O* 30
Le Monde du Voyage,
Serpette, St-O 53
Danièle Bouillot,
Antica, St-O 57
Thierry Amblard,
Dauphine, St-O 68
156 *rue des Rosiers, St-O* 76
Scarlett, *Vanves* 89

Bebe, *Alfies* 18
Kit Smith, *Covent Garden* 52
Linda Bee, *Grays* 58
X.S. Baggage Co.,
Antiquarius 70
Viva Barnett, *Portobello* 76

HARDWARE
Stall 5, *Vernaison, St-O* 13
Art et Cristal,
Vernaison, St-O 13
Stall 12, *Vernaison, St-O* 14
Stall 46, *Vernaison, St-O* 15
Stall 74, *Vernaison, St-O* 16
Stall 168, *Vernaison, St-O* 21
Le Marché des Antiquaires,
rue Jules Vallès, St-O 78

Dudley and Genie, *Alfies* 19
Richard Perry, *Bermondsey* 29
 CURTAIN POLES
 Gillian Danz, *Alfies* 18

HATS
Un Parfum d'Aventure,
Vernaison, St-O 15
Stall 78, *Vernaison, St-O* 16
Francine,
Vernaison, St-O 18
Stall 40, *Jules Vallès, St-O* 36
Chantal Dagommer,
Paul Bert, St-O 41
Danièle Bouillot,
Antica, St-O 57
Boutique Lydia,
Dauphine, St-O 69
Stall 10,
Lécuyer-Vallès, St-O 73
156 *rue des Rosiers, St-O* 76

Violette et Sarah,
rue Paul Bert, St-O 77
Métier Costumier,
Viaduc des Arts 96
Jean-Charles Brosseau,
Viaduc des Arts 98

Bebe, *Alfies* 18
Marie-Louise of Marylebone,
Alfies 20
Sarah and Jo, *Portobello* 77

HORSERIDING see **SPORT**

HUNTING see **SPORT**

ICONS
Garry, *Biron, St-O* 28

IRONWORK see
METALWARE

ISLAMIC ART
Shiraz Antiques, *Grays* 60
Sultani Antiques, *Grays* 60
Henry Brownrigg, *Portobello* 81

JEWELRY
Stall 83, *Vernaison, St-O* 15
Au Grenier de Lucie,
Vernaison, St-O 18
Stall 153, *Vernaison, St-O* 20
Mireille Favre,
Vernaison, St-O 20
Garry, *Biron, St-O* 28
Biron 28, *Biron, St-O* 28
Hélène Jordan, *Biron, St-O* 30
Stall 202, *Biron, St-O* 33
Sylvie Corbelin,
Paul Bert, St-O 45
Patricia Timsit,
Serpette, St-O 52
Saint-Ouen Antiquités,
Serpette, St-O 52
Diamantina, *Dauphine, St-O* 69
Yves Baruchel, *Vanves* 86
Claire Lavoine, *Vanves* 87
Abec, *Vanves* 89
Patrice Bodzen, *Vanves* 89
Catherine Manoci, *Vanves* 89

Raul Arantes,
Camden Passage 42
Kit Smith, *Covent Garden* 52
Aura Antiques, *Grays* 58
A. Douch, *Grays* 58
Shapiro & Co., *Grays* 60
Vinci Antiques, *Grays* 61
Delehar, *Portobello* 82
Carlo Fuller, *Portobello* 84
Nadia, *Portobello* 87
Pat Novissimo, *Portobello* 88
 COSTUME JEWELRY
 Galerie ABC,
 Vernaison, St-O 15
 Au Grenier de Lucie,
 Vernaison, St-O 16, 18
 Brudasz, *Biron, St-O* 30
 Olwen Forest,
 Serpette, St-O 53
 Boutique Lydia,
 Dauphine, St-O 69
 Robert Jonard et Brigitte
 Olivier, *Vanves* 88
 Patrice Bodzen,
 Vanves 89

Cécile et Jeanne,
   Viaduc des Arts 96

Cristobal, *Alfies* 18
Francesca Martire, *Alfies* 20
Linda Bee, *Grays* 58
The Gilded Lily, *Grays* 59
Steinberg & Tolkein,
   Antiquarius 71
Betty and Len Wiltshire,
   Portobello 91
Diana Laurie,
   Spitalfields 100
TRIBAL JEWELRY
Les Chevaux du Vent,
   Vanves 89

Owen Hargeaves,
   Covent Garden 51
Henry Brownrigg,
   Portobello 81
Nicholas Donn,
   Portobello 82

KEYRINGS
Françoise Chappuy,
   Vernaison, St-O 17

KITCHENALIA
Olga Horde, *Vernaison, St-O* 17
Stall 25, *Jules Vallès, St-O* 36
Nicole Aker, *Malassis, St-O* 63
Stall 179, *Dauphine, St-O* 69
Au Roi des Antiquaires,
   rue Jules Vallès, St-O 77
Monnier, *Vanves* 87
Josette et Gilbert Antoine,
   Vanves 88
Louise Royer, *Vanves* 88
L'Atelier du Cuivre et de
   l'Argent, *Viaduc des Arts* 98

Kitchen Bygones, *Alfies* 20
Paola and Iaia, *Alfies* 21
Jonathan's Belowstairs,
   Camden Passage 44
H&C, *Covent Garden* 50
Kim Sinclair, *Portobello* 89
Emma Bernhardt, *Portobello* 92
Lucy Everett, *Spitalfields* 100
Odyssey, *Columbia Road* 103
   BREADBOARDS
   Rosslyn Neave,
      Bermondsey 29

KITSCH
Françoise Chappuy,
   Vernaison, St-O 17
Béatrice Cuvelier,
   Vernaison, St-O 22
Au Bonheur du Jour,
   Dauphine, St-O 67

Jessica Ward, *Alfies* 22
Emma Bernhardt, *Portobello* 92
Diana Laurie, *Spitalfields* 100

LACE *see* **TEXTILES**

LIGHTING
   CHANDELIERS
   Art et Cristal,
      Vernaison, St-O 13
   Stall 12, *Vernaison, St-O* 14
   Robert et Fils,
      Vernaison, St-O 14
   Stall 27, *Vernaison, St-O* 14

Stall 46, *Vernaison, St-O* 15
Stall 105bis,
   Vernaison, St-O 17
Stalls 241–43,
   Vernaison, St-O 22
F. Bruyneel, *Biron, St-O* 28
Yvette Robert,
   Biron, St-O 28
Stany Hoffmann,
   Biron, St-O 29
Philippe Lachaux,
   Biron, St-O 32
Stall 54,
   Jules Vallès, St-O 36
Carpentier,
   Paul Bert, St-O 40
La Martinière,
   Paul Bert, St-O 41
Stall 239, *Paul Bert, St-O* 43
Lits et Lampes,
   Paul Bert, St-O 45
Stall 27, *Serpette, St-O* 51
Carmina Antiquités,
   Serpette, St-O 52
Stall 41, *Serpette, St-O* 53
Jean-Yves Barczyk,
   Serpette, St-O 53
Renaud Vuaillat et
   Xavier Chollet,
   Serpette, St-O 53
Stall 17, *Serpette, St-O* 55
Stall 18, *Serpette, St-O* 55
Attitudes,
   Malassis, St-O 65
ABJ, *Dauphine, St-O* 69
Stall 16,
   Lécuyer-Vallès, St-O 73
L'Entrepôt,
   rue des Rosiers, St-O 75
Baguès, *Viaduc des Arts* 96

Carlton Davidson Antiques,
   Camden Passage 42
Baroque 'n' Roll,
   Lillie Road 68
LAMPS AND WALL BRACKETS
Stall 95, *Vernaison, St-O* 17
Stalls 241–43,
   Vernaison, St-O 22
Yvette Robert,
   Biron, St-O 28
Stall 190, *Biron, St-O* 32
Stall 78,
   Jules Vallès, St-O 37
Stall 41, *Paul Bert, St-O* 41
Stall 59, *Paul Bert, St-O* 41
Attitudes, *Malassis, St-O* 65
P.B., *Dauphine, St-O* 70
Au Roi des Antiquaires,
   rue Jules Vallès, St-O 77
Les Templiers, *Vanves* 87
Le Via, *Viaduc des Arts* 96
Baguès, *Viaduc des Arts* 96
Dix Heures Dix,
   Viaduc des Arts 98

David Burrows, *Alfies* 18
Dudley and Genie, *Alfies* 19
Francesca Martire, *Alfies* 20
Geoffrey Robinson, *Alfies* 22
Rojeh Antiques, *Alfies* 22
Susie Cooper Ceramics,
   Alfies 22
CO_2, *Camden Lock* 36
The Corner Room,
   Camden Passage 42

Carlton Davidson Antiques,
   Camden Passage 42
Decodence,
   Camden Passage 43
John Goodison and
   Chris Paraskeva,
   Camden Passage 43
Shane Meredith,
   Camden Passage 44
After Noah,
   Camden Passage 45
twentytwentyone,
   Camden Passage 45
Aram Designs,
   Covent Garden 53
Decorative Antiques,
   Lillie Road 69
Catherine Nimmo,
   Lillie Road 69
Chelsea Gardener,
   Antiquarius 71
Les Coussis du Chien,
   Portobello 76
Stephen Osborn,
   Portobello 77
Bazar Antiques &
   Decorative Items,
   Portobello 92
Roughneck & Thug,
   Spitalfields 101
Odyssey,
   Columbia Road 103

LINEN *see* **TEXTILES**

LUGGAGE
Luggage, *Vernaison, St-O* 18
Stall 194ter, *Biron, St-O* 33
Voyages, *Serpette, St-O* 53
Le Monde du Voyage,
   Serpette, St-O 53
Thierry Amblard,
   Dauphine, St-O 68

X.S. Baggage Co.,
   Antiquarius 70

MEDIEVAL ART
Nigel Mills, *Covent Garden* 51
Jane Stewart, *Grays* 60
Marc-Antoine Du Ry,
   Portobello 83

METALWARE
L'Entrepôt,
   rue des Rosiers, St-O 75
Mazeaux, Aux Vieux Métaux,
   rue Jules Vallès, St-O 77
René Marie, *Vanves* 88

Richard Perry, *Bermondsey* 29
Shane Meredith,
   Camden Passage 44
David Levi Antiques,
   Portobello 86
   BRASS AND COPPER
   Dudley and Genie, *Alfies* 19
   R.A. Barnes, *Portobello* 80
   Noel and Elizabeth Pullman,
      Portobello 89
   CHROME
   Stable Five,
      Camden Lock 36
   FIREGUARDS
   Stall 59,
      Paul Bert, St-O 41

115

Marc Bouchetard,
Paul Bert, St-O 43
Le Savoir Fer,
Serpette, St-O 51
L'Entrepôt,
rue des Rosiers, St-O 75
Mazeaux, Aux
Vieux Métaux,
rue Jules Vallès, St-O 77

Noel and Elizabeth Pullman,
Portobello 89
IRONWORK
Stall 163, *Vernaison, St-O* 21
Stall 176,
Vernaison, St-O 21
Philippe Lachaux,
Biron, St-O 32
Jean Beaumarié,
Paul Bert, St-O 41
Christophe Gaignon,
Paul Bert, St-O 42
Marc Bouchetard,
Paul Bert, St-O 43
Le Savoir Fer,
Serpette, St-O 51
Jean-Yves Barczyk,
Serpette, St-O 53
L'Entrepôt,
rue des Rosiers, St-O 75
La Boutique 75,
rue des Rosiers, St-O 75
SEMA,
rue Paul Bert, St-O 76
Mazeaux, Aux
Vieux Métaux,
rue Jules Vallès, St-O 77
René Marie, *Vanves* 88
PEWTER
Hilary Kashden,
Covent Garden 51
Jane Stewart, *Grays* 60
ZINC
Stall 74, *Vernaison, St-O* 16

MILITARIA
Novella, *Vernaison, St-O* 13
Un Parfum d'Aventure,
Vernaison, St-O 15
Stall 74bis, *Vernaison, St-O* 16
Stall 78, *Vernaison, St-O* 16
La Tranchée Militaire,
Malik, St-O 25
Stall 40, *Jules Vallès, St-O* 36
Stall 52, *Jules Vallès, St-O* 36
Choisi pour Vous,
Jules Vallès, St-O 37
Stall 80, *Jules Vallès, St-O* 37
Renaud Tessier,
Paul Bert, St-O 45
Stall 4, *Serpette, St-O* 51
La Garde, *Serpette, St-O* 51
Surplus Militaire Garba,
rue Jules Vallès, St-O 78
Surplus Simon,
rue Jules Vallès, St-O 78
Métier Costumier,
Viaduc des Arts 96

Richard Perry,
Bermondsey 29
London Military Market,
Camden Passage 41
Steven Wheeler,
Covent Garden 52
Don Bayney, *Grays* 58

Gordons Metals Ltd,
Grays 59
Anthony Jack, *Portobello* 86
David Lewin, *Portobello* 86

MIRRORS
Stalls 241–43,
Vernaison, St-O 22
Blandine Lefèvre, *Biron, St-O* 31
Stall 150, *Biron, St-O* 31
Philippe Lachaux,
Biron, St-O 32
Carpentier, *Paul Bert, St-O* 40
H.P., *Paul Bert, St-O* 41
Stall 239, *Paul Bert, St-O* 43
Laurence Lenglare,
Paul Bert, St-O 43
Patrice Mayer,
Paul Bert, St-O 44
Christophe Reynal,
Paul Bert, St-O 45
Stall 26, *Serpette, St-O* 51
Stall 27, *Serpette, St-O* 51
Mahé, *Serpette, St-O* 52
Dominique Heidenger,
Serpette, St-O 54
Marie-Eve Rosenthal,
Serpette, St-O 54
Michèle Perceval,
Serpette, St-O 55
Stall 30, *Malassis, St-O* 61
ABJ, *Dauphine, St-O* 69
P.B., *Dauphine, St-O* 70
La Galerie des Glaces,
rue des Rosiers, St-O 75
Miroirs,
rue des Rosiers, St-O 75
Eric Heitzmann,
rue Paul Bert, St-O 77

David Burrows, *Alfies* 18
Rojeh Antiques, *Alfies* 22
Carlton Davidson Antiques,
Camden Passage 42
Shane Meredith,
Camden Passage 44
Andrew Bewick and Jonathan
Lee, *Lillie Road* 69
Decorative Antiques,
Lillie Road 69
Catherine Nimmo,
Lillie Road 69

MODERN DESIGN see also
FURNITURE
Eric Lentz, *Paul Bert, St-O* 43
Vingtième Siècle,
Paul Bert, St-O 45
Fantazio, *Vanves* 87

Francesca Martire, *Alfies* 20
Bruna Naufal, *Alfies* 21
CO₂, *Camden Lock* 36
The Home Service,
Camden Lock 36
Planet Bazaar, *Camden Lock* 36
Stable Five, *Camden Lock* 36
Unit 78, *Camden Lock* 36
Decodence,
Camden Passage 43
After Noah,
Camden Passage 45
twentytwentyone,
Camden Passage 45
Aram Designs,
Covent Garden 53

Les Coussis du Chien,
Portobello 76
Paul Lau, *Portobello* 77
Andreas Schmid,
Spitalfields 101
Odyssey, *Columbia Road* 103
FORNASETTI
Francesca Martire, *Alfies* 20

MOTORCYCLES
Victory Motorcycles,
Camden Lock 37

MUSICAL INSTRUMENTS
Novella, *Vernaison, St-O* 13
Allain Cadinot,
Viaduc des Arts 97
Roger Lanne,
Viaduc des Arts 97

NATURAL HISTORY
Cranborne Antiques,
Portobello 82
Michael Telfer-Smollett,
Portobello 90

**NAUTICAL OBJECTS
AND ANTIQUES**
Brophy, *Biron, St-O* 30
Stall 173, *Biron, St-O* 32
Brick à Barc, *Malassis, St-O* 62
L'Armada, *Dauphine, St-O* 70
Monnier, *Vanves* 87

Peter Laurie, *Bermondsey* 29
Titanic, *Old Crowther* 68
B.A. Neal, *Portobello* 87

NEWSPAPERS
Stall 47, *Vernaison, St-O* 15
Nicolas Rémon,
Vernaison, St-O 19
Stall 181, *Vernaison, St-O* 21
temporary stalls,
Marché du Livre Ancien 101

NINETIES
CO₂, *Camden Lock* 36

**ORIENTAL ART
AND CERAMICS**
Annie Minet, *Biron, St-O* 29
Stall 179, *Biron, St-O* 32
Lucien Pineau,
Serpette, St-O 54
Trace de Chine,
Antica, St-O 57
Trésors de Perse,
Malassis, St-O 61
Stéphane Bardot et Patricia
Attwood, *Malassis, St-O* 61
Exotic Kalagas,
Dauphine, St-O 70
Kimono-Dô, *Montreuil* 83
Les Chevaux du Vent,
Vanves 89

Don Bayney, *Grays* 58
Guest and Gray, *Grays* 59
Wheatley Antiques, *Grays* 60
Linda Wigglesworth, *Grays* 61
Geoffrey Waters,
Antiquarius 70
R.A. Barnes, *Portobello* 80
Henry Brownrigg,
Portobello 81

Jo De Sousa Macedo,
 Portobello 82
The Nanking Porcelain
 Company, *Portobello* 87
Alastair Thomas, *Portobello* 90
 BUDDHISM
 Aura Antiques, *Grays* 58

PAINTINGS
Stall 29, *Vernaison, St-O* 14
Au Grenier de Lucie,
 Vernaison, St-O 16
Stall 193, *Vernaison, St-O* 21
Garry, *Biron, St-O* 28
Paul Milgen, *Biron, St-O* 29
Gilbert Fischer, *Biron, St-O* 29
Hélène Jordan, *Biron, St-O* 30
Stall 125, *Biron, St-O* 30
Stall 54, *Jules Vallès, St-O* 36
Stall 215, *Paul Bert, St-O* 42
Transparences,
 Rosiers, St-O 49
Mahé, *Serpette, St-O* 52
Stall 12, *Serpette, St-O* 54
Lucien Pineau,
 Serpette, St-O 54
Hier… Encore, *Antica, St-O* 57
Carte Blanche,
 Malassis, St-O 61
Marie-Thérèse Nays-Favre,
 Malassis, St-O 63
Daniel Longueville,
 Dauphine, St-O 68
Maison Beys,
 rue des Rosiers, St-O 75
La Boutique 75,
 rue des Rosiers, St-O 75
La Petite Maison aux Puces,
 rue Paul Bert, St-O 76
Danièle Engliz-Bey, *Vanves* 87
René Marie, *Vanves* 88
Philippe Lambert, *Vanves* 89
Poisson, *Vanves* 90

Greg Li and Edward Holden,
 Alfies 20
Madeline Crispin Antiques,
 Alfies 23
Gordon Gridley,
 Camden Passage 43
Carter & Brady, *Portobello* 82
Charles Daggett Gallery,
 Portobello 82
Colin Gross, *Portobello* 85
Susana Montiel, *Portobello* 87
 TAPESTRY CARTOONS
 Lhomond,
 Vernaison, St-O 13
 Stalls 167–68,
 Biron, St-O 32
 Sylviane Cristobal,
 Malassis, St-O 61
 WATERCOLOURS
 Patrice Salet,
 Vernaison, St-O 17
 Pierre Jonchères,
 Vernaison, St-O 18
 Françoise Renoult,
 Serpette, St-O 53
 Isabelle Feugère,
 Dauphine, St-O 69
 La Petite Maison
 aux Puces,
 rue Paul Bert, St-O 76
 Danièle Engliz-Bey,
 Vanves 87

Philippe Lambert,
 Vanves 89

Barry Landsman, *Alfies* 20
Charlie, *Bermondsey* 28
Carter & Brady,
 Portobello 82
Ester Chigine, *Portobello* 82

PANELLING see WOOD

PENS see DESKS

PEWTER see METALWARE

**PHOTOGRAPHS AND
PHOTOGRAPHIC
EQUIPMENT**
Mourad Amezal,
 Malassis, St-O 60
Au Bonheur du Jour,
 Dauphine, St-O 67
Au Passé Simple,
 Dauphine, St-O 70
Stall 12,
 Lécuyer-Vallès, St-O 73

Kay Books, *Bermondsey* 29
Manuela Hofer,
 Camden Passage 45
The Photographers' Gallery,
 Covent Garden 53
Historical Impressions,
 Portobello 85

PIPES
Stall 195, *Vernaison, St-O* 22
Gérard Leprêtre,
 Dauphine, St-O 70

PLASTIC
Stall 41, *Paul Bert, St-O* 41
Stall 180, *Paul Bert, St-O* 42
Vingtième Siècle,
 Paul Bert, St-O 45

Emma Bernhardt,
 Portobello 92
Lucy Everett, *Spitalfields* 100
Odyssey, *Columbia Road* 103
 BAKELITE
 Paola and Iaia, *Alfies* 21
 Decodence,
 Camden Passage 43

POSTCARDS
Stall 188, *Vernaison, St-O* 21
Stall 195, *Vernaison, St-O* 22
D'Autreppe,
 Vernaison, St-O 22
Renaud Tessier,
 Paul Bert, St-O 45
Aire du Temps,
 Malassis, St-O 62
Normand, *Dauphine, St-O* 68
Alpha Collections,
 rue des Rosiers, St-O 76
Sylvie Cablat, *Vanves* 90

Cheryl All, *Covent Garden* 50

POSTERS
Stall 47, *Vernaison, St-O* 15
Stall 148, *Vernaison, St-O* 19
Philippe, *Vernaison, St-O* 20
Jane Moufflet,
 Biron, St-O 27

Stall 140, *Biron, St-O* 31
Rétro Pub, *Dauphine, St-O* 68
Au Passé Simple,
 Dauphine, St-O 70
L'Atelier Robin Tourenne,
 Viaduc des Arts 96

Posters for Collectors,
 Grays 60
At the Movies,
 Antiquarius 69
Liz Farrow, *Portobello* 83

POTTERY see CERAMICS

PRINTS AND ENGRAVINGS
Stall 65, *Biron, St-O* 29
Stall 83, *Biron, St-O* 29
Olivier Deboscker,
 Paul Bert, St-O 43
M.L.V., *Paul Bert, St-O* 44
Walfredo Barth,
 Cambo, St-O 47
Anne-Marie Despas,
 Serpette, St-O 53
Librairie du Louvre,
 Malassis, St-O 64
Au Réverbère,
 Dauphine, St-O 67
Luc Bouveret,
 Dauphine, St-O 69
Papiers Anciens,
 Dauphine, St-O 70
Anthare de Schuyter,
 Dauphine, St-O 70
Jean-Louis Heitzmann,
 Vanves 86
temporary stalls,
 Marché du Livre Ancien 101

Robin Gardiner, *Alfies* 19
Kay Books, *Bermondsey* 29
print dealer, *Bermondsey* 30
Sandy Field, *Covent Garden* 50
Patrick Boyd-Carpenter,
 Grays 58
Emerich Vidich, *Antiquarius* 70
Ester Chigine, *Portobello* 82
Cranborne Antiques,
 Portobello 82
Julie Gregory, *Portobello* 85
 CHROMOLITHOGRAPHS
 Stalls 128–29,
 Dauphine, St-O 69
 Marie Moulis, *Vanves* 88

RADIOS AND HI-FI
Antik Art, *Vernaison, St-O* 15
Stall 12,
 Lécuyer-Vallès, St-O 73
Docks de la Radio,
 rue Jules Vallès, St-O 78

Decodence,
 Camden Passage 43

RECORDS
Au Passé Simple,
 Dauphine, St-O 70
Discophilie,
 rue des Rosiers, St-O 76
Alpha Collections,
 rue des Rosiers, St-O 76
Docks de la Radio,
 rue Jules Vallès, St-O 78
Copa Music,
 rue Jules Vallès, St-O 78